JUSTICE

by

John Corbett

Manufactured In The United States Of America

ISBN: 978-0-578-00033-6

This publication is designed to
provide information to help
settle or win your complaint.

It is sold with the understanding
that the publisher is not a
substitute for legal
advice.

If legal advice is required, a
competent attorney should
be retained.

John Corbett does not
accept any responsibility for
liabilities resulted from
the actions of any
parties involved.

TABLE OF CONTENTS

INTRODUCTION

This manual has been published to assist you in hopefully winning your case of discrimination or sexual harassment against your employer. However, it should not be used as a complete substitute to competent legal professional help. Attorneys charge a lot of money to handle job complaints. Unfortunately, when we are faced with discrimination and sexual harassment, we are never prepared. Whether your complaint is based upon race; color; religion; sex (including sexual harassment); age (40 years of age or older); national origin; physical or mental disability; or as a retaliation for opposing any practice made unlawful by federal discrimination laws or for participating in proceedings under those laws you will have to be well knowledgeable about discrimination complaints. Your employer will be well prepared to defend themselves against your charges.

When I thought about filing a discrimination complaint against my employer, I first tried to educate myself on procedures and laws of Equal Employment Opportunity complaints. I found out that there is very little information available in public libraries or even in law libraries on how to prepare a case against your employer. Your employer is certainly not going to assist you in winning complaint against them. Most people are naïve to think so. I consulted many attorneys and unfortunately found out that they do not specialize in discrimination cases. For various reasons many attorneys do not want to take cases of discrimination. Many of those reasons they say why they do not want these cases are because the cases are difficult to prove. They are also very timely and not enough money is involved in them. They are also afraid of the system which institutionally discriminates against you. Many lawyers will take their client's money as a retainer knowing very well they do not intend to effectively prepare your case.

It will be ultimately up to you to know your rights and learn how to prepare your case. You will also need to know how to maintain it in the system. You will learn that ultimately no one cares deeply about your case or your life but you.

When you formerly charge your employer, you will have engaged in a battle that will ultimately effect you for the rest of your life. You must be prepared like you are going to war.

Now you probably asking, "How does he know so much and how did he acquire this knowledge?" This knowledge came to me by experience which I have been told is the best teacher. In 1984, while employed by Department of the Army as a civilian employee, I was engaged in racial discrimination. I tried to do everything possible to advert from filing a formal charge of discrimination. I consulted my superiors on all levels and received consultations from the local Equal Employment Opportunity Office where I was employed. I received no resolution or respect for my complaint. After about two years after my informal talks with my employer, I decided to file a formal complaint of race discrimination. My employer was affecting my health. When involved in discrimination, one will find out that there will be many reasons for going formally and least of all, it will be about money or a promotion.

When I formally charged my employer with discrimination, I was dismissed from my job for filing that charge. The EEO office did not welcome my complaint and took other retaliatory measures against me to try to dismiss the complaint. They refused to assist me in articulating my complaint in the agency. I eventually had to file a complaint against the EEO office for violating my rights as a federal employee. After many appeals, in 1987 I won a decision against the Department of the Army for terminating my job without proper appeal rights. In 1994, I won another decision against the Department of the Army for discriminating against me in the processing of my complaint before I was dismissed.

It took me several long years to win my case of discrimination because I didn't give up. If I had known this information that I have assembled for you, I would have won my case very sooner.

Many people do not like to speak about or challenge discrimination. None of my counsel was aggressive and direct in providing me with information that I needed to know.

I hope this manual will give you courage and inspiration to continue your case. It won't be easy, but nothing worthwhile is easy. If you prepare your case well, you will win. Remember, people who fail to plan, plan to fail. Good luck!

KNOWING HOW TO TALK TO YOUR SUPERVISORS WHEN YOU EXPERIENCE ADVERSE ACTIONS

No one can predict human behavior or answer why people act the way they do. It is unfortunate if you have a supervisor who has rude behavior and directs it toward you. If he treats everyone rude and does not violate the job regulations or employment laws, you may not have any recourse but to transfer away from him or her. Never quit a job that you really want without a fight. But if your superiors treat you different than others consistently, you will have to talk to them at some point.

Let's discuss the do's and don'ts you should follow when you talk to your supervisor or other superiors.

1. Document all of your concerns with the date, time and individuals involved. It is important that you sign your document with your signature and not typed signatures.
2. Always have a representative or witness with you during any stage of your complaint. Also have a representative or witness present with you when you talk about concerns that you know may not be resolved and lead to a complaint.
3. If you and your superiors agree to a resolution to your concerns or your complaint, have them to put the resolution in writing and you and your supervisors sign it with the present date.
4. Never appear angry or hostile when you meet with your supervisor or other superiors.

5. Rehearse what you want to say so that you can say everything you want to say and not have to pause to let your superiors enter before you finish. Having notes of your concerns present with you will help you to remember what you want to say. If your superiors are able to break in on your thought pattern, they will try to diminish your concerns and shrug them off as you being mistaken or you and the opposing person having a communication problem.
6. Be brief and concise about your concerns. Always be professional and insist on a sit down meeting to be relax and talk about your concerns.
7. Never threaten your supervisor with plans of filing a complaint. It is very important that you do not let your supervisor know how to block your complaint. Never discuss planning to file a complaint with your coworkers or anyone else in the company or agency. Management will be well prepared to defend themselves if they learn about your plans before you file your complaint.
8. Never point out other employees whom you feel are being treated better than you before you file your complaint. Keep your complaint focused solely on yourself. If you can resolve your concerns with a discussion, it will be to your advantage. No one really wants to file a complaint, so an informal resolution is what you really want.
9. Thank your supervisor for listening to your concerns. If you are dissatisfied with the outcome of the meeting, arrange a meeting with the next level supervisor. If your dissatisfaction persists and you know you

have a good complaint, you should file one against your immediate supervisor.

10. When you formally file a complaint, the formal complaint form will request that you state a specific action or reason for filing your complaint. You may state a specific reason for filing but always make the charge or charges broad enough to incorporate negative incidents to support the charge.

Example:

Correct

I, John Doe, was denied a promotion to the next grade level because of my race, sex, etc.

Incorrect

I, John Doe, was denied a promotion to the next grade level in 2004 because of my race, sex, etc.

By putting a time frame or narrowing the charge will limit the unfavorable incidents that may have happened before or after 2004. You will have to show that the discriminatory conduct has persisted over a period of time and not one incident. This will be the most important part of any case, having a sufficient charge. This was the biggest error I made when I first filed my case.

PROCEDURES FOR PROCESSING COMPLAINTS OF DISCRIMINATION AND SEXUAL HARASSMENT

Many states have different methods of investigating complaints of discrimination and sexual harassment before you contact the Equal Employment Opportunity Commission. In many states the procedure is very similar to the federal employment procedure. If your state has a different investigative procedure in the informal stage from the federal procedure which I have listed below, it probably differs by very little because the federal government established the laws for investigating all EEO complaints.

The federal procedure according to 29 Code of Federal Regulations 1614 is based upon race; color; religion; sex; including sexual harassment; age (40 years of age or older); national origin; physical or mental disability or as a retaliation for opposing any practice made unlawful by federal discrimination laws or for participating in proceeding under those laws is:

Step # 1

Contact an Equal Opportunity Counselor (EEO) within 45 days of an alleged discriminatory event or in the case of a personnel action, within 45 days of the effective date, to file an informal discrimination complaint.

The EEO counselor is not a representative for either management or the complainant. The EEO counselor should be a neutral party trained to gather facts and attempt to resolve your complaint. In order for any EEO counselor to do a fair job on your case, you should provide pertinent information that will bring a resolution to the complaint.

Listed are six critical elements that all complainants should provide to the EEO counselor.

1. Tell the counselor the reason why you feel that you should file a complaint.
2. Tell the counselor the issues surrounding why you believe you were discriminated against.
3. Identify Who? What? Where? When? Why? And how the event or events occurred.
4. Provide copies of all relevant documents to the EEO counselor.
5. Identify all names of potential witnesses who may have relevant information to your complaint.
6. Tell the counselor what you want as relief to your complaint.

The counselor cannot accept a complaint that has happened after 45 days of the incident or incidents happened in order for you to go formal.

The EEO counselor has 30 days in which to conduct informal counseling and attempt resolution, unless both the EEO counselor and the complainant agree in writing for an extension of not more than 60 days. Management should be working closely with the EEO counselor in discussing the alleged discriminatory events and attempting resolution. At the end of the counseling process, the EEO counselor will prepare a report of the fact-findings and the actions taken to attempt resolution. The EEO counselor does not express personal opinions or renders a decision on whether or not discrimination occurred.

Step # 2

If the complainant is not resolved at the EEO counseling stage, the complainant will be given a final interview notice informing him/her of the right to file a formal discrimination complaint. The complainant has 15 calendar days from receipt of the final interview notice to file a formal discrimination complaint to the EEO director.

Step # 3

Formal discrimination complaints are reviewed by the EEO director's office to determine whether or not they can be accepted, in accordance with the EEOC regulation.

If a complaint is dismissed, the complainant has the right to appeal the dismissal to the EEOC within 30 days of receipt of the dismissal.

Discrimination complaints which are accepted will be investigated by an independent investigator from outside the agency. According to the EEOC regulation, investigations should be completed within 180 days of filing the complaint. The complainant should remember that the burden of proof remains on him/her to prove discrimination. Therefore, it is important to cooperate in a timely manner with the investigator so that a complete and factual record can be completed.

Step # 4

When the investigation is complete, the complainant will get a copy of the report of the investigation, along with notification that within 30 calendar days, he or she may request a hearing before an administrative judge of the EEOC or a Final Agency Decision (FAD) from the EEO director without a hearing.

If the complainant does not request a hearing within 30 days, the EEO officer may adopt the proposed disposition of the complaint as the decision of the agency. The complaint is then forwarded to the head of the agency for the agency's final decision.

If the complainant asks for a hearing, the agency requests the Equal Employment Opportunity Commission to assign an administrative judge to conduct a hearing.

The complaint file is reviewed to see if the file is completed.

If the file is incomplete, the reviewer may remand the complaint back to the agency for further processing before the hearing is conducted.

The head of the agency makes a final decision, based on the file, giving the complainant a copy of the administrative judges recommended decision and the verbatim transcript of the hearing. If the agency rejects or modifies the recommended decision, it must state its reason and provide a copy to the complainant.

Step # 5

The agency has 180 days in which to issue findings of fact and conclusion of law. The agency then has 60 days to accept, reject, or modify these conclusions and to issue a final agency decision.

Step # 6

The complainant has a right to appeal the final agency decision within 30 days of receipt of the decision or file a civil action in a U.S. District Court within 90 days.

Step # 7

If the complainant appeals to the Equal Employment Opportunity Commission and is dissatisfied with the decision from the commission, he or she may then file a civil action in federal district court within 90 days.

The complainant may file a civil action in federal district court if a letter of final action on the complaint is not taken by the agency within 180 days of filing or if a final action is not taken on an appeal to the commission within 180 days of filing.

Note: The filing of an EEO complaint is a personal matter and you may be disciplined for using government or your business's property. The use of government or a business's property must be authorized.

THE MEDIATION PROCESS

The Equal Employment Opportunity Commission has offered a new form of mediation, Alternative Dispute Resolution (ADR), as an alternative to the traditional investigative or litigation process. Mediation is an informal process in which a neutral third party assists the opposing parties to reach a voluntary, negotiated resolution of a charge of discrimination. The decision to mediate is completely voluntary for thc charging party and the employer. Mediation gives the parties the opportunity to discuss the issues raised in the charge, to clear up misunderstandings. It is also used to find areas of agreement and then incorporate those areas of agreement into resolutions. A mediation does not resolve the charge or impose a decision on the parties to agree on a mutually unacceptable resolution. The mediation process is strictly confidential. Information disclosed during mediation will not be revealed to any one, including other EEOC employees.

Mediation is an efficient process that saves time and money. Since each EEO complaint process costs federal agencies thousands of dollars, agencies should be willing to fully fund any expedited alternative dispute resolution procedure. Successful mediation avoids a time consuming investigation and costly expense, achieving a prompt resolution to the charge. The majority of mediations are completed in one session, which usually lasts from one to five hours.

An EEOC representative will contact the employer concerning their participation in the program. If both parties agree, a mediation session is conducted by a trained mediator. It is not necessary to have an attorney in order to participate in EEOC's mediation program, either party may choose to do so. It is important that persons attending the mediation process have authority to resolve the dispute. If mediation is unsuccessful, the charge is investigated in the traditional agency EEO process.

Mediation sessions are not tape recorded or transcribed. Notes taken during the mediation are discarded. Settlement agreements secured during mediation do not constitute an admission by the employer of a violation of laws enforced by the Equal Employment Opportunity Commission.

PROCESSING COMPLAINTS THROUGH THE FEDERAL SECTOR, PART 1614, EEOC REGULATIONS

- This manual is found at your local library, university, or college library and your local law library. The federal guidelines for processing complaints may change from time to time. You should be familiar with this process at all times to monitor the processing of your complaint.

TIME FRAME FOR FILING EEO COMPLAINTS

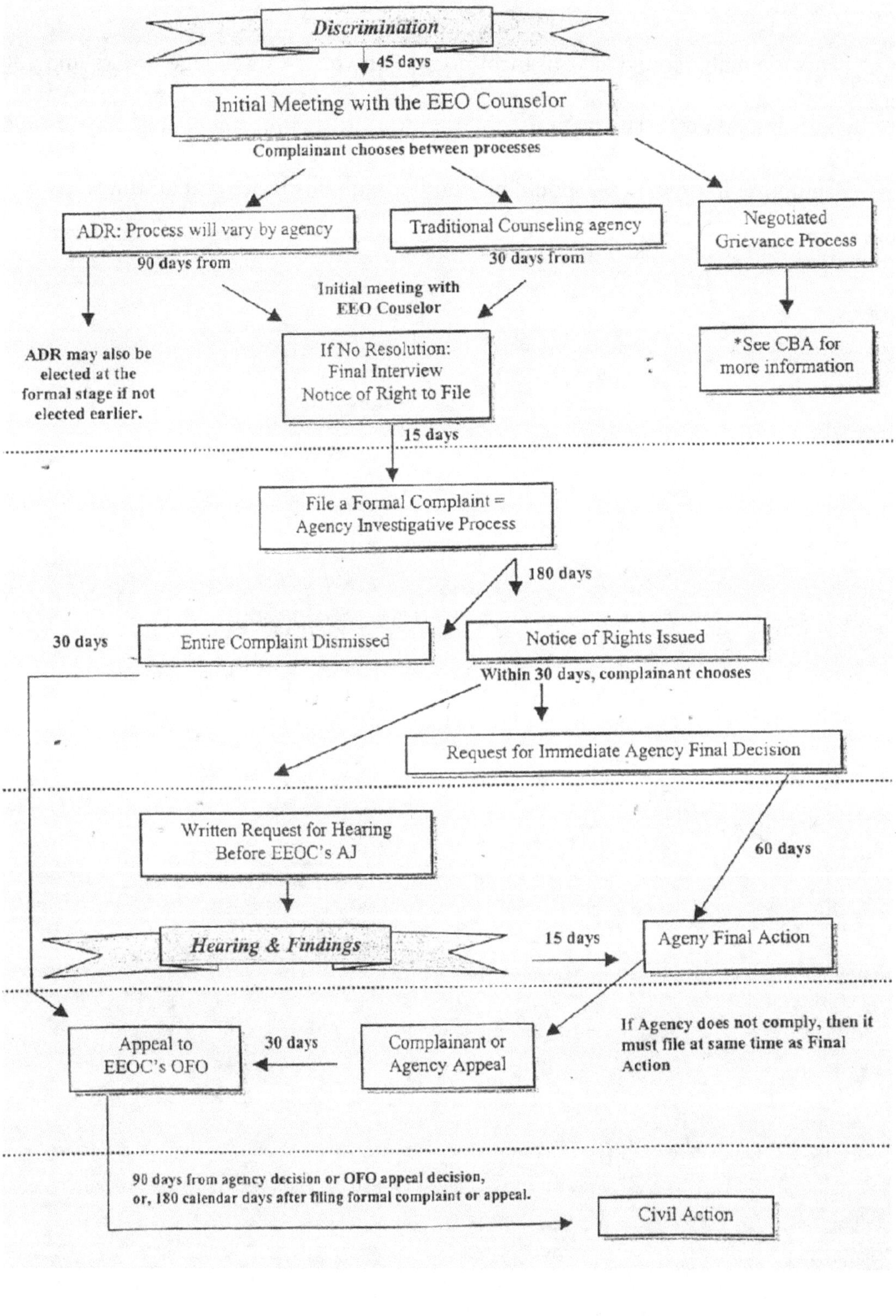

DISCOVERY RIGHTS

During the period after a hearing request and before the hearing, the complainant and the agency have the right to seek discovery. There are very strict guidelines that need to be abided by during the discovery process. The guidelines are completely under the control of the administrative judge. Typically, they look like this: first, within 10 calendar days after the administrative judge's receipt of thc complaint file from the agency (Notice: not from the date the EEOC received the hearing request), the administrative judge must send all parties, including the complainant, notice of the right to seek discovery. Next, within 10 calendar days of receipt of the notice, the complainant must file with the EEOC administrative judge either a stipulation (or written agreement) of the parties permitting discovery or a request for authorization to commence discovery (if the parties could not reach agreement on scope and method of discovery). The stipulation or request should address what types of discovery and how much of each type of discovery each party seeks. Absent specific authorization from the administrative judge, neither party may propound more than one (1) set of interrogatories (written requests) containing no more than 30 questions (no subpart allowed), and no more than 30 requests for admission of facts. There does not appear to be any limit on the number of depositions either party may take, although each party must pay for any depositions they request. However, employees will get official time pay for any deposition in which they are involved. Nor does there appear to be a limit on the number of requests for production of documents, although each request must be specific, identifying the document or type of document requested.

If the complainant and the agency have stipulated to the amount of discovery to which each is entitled, they must begin to exchange discovery requests within ten (10) days of receipt of the administrative judge's initial notice of the right to conduct discovery. If they have not agreed on the method and scope of discovery and instead need to submit a request to the administrative judge, then the judge must, within ten (10) days of receipt of the request, issue an authorization that describes the amount of discovery and type to which each is entitled. In either case, when the complainant begins discovery, he or she should address the discovery requests to the agency, not to the EEOC administrative judge.

There are also time limitations associated with responding to discovery requests. The opposing party or representative must respond to the request for discovery within fifteen (15) calendar days from the date of receipt of the request. A response can either be:

- Compliance with the request
- Written opposition to the request stating, with respect to each interrogatory, request for admission, or request to produce documents, that the request is irrelevant, over burdensome, repetitious, or privileged;
- A written agreement or stipulation of the parties that prevent the need for the response (for example, if the parties stipulate to a given fact that prevents the need for production of documents as to that fact); or
- A request for an extension of time to comply or to produce a written agreement not to exceed fifteen (15) calendar days.

If either the complainant or the agency fails to respond to discovery within fifteen (15) calendar days of receipt of the request, the other party may file a motion to compel discovery. This motion must be filed within five (5) calendar days after the expiration date for responding to a request for discovery. It must be filed with EEOC administrative judge and it must contain a certification that a copy was served on the opposing party. The opposing party must file any opposition within 10 calendar days of service of the motion and must also certify that a copy was mailed to the party who first filed the motion.

Within ten (10) calendar days after the opposition to the motion was filed, the administrative judge must rule on the motion. In the alternative, the judge may order that documents, witnesses, or other evidence at issue be produced at the hearing. If the judge approves the motion, he or she will issue a written order to comply. Compliance with the order must occur within fifteen (15) calendar days of the order. When either party fails to respond to proper request for information or witnesses, the administrative judge may draw adverse inferences, exclude other evidence, issue a decision against the interest of the party, or take other appropriate action. In addition, the administrative judge may determine individually, or upon request of a party, that some of all facts are not in dispute, and issue a summary decision on the matters (thus limiting the scope of the hearing) after giving the parties an opportunity to respond in writing.

Finally, discovery must be completed within ninety (90) calendar days from the commission receipt of a request for a hearing.

SAMPLE DISCOVERY FORMS

The following pages contain sample discovery forms for the complainant and/or his or her representative to use in assisting them in creating appropriate discovery requests. Included here are forms for interrogatories, requests for admission, requests to produce documents, and a sample motion to compel discovery.

The complainant and the agency are generally entitled to no more than one (1) set of interrogatories that contain no more than thirty (30) questions, no more than one (1) set of requests for admission that contain no more than thirty (30) questions and also depositions and relevant requests for production of documents. Interrogatories should be used when the complainant wishes the agency to provide answers to questions that generally involve more than a "yes" or "no" answer. Requests for admission should be used when, on a relatively major issue, the agency can provide either an "admit" or "delay" response. Because there is a limit on the number of requests for admission, the complainant should try to be fairly certain that the agency will have to "admit" the request. Requests for documents should be used when the complainant wishes to obtain documents. Depositions should be used when the complainant's representative needs to have an oral question and answer session with a witness under oath. Depositions should be used sparingly because of the expense involved to the complainant. A motion to compel should be filed with the EEOC administrative judge and served on the agency in the event the agency is refusing to provide the appropriate discovery responses.

The discovery request forms provided in this manual are merely sample discovery requests. You should tailor your request to provide the best information for your complaint. The complainant and his or her representative should read through the interrogatories, requests for admission, and request for production of documents and individualize them to the extent necessary. The complainant and his or her representative should feel free to deviate from the questions provided adding additional questions where appropriate (for example, the complainant's representative should exclude questions that do not seem relevant to the complaint and even some that the complainant is certain he or she already knows the answer the agency will give). The motion to compel should explain why the discovery is calculated to produce or lead to the production of material evidence that is not repetitious of facts or documents information already in the complaint file, is not privileged or restricted information, and is not overly burdensome.

BEFORE THE
EQUAL EMPLOYMENT OPPORTUNITY COMMISSION

NAME OF COMPLAINANT (fill in)	:	
Complainant,	:	
VS.	:	EEOC HEARING CASE NO. (fill in)
AGENCY HEAD (fill in) Title (fill in) Agency Name (fill in) Agency.	:	

INTERROGATORIES

The Complainant, through his/her designated representative, requests that the agency respond to the following written interrogatories under the provisions of 29 C.F.R. 1614. You are required to answer these interrogatories separately and fully in writing, under oath. You are required to respond to these interrogatories no later than fifteen (15) calendar days after receipt of the interrogatories.

All of the following interrogatories shall be continuing in nature until the date of the hearing, and you must supplement your answers as additional information becomes known or available to you:

1. State the name, identity, location, address, and telephone number of any and all witnesses who will testify in person and/or via affidavit or deposition on behalf of the agency at the EEOC administrative hearing.

2. State the relationship of these witnesses to the agency's case.

3. State the name, identity, location, address, and telephone numbers of any and all individuals who witnessed (<u>fill in the key event or events, if appropriate</u>) or who otherwise have information that is relevant to the issue involved in this hearing, but are not listed in response to interrogatory No. 1, above.

[Remember: You are limited to only 30, so choose Sample interrogatories selectively]

4. State any and all qualifications necessary for the position of (fill in the name of the position to which you were not promoted or position for which you were not hired).

5. With respect to each formal complaint of discrimination filed against the agency in (fill in city or state location, unless the agency is relatively small) since January 1, 2005, state the name, (choose as many of the following as you believe are relevant) sex, race, ethnicity, and national origin of the Complainant, the last known address, the date and charge number, the recommended decision of the EEOC administrative judge, if any, and the action, if any, taken by the agency.

6. Describe every lawsuit filed in federal court against the agency involving charges of discrimination in employment since 2005 indicating the disposition of each.

7. State whether, at any time after January 1, 2005, any job or job series (a series of jobs through which employees are sequentially promoted) were restricted to (a certain sex, race, religion, ethnicity – choose whichever categories are appropriate for the complaint), by any rule, procedure, custom or practice, or by any other means or were in fact all one (sex, race, religion, ethnicity) at any time after January 1, 2005.

8. If the answer to interrogatory no. 7 is in the affirmative, further describe each and every situation in which it occurred, including department name and location, the jobs so restricted, whether or not the restrictions were at any time removed or the disparity corrected, and the nature of any rights granted to incumbent minority or female employees.

9. Describe all the requirements for the position(s) of (fill in any job relevant to the complaint), including educational requirements, work experience requirements, recommendations of superiors and/or managers (if so, state the criteria used and indicate the person or persons who made or make such reports), transfer or promotion rights, and other requirements.

10. State whether there have been any changes in requirements for position(s) of (fill in the same jobs you listed in interrogatory no. 9), and describe all such changes.

[Remember: You are limited to only 30, so choose Sample interrogatories selectively]

11. Identify all persons who participated in the decision not to promote the Complainant to the position of (fill in appropriate position) by stating name, job title, address, telephone number, current employment status with the agency, and the reason each gave for the denial.

12. State the method of recruitment for new employees. If there is no particular method, state any and all ways that new employees are notified of open positions at the agency.

13. List by name and location all newspapers and publications in which (fill in name of agency and location) regularly advertises for the filling of job vacancies.

14. List the names, addresses, telephone numbers and current job status at the agency of any and all employees whose job duties included preparing, posting, or administering the preparation or posting of available employment opportunities at (fill in the agency and location) for the period (fill in applicable time period).

15. State the name and address of the person who filled the position of (fill in the name of the position to which you were not promoted or position for which you were not hired).

16. Describe the qualifications of the person you named in interrogatory no. 18 for the position of (fill in the name of the position to which you were not promoted or position for which you were not hired).

17. Identify all persons who held the position of (fill in appropriate position) during the period of (fill in appropriate time period) by stating date of birth, sex/race/national origin/etc., date on which employment commenced, qualifications, prior employment record, starting salary, job ratings, any special training, including whether each person attended any school or course and if so, when and by whom such training was provided.

18. State whether any persons named in the interrogatory no. 20 were promoted or demoted during the Period. If so, state in detail the reasons for such promotion or demotion.

19. Identify all person denied promotion within the agency at (fill in location) who were over 40 years of age at the time of the denial/female/Black/etc. and for each state name, address, position occupied at time of denial, and reason for denial.

[Remember: You are limited to only 30, so choose Sample interrogatories selectively]

20. State for each year, the number of applications, the age/sex/race/etc. of each applicant for employment filed commencing with (fill in appropriate date) and for each year thereafter at the agency in (fill in location), and the action taken with respect to each application.

21. State separately for each year, the number of employees and their age/sex/race/national origin/etc., whether they were discharged, terminated or laid off, including temporary lay-offs, with the agency at (fill in location) commencing with (fill in appropriate date) and for each year thereafter.

22. Does the agency have a policy or procedure for transfer of employees from one department or operational unit to another department or operational unit? If so, please describe.

23. Until the date Complainant ceased employment/was demoted at the agency, were there any complaints relating to his/her ability to do his/her work? If so, please detail and include name, address, telephone number and current employment status with the agency of the person making the complaint.

24. Who was present when Complainant was laid off/discharged/demoted?

25. What was said and by whom to Complainant when he/she was laid off/discharged/demoted?

26. Why did Complainant's employment terminate (or why was Complainant demoted)?

27. On what facts do you rely to prove your denial that Complainant was discharged/demoted/not hired because of his or her race/sex/age/national origin/ethnicity/handicap?

28. Name any and all persons involved in the decision not to accommodate Complainant's handicap at the agency. Please also include their addresses, telephone numbers and current employment status with the agency.

29. On what bases did the agency determine that the Complainant's handicap could not be reasonably accommodated?

30. Describe the essential functions of the position of (fill in position for which Complainant did not receive appropriate accommodation).

[Remember: You are limited to only 30, so choose Sample interrogatories selectively]

31. Describe the different possible accommodations the agency considered in making its determination about accommodating the Complainant and explain the reason(s) for rejection of each alternative accommodation.

32. At any time between (fill in time period surrounding decision not to accommodate Complainant's handicap), were there any funded, vacant positions within the agency at (fill in location)? If so, please name positions and describe essential functions of each position?

33. At any time before Complainant's termination/demotion was Complainant given a "firm choice" between treatment for his or her alleged alcoholic condition and termination/demotion? If so, by whom, when, and what precisely was the Complainant told?

34. State under what circumstances the agency decided not to permit, as a reasonable accommodation, leave for the Complainant to obtain suitable living arrangements and after-care treatment following her hospitalization for alcohol and substance abuse.

35. State what efforts have been made during the past (fill in applicable years) years by the agency to accommodate appellant's alcoholism and substance abuse.

36. Identify all formal training (by dates, length of training, and substance of training) offered to managers of the agency within the last five years that trained on any of the following: identification, accommodation or treatment of troubled employees or employees perceived to have alcohol or substance dependencies.

37. State the names of any and all of Complainant's supervisors or managers who attended any of the training sessions identified in response to interrogatory no. 39, and identify the training session each attended and the date of attendance.

38. Does the agency have any height or weight requirements in effect for the position of (fill in appropriate position)? If so, please describe.

[Remember: You are limited to only 30, so choose Sample interrogatories selectively]

39. Identify specifically all documents, records or other materials used in preparing your answers to or containing information relating to matter raised in the preceding interrogatories, setting forth such information separately for each interrogatory and indicating location and custodian of the document.

40. Regarding the Requests For Admission served upon the agency on (fill in date), for each denial or partial admission, state with specificity the reason the statement cannot be admitted as true. Identify all evidence that would support the reasoning for each denial or partial admission.

____________________________ ______________________________________

Date

Complainant's Representative (fill in)
Address and Phone Number (fill in)

CERTIFICATE OF SERVICE

I hereby certify that a copy of the foregoing was mailed this (fill in) day of (fill in), 20___, to the agency's representative, (fill in name).

____

(Fill in Complainant's Representative's Name)

BEFORE THE
EQUAL EMPLOYMENT OPPORTUNITY COMMISSION

NAME OF COMPLAINANT (fill in) Complainant,	:	
VS.	:	EEOC HEARING CASE NO. (fill in)
AGENCY HEAD (fill in) Title (fill in) Agency Name (fill in) Agency.	:	

REQUESTS FOR ADMISSION

The Complainant, through his/her (choose one) designated representative, requests that the agency admit or deny the following requests for admission under the provisions of 29 C.F.R. 1614. You are required to respond to these requests for production of documents no later than fifteen (15) calendar days after receipt of these requests.

1. Of the (fill in number) employees, only (fill in number) were Black/female, etc., at (fill in location).

2. There were only (fill in number) Black/female, etc. employees in GS positions above (fill in appropriate position grade) out of (fill in number) employees in GS positions above (fill in same position grade as above) at (fill in agency) in (fill in location).

3. There were no Black/women, etc., in supervisory positions from the year (fill in year) to (fill in year) at (fill in agency) in (fill in location).

4. Only (fill in number) minority employees received promotions in the twelve month period from (fill in appropriate date) to (fill in appropriate date) at (fill in agency) in (fill in location).

(Remember the limit of 30 Admissions)

5. The first Black/female, etc. was employed by (fill in agency) in (fill in location) in the year (fill in appropriate year).

6. No Black/female, etc. was ever a member of a promotion panel which rated Complainant for promotional vacancies for which he/she applied within (fill in agency).

7. (Fill in Complainant's supervisor's name) never selected a Black/female to fill a position at the GS-(fill in grade) or above during any of the times he/she served as (fill in title of supervisor) at (fill in agency).

8. Each of the following Blacks/females applied unsuccessfully on one or more occasions for promotional vacancies within (fill in agency name) agency between (fill in appropriate year) and (fill in appropriate year).

(List Names).

9. (Fill in name of supervisor to receive EEO Officer recommendations) received the recommendations of (fill in EEO Officer's name), EEO Officer dated (fill in appropriate date), regarding the discrimination complaint of Complainant.

10. (Fill in supervisor's name) was asked by (fill in EEO Director's name), EEO Director to assure that Items (fill in recommendations that EEO office made to agency to ensure equal employment for Complainant) be given priority attention.

11. Complainant and (fill in appropriate name) have had the same job code and job title or classification since (fill in appropriate date), i.e. (fill in position).

12. When (fill in appropriate name) and the Complainant were hired as (fill in name of position), they were not required to meet different requirements in terms of job skills or qualifications for their jobs.

13. The difference in compensation/wages paid to (fill in appropriate name) and the Complainant is not explained by seniority, skill, effort or responsibility required to perform the job, or working conditions.

14. Complainant is a "handicapped person" as defined by 20 C.F.R. Section 1614.203 due to alcohol and substance abuse addictions.

(Remember the limit of 30 Admissions)

15. Complainant is a "qualified handicapped person" as defined by 29 C.F.R. Section 1614.203 due to alcohol and substance abuse addictions.

16. Complainant was not give a "firm choice" between disciplinary action and treatment, prior to the agency's disciplinary action.

17. Complainant successfully completed the alcohol and substance abuse treatment program on (fill in appropriate date).

18. Complainant attempted to return to work at the agency on (fill in appropriate date) and was denied return.

______________________________ ______________________________

Date Complainant's Representative (fill in)
Address and Phone Number (fill in)

CERTIFICATE OF SERVICE

I hereby certify that a copy of the foregoing was mailed this (fill in) day of (fill in), 20___, to the agency's representative, (fill in)______________________.

____

(Fill in Complainant's Representative's Name)

BEFORE THE
EQUAL EMPLOYMENT OPPORTUNITY COMMISSION

NAME OF COMPLAINANT (fill in) Complainant,	:	
VS.	:	EEOC HEARING CASE NO. (fill in)
AGENCY HEAD (fill in) Title (fill in) Agency.	:	

REQUESTS FOR PRODUCTION OF DOCUMENTS

The Complainant, through his/her (choose one) designated representative, requests that the agency produce the following documents or things for inspection or copying under the provisions of 29 C.F.R. 1614. You are required to respond to these requests for production of documents no later than fifteen (15) calendar days after receipt of these requests.

1. All written statements made by any individual or documents relevant to the allegations contained in the complaint.

2. All writings or documents that the agency intends to use at the hearing.

3. Any and all work performance evaluations of the Complainant.

4. Any and all writings or documents pertaining to the reduction in force instituted from the period (fill in the applicable time period).

5. Any and all writings or documents pertaining to the Complainant's performance of his or her job duties with the agency.

6. Any and all writings or documents pertaining to the selection of the individual for the position of (fill in applicable position) over the other applicants at the agency at (fill in appropriate location).

7. Any and all employment applications filed at the agency at (fill in appropriate location) from (fill in appropriate date) to the present.

8. Any and all employment application forms used at the agency at (fill in appropriate location) from 2005 to the present.

9. Any and all personnel files on past and present people in the position of (fill in appropriate position) from 2005 to the present at the agency in (fill in appropriate location).

10. Any and all manuals, guidelines, written memoranda pertaining to advertisement for, application, selection, and promotion for the position of (fill in appropriate position) at the agency.

11. Any and all confidential files kept on each person in the position of (fill in appropriate position) at the agency at (fill in appropriate location).

12. Any and all current agency regulations and orders, instructions, or other directives relating to the treatment and rehabilitation/accommodation of individuals employed by the agency afflicted with alcoholism.

13. Any and all manager's handbooks and guides issues by the agency containing guidance on employee discipline.

14. Any and all manager's handbooks and guides issued by the agency containing guidance on the identification, and/or treatment, and/or counseling of employees suspected or known to suffer from alcohol or drug addiction problems.

15. Any and all records maintained by the agency (including medical records) concerning the treatment and counseling of Complainant's alcohol and drug problems.

_______________________________   _______________________________

Date

Complainant's Representative (fill in)
Address and Phone Number (fill in)

CERTIFICATE OF SERVICE

I hereby certify that a copy of the foregoing was mailed this (fill in) day of (fill in) ____________, 20__, to the Agency's Representative, (fill in)_________.

____

(Fill in Complainants Representative Name

BEFORE THE
EQUAL EMPLOYMENT OPPORTUNITY COMMISSION

NAME OF COMPLAINANT (fill in) Complainant,	:	
VS.	:	EEOC HEARING CASE NO. (fill in)
AGENCY HEAD (fill in) Title (fill in) Agency.	:	

MOTION TO COMPEL RESPONSE TO WRITTEN INTERROGATORIES

The Complainant, through his or her designated representative moves that the EEOC Administrative Judge issue an order compelling the agency to respond to the Complainant's (fill in date the interrogatories were dated) Interrogatories.

The Interrogatories (a copy of which is attached) were served on the agency on (fill in date). The agency has not filed objections to them within the appropriate fifteen calendar day period/has objected to interrogatory numbers on the following bases:

(Fill in appropriate interrogatory numbers and agency's bases for objection).

The information sought by these interrogatories is calculated to produce or lead to the production of material evidence. (Fill in explanation specific to the interrogatories).

The interrogatories are not repetitious of facts or documents already in the complaint file because (fill in explanation specific to the Interrogatories).

The interrogatories do not seek privileged or restricted information because (fill in explanation specific to the interrogatories).

The interrogatories are not overly burdensome because of (fill in explanation specific to the interrogatories).

CERTIFICATE OF SERVICE

I hereby certify that a copy of the foregoing was mailed this ______ day of ______________, to the agency's representative, __________________________.

______________ ____________________________________

Date (Fill in Complainants Representative Name

Address and Phone Number

FEDERAL EEO COMPLAINT PROCESSING THROUGH THE AGENCY EEO COUNSELOR

A federal employee has to file his or her complaint through their agency EEO counseling process. This will be the first critical stage of filing your complaint.

Many agency EEO counselors will appear to be impartial when you first contact them but they only befriend you to minimize your complaint. I was naïve to think that federal agencies follow strict laws that adhere to discrimination complaints. But I was dead wrong and it resulted in my complaint being dismissed for my lack of knowledge of their bias against me. They are "wolves in sheep's clothing."

The federal agency has a duty and legal right to follow the law but they do not. My case suffered because of repeated violations of the law. I have talked with and counseled many people in my community who have experienced the same problems. One of the reasons they are untrustworthy is because they feel their loyalty is to the agency and not the law.

One area of your complaint processing is the critical stage of articulating your complaint. The agency EEO director is supposed to help you articulate your complaint by law if you are not represented by your local grievance process (union). I talked briefly about this area of your complaint in an earlier section.

I was not a member of the local union and I needed the help of the EEO counselor to correctly file my complaint. My agency vehemently refused to assist me in articulating my complaint and I ultimately had to file a complaint against them. If I had not done this, I would have never won my complaint. If they refuse to help you and you don't complain, you will not win your complaint. The agency director will dismiss your complaint and believe that you did not request assistance.

My agency violated the law at every stage of my complaint and I had to report the continuous violations and have EEOC monitor that they were complying with the law. Evidence of my agencies failures is included in this course manual.

The EEO counselor has a duty to inform you on how you want to proceed on your complaint. You will have a choice to file your case of discrimination with the local EEO office or the local grievance procedure. Your election will be made with the EEO counselor during the first meeting. To be more informed on the election process, you should read Code of Federal Regulations, 29 C.F.R. S1614.105. This section is not long and you should be very knowledgeable of this section.

Before 1995, many agency EEO directors and counselors were using complainants' ignorance of the law to dismiss their complaints.

One of the reasons I filed a complaint against my agency EEO director was that I knew I had the right to be informed in the federal process according to federal administrative law.

The Federal Sector Certification Form to inform you on how to proceed should be similar to the following.

CERTIFICATION

I, _________________________ (aggrieved person), hereby certify that _____________________________ (EEO counselor) has informed me of the possible applicability of 5 U.S.C. 7121 (d) to my allegation(s) of discrimination and has communicated to me the substance of Title 29 C.F.R. S1614.301 and has furnished me a copy of this notice. I understand that the original or a copy of this notice will be made a part of the EEO counselor's report as evidence of the EEO counselor's compliance with Title 29 C.F.R. S1614.105.

______________________	______________________________________
(Date)	(Aggrieved Person)
______________________	______________________________________
(EEO Counselor)	(Aggrieved Person's Representative)

NON-FEDERAL PROCESSING OF EEO COMPLAINTS

Non-federal employees, meaning employees in the private sector, are also required to file a complaint through their area or district office.

You must file a charge within 45 days of the date of the charge. After serving the charge on the opposing party, EEOC will conduct an informal investigation which is not binding on either party. After completing the investigation, EEOC is directed by statute to determine "reasonable cause." If "reasonable cause" is determined, EEOC is directed to informally resolve the charge through mediation. If mediation produces an acceptable solution by both parties, then EEOC will dismiss the complaint. If no acceptable solutions is produced through mediation, then EEOC is empowered to file a suit on behalf of the complainant.

If no "reasonable cause" is determined, then the complainant has the right to file a suit on his or her behalf. The complainant has 90 days to file a complaint in its appropriate court to adjudicate the charge. EEOC's determination of no "reasonable cause" does not limit review in court as any other civil complaint would proceed.

Non-federal employees do not have a lengthy administrative procedure that follows them to court as afforded to federal employees. But because of federal regulation not closely practiced in private companies, discrimination is usually more overt and openly practiced.

Compensatory and punitive damage awards far exceed what is allowable in the federal sector.

Employees in the private sector are empowered to have a very strong complaint in the beginning stage. The private companies may appeal the court's judgment but in federal court the court's judgment is final in accordance with federal laws.

LEARNING THE POLICIES AND PROCEDURES OF YOUR EMPLOYER

You must take the time to learn the policies and procedures of your employer to fully know your rights as an employee.

Many of us as employees briefly read the policies and procedures when we are hired in on a job. With the daily routine of your jobs, you cannot take for granted that you still know all of the information you have read. Among the many reasons that you should know this information is that many management officials do not know their own personnel policies and procedures. Your case can be easily won if your employer violates the company or agency's policies and procedures.

If this information is not readily available to you at your office or if you have been terminated, immediately request all policies and procedures in writing to be available to you.

When your complaint comes before the Equal Employment Opportunity procedure, request all EEO guidelines from your office, state, and the Equal Employment Opportunity Commission in Washington. If your employer learns that you do not know your rights, they will use this against you. Your right to counsel from an attorney will be given to you during your complaint stage.

RECOGNIZING SUBTLE FORMS OF DISCRIMINATION, DISPARATE TREATMENT AND UNWANTED ADVANCES OF SEXUAL HARASSMENT

When you become a new employee of a company or receive a promotion, there will always be someone watching you from a distance to determine whether they will like you or not. We cannot control how other people feel about us and we have to learn how to deal with resentment the best way we can. You as an individual will have to learn what is best for you and know the difference between right and wrong. Eventually, one of those people who has been watching you from a distance will become your superior. They won't like you because they have never had the courage to improve their self-esteem.

Many people will suggest to you to play the game, politic or get them to like you in some other way. Politicking has become a major survival tactic used by employees who desperately want to succeed. No one can tell another person what to do to survive in the job market because it is a dog eat dog world. I personally don't believe in politicking because it won't make you feel good about yourself once your career is over. The best advice I received from a retired person when I first entered the job market was to be yourself. But if a person naturally has a gift to successfully politic and receives no mental problems from it, then I say play the game to the best of your ability. Also, you probably know that politicking is the nice way to say brown-nosing!

Sexual harassment is about power and control of another person. Many people who practice sexual harassment enjoy the feeling of control more than the sexual nature of the experience. Sexual harassers may be women with power over men as well as men with power over women. In the last few years, the Supreme Court has articulated the level of harm that must exist in a sexual harassment claim to succeed. Harris v. Forklift. The Supreme Court also articulated the pretext for intentional discrimination in the case of Mary's Honor Center v. Hicks.

Identifying sexual harassment will be no problem at all for someone who will experience unwanted sexual advances which creates a hostile environment for them. In cases of sexual harassment, never go out alone with a potential victimizer. If you are seen frequently out to lunch or on other occasions, it will make you look as if you were a willing participant in whatever action you say happened. We all remember that Anita Hill made her mistake by following Clarence Thomas from one job to another. Her actions would not allow a case of sexual harassment to be probably won. Sexual harassment cases can be some of the easiest cases to win in civil court.

The Equal Employment Opportunity Commission states what constitutes sexual harassment as "unwanted sexual advances, requests for sexual favors and other verbal or physical conduct of a sexual nature constitutes sexual harassment. When submission to or rejection of this conduct explicitly or implicitly affects an individual's employment, unreasonably interferes with an individual's employment, unreasonably interferes with an individual's work performance or creates an intimidating, hostile or offensive work environment."

In 1986, the United States Supreme Court ruled that a Washington, D.C. bank employee, a black female, was a victim of sexual harassment in a landmark decision case. She accused her supervisor of fondling her in front of other employees, following her into the ladies room, and even raping her on several occasions. In the same year, an Ohio woman won 3.1 million dollars in a judgment against an employer who asked her to perform oral sex or lose her job.

I would also suggest that a new female employee wear conservative clothes that don't suggest that you have an abnormal sexual appetite. Your victimizer will certainly bring up your clothing if it is not appropriate.

Sexual harassment is not experienced exclusively by female employees. Many men experience sexual harassment from their female bosses. Our society has never taken a close look at offenses to men by women. But, in the job market where there are many happily married men with families, persistence by an overbearing female boss can be a real problem.

You will notice subtle forms of discrimination, for example, not being informed of meetings, over-judging your work, and other forms of bias treatment in the office if you refuse some superior's sexual advances. The best way to counter these subtle forms of disparate treatment if they occur is to closely watch and document the treatment of others. You should also be assertive with responses telling your supervisors that you have noticed differences in treatment of other employees. If you wait until harassment or disparate treatment builds up, you may not be able to address the issues calmly and may resort to irrational behavior. You do not want to give your superiors justifiable reasons to terminate your employment.

In age discrimination cases, we are finding more employers are replacing older workers with less-experienced younger workers. Employers are doing this because they can pay younger workers a salary that is considerably less than the older worker's salaries. Age discrimination cases have not been litigated to the extent of race and sex discrimination cases. These cases can be won by individual complaints but they are more likely to be won easier by group class complaints. When you compile information against your employer, it would be best to keep your information at home and not the office. You do not want to run the risk of having your information exposed to others. Your employer may learn of your case before you file it. Your employer should only learn that you are filing a case against them when you have gathered all of your information.

The EEO definition of illegal sexual harassment included the three basic types of sexual harassment, hostile environment, and sexual favoritism. Sexual harassment occurs when a supervisor or someone else with authority over an employee makes unwelcome sexual advances and states or implies that the employee must submit if the employee wants to receive or keep a job benefit. Hostile environment sexual harassment occurs when an employee is subjected to unwanted sexual conduct based on sex that is so pervasive or severe that it creates an abusive or hostile work environment. Sexual favoritism and sexual harassment will occur when there is a pervasive workplace pattern of rewarding employees who consensually submit to sexual demands, which then penalize those who do not submit or were not target of the demands.

RECOGNIZING RACIAL, ETHNIC, RELIGIOUS, AND CULTURAL HARASSMENT

It is very unfortunate that in many ways we have returned to some of the ways groups of people were treated in the 1960's. Many of us thought those days were long gone and America was ready to lead other countries to a new world of humanitarianism. But it is sad to see in many parts of the country many people are not practicing decent humanity towards each other.

There are many people on many jobs that are bringing their bigotry to work as a form of recreation. Some of the people will tell you that they think it is no harm done and it is all in great fun. I don't have to tell you what may be offensive to you.

The best way to deal with these forms of harassment when you first encounter it is to not let the alarm go off in your head so that you can not think. You should report it to your superior when you see it and wait to see what happens.

In most cases, nothing will be done if you have an "ol' boy" network in place. If this is the case, you will have to develop a strategy to deal with it and file a complaint if it persists. If you see material that is offensive on the bulletin boards or in offices, make a copy of it and place it back where you found it. Do not let anyone see you placing this material back where you found it because you may be perceived as the culprit. If it comes across your desk, I would make a copy of it and keep the copy placed on your desk. There are probably many other copies floating around. You will not need to report every piece of material individually to your supervisor if you have already told him or her you have witnessed offensive material in the job environment. If they take your informal complaint seriously, then someone should be secretly investigating it. You have given them the opportunity to correct the problem. If this material is directed at you personally, then you should do your own investigating after you have reported it to your supervisor. If you are in a non-sensitive working area (ex. non-secret, non-top secret) and you have a person or persons making derogatory comments to you personally, you should try to record their conversations. There are many small pocket-size tape recorders with hi-gain microphones that will be able to pick up their conversations. If you have an hour long tape in it, simply turn it on and keep it on in the presence of your suspect.

You should tell others who you know that you can trust to witness some of the derogatory incidents that you encounter. The person that you tell about these incidents must be someone that you really know that you can trust. You may have a hard time finding someone that you can trust because many people are like chameleons in that they adapt to everyone who is around them to try to get ahead in an unhealthy environment.

I strongly believe these types of cases can be proven very easily if you gather enough information before you go formal. Most agencies and companies are not going to thoroughly investigate on their own to build a case for you. If you think they are, then you will put yourself in a no-win situation.

The most important thing one can do to build your case is to keep a diary or notes on calendars noting the negatives one experiences on their job. Make sure you keep the time, date, and opposing person of the negative actions you receive. You should also watch or be aware of your co.-workers progress if you feel that they are advancing in training and promotions more than you.

RECOGNIZING AGE DISCRIMINATION CASES

We have all heard the new corporate term downsizing. The companies say that it is a cost effective way to run their companies in a lean and competitive way in the new millennium. No one will argue that a company should have at its top agenda, saving money. But if a company is making enormous profits every year and people are laid off or forced to resign, maybe there is another problem the company has.

Many companies feel that it is more profitable to employ younger workers and let older workers go. Older workers usually have attained big salaries and companies feel they are liabilities rather than assets. If you are a middle age worker, you should always look for the signs of age discrimination because it may affect you before you know it is coming. Middle management and top management employees have often received great praise for their jobs, received hefty bonuses and other perks the company has to offer for being near the top. So when the same top management tells you that your job is being eliminated and they cannot find a place for you, your world will begin to tumble down. You will be frightened and panic-stricken to the point of immobility.

Never think that you have it made and you are financially secure when you work for someone else. This can be far from reality. In the real world, the person at the top is usually insecure and thinks that he or she will be knocked off the top by you. He or she would rather see you leave than deal with the unknown factors in the future.

So how will you recognize age discrimination if it happens to you? Age discrimination cases can be some of the easiest discrimination cases to win if you know the signs and the law against age discrimination. Many times older employees are forced to resign and younger employees are transferred to other jobs when downsizing occurs in companies. Some of the more obvious signs are learned when you hear talk like, "We are going to have to get some young blood in here," or "Some of these old heads are going to have to go." Whatever you hear, keep documentation of negative connotation to age so that you will be prepared when you file your complaint.

Many older workers who face age discrimination cannot defend themselves because they have felt they were a part of the system. When they begin to feel they have been betrayed, their self-esteem will begin to crumble. Most of the time they will settle for a modest severance package than fight for their rights. But if you are prepared to take on an age discrimination case, fight it until you prevail.

DISCRIMINATION AGAINST INDIVIDUALS WITH DISABILITIES

Many people with disabilities prefer to be called "individuals with disabilities" rather than "handicapped," the Rehabilitation Act of 1973, the act that protects federal employees with disabilities.

The Rehabilitation Act of 1973 (Section 501, 29 U.S.C. 791) requires agencies to reasonably accommodate the needs of qualified federal employees and applicants with a known "handicapping condition." The Rehabilitation Act may require the agency to change or adjust the position or the workplace to enable the individual to perform the essential functions of the position.

The employee or applicant must satisfy two requirements to receive the protection of the Rehabilitation Act. First, he or she must be a qualified person, as the act defines that term, second, the employee or applicant must have a handicapping condition, as defines that term.

The term qualified person means a person who, with or without reasonable accommodation, can perform the essential functions of the position without endangering the health and safety of the individual or others. In addition, the individual must, depending on the type of appointing authority being used, (1) meet the experience and/or educational requirements (which may include passing a written test) of the position in question, or (2) meet the criteria for appointment under one of the special appointing authorities for handicapped persons.

A person with a handicapping condition is one who: (1) has a physical or mental impairment which substantially limits one or more of such person's major life activities (for example, walking, standing, or lifting); or (2) has a record of such impairment (that is, has a history of, or has been classified as having an impairment); or (3) is regarded as having such an impairment (for example, conditions people mistakenly believe are limiting, such as a facial disfigurement, or an involuntary head jerk).

There are many different impairments that may qualify as handicapping conditions. Examples include: HIV and AIDS, alcohol and drug addictions, (the person must have stopped his or her use of illegal drugs); nervous breakdown; diabetes, carpal tunnel disease, sickle cell anemia; deafness, blindness, and wheelchair bound. A disability is an impairment that substantially limits a major life function.

There are many examples of reasonable accommodation the agency may provide. The individual who qualifies for protection under the Rehabilitation Act should bear in mind, however, that the agency has the right to choose the accommodation it wishes to provide, as long as the accommodation enables the individual to perform the essential functions of the job. The employer or applicant should provide as much input as possible to assist in the decision over what accommodation the agency should make, since the employee or applicant may know best the accommodation that will enable him or her to perform most efficiently on the job.

Examples of reasonable accommodation include: providing a reader or sign language interpreter (for the blind or deaf); making the workplace readily accessible (building a ramp, changing the desk height, modifying toilet facilities, providing cups at the water fountain); restructuring the job or reassigning some of the marginal job functions; redesigning or adapting equipment (providing instructions in Braille, providing a shoulder rest); and, as a last resort, reassigning the employee to a funded, vacant position.

Alcoholism is considered a handicapping condition, and therefore warrants reasonable accommodation. For example, if there is reason to suspect that an employee may be an alcoholic, the employee may be referred to employee assistance counseling and be granted leave if he or she enters a rehabilitation program. However, there have been important recent changes in the area of the law. The law used to require that no disciplinary action may be taken against a qualified alcoholic employee until the employee has been given a "firm choice," rehabilitation or discipline. Unfortunately, recent decisions by the EEOC and the MSPB eliminates the agency's obligation to provide a "firm choice" to alcoholic employees prior to imposing discipline for disability-related conduct. Therefore, agencies are no longer obligated to provide accommodation to an employee who raises alcoholism for the first time as an excuse for misconduct or performance deficiencies which warrant removal.

In the case of Johnson v. Babbitt, EEOC Petition No. 03940100 (March 28, 1996), the EEOC determined that while agencies are clearly obligated to reasonably accommodate qualified employees who are disabled by alcoholism, they are no longer required to provide the reasonable accommodation of a firm choice under Section 501 of the Rehabilitation Act. Agencies may now hold alcoholic employees to the same requirements for acceptable conduct and performance to which it holds all other employees. However, the Johnson decision still requires agencies to accommodate qualified employees who are disabled by alcoholism, and it specifically recognizes that a flexible work schedule or leave to accommodate an employee's treatment is still required as one form of reasonable accommodation. Furthermore, while a firm choice is no longer mandated by law, agencies may continue to provide firm choice as an option.

An MSPB decision, Kimble v. Navy, MSPB Docket No. SF-0752-95-0404-1-1, June 11, 1996, adopted the EEOC's ruling in Johnson and paved the way for agencies to formulate individual firm choice offers to employees on a case-by-case basis.

The new decisions eliminate the "firm choice" doctrine from all future EEOC and MSPB cases and have also influenced the courts. In Burch v. Coca-Cola, Co., No. 95-10990, employers are neither required to provide a firm choice between treatment and discipline nor required to provide a retroactive accommodation by excusing pre-accommodation misconduct.

The requirements for establishing a violation of the Rehabilitation Act are basically the same as other disparate treatment discrimination complaints. In order to establish a violation of the Rehabilitation Act, the complainant must first establish a prima facie case. This means that the complainant must show by a preponderance of the evidence that: (1) he or she has a handicapping condition; (2) he or she is a qualified person; (3) an adverse employment action occurred; and (4) the handicapping condition caused the conduct or performance about which the agency complains. Once the complaint establishes a prima facie case, the agency must articulate a legitimate, non-handicap reason for its action. The agency may also attempt to demonstrate that accommodation would impose an "undue hardship" on the agency. "Undue hardship" is a very difficult standard for the government to meet. The complainant must then show that the agency's reasons are pretexual, and/or that the accommodation would be reasonable.

The process of filing a Rehabilitation Act complaint is the same as that for any other discrimination complaint. For instance, the victim could file a complaint with the Equal Employment Office and then raise the allegation before an administrative law judge of the Merit Systems Protection Board.

Under the 1991 Civil Rights Act, if your agency intentionally discriminates against you and you are a qualified person with a handicapping condition, you may be able to recover up to $300,000 in compensatory damages plus back pay and attorney's fees. Typical forms of compensatory damages may include economic damages (such as medical costs, lost benefits, and other "out of pocket" expenses) and non-economic damages (such as pain and suffering and emotional distress). However, there is an exception. If the agency makes a good faith attempt to reasonably accommodate a qualified person with a handicapping condition, compensatory damages are not available.

Since 1973, federal employees with disabilities have been protected against discrimination by virtue of the Rehabilitation Act of 1973. However, the Rehabilitation Act of 1973 only protected federal employees, or private sector employees. Congress attempted to remedy this disparity between federal and private sector employees by passing into law the American with Disabilities Act of 1990. The ADA was based in large part on the Rehabilitation Act of 1973. The ADA provided protection for state and local government employees as the majority of private sector employee. Federal employees are not covered by the ADA since they are still covered by the Rehabilitation Act. Since the ADA was passed into law, many courts have interpreted passages of the ADA. The court interpretations of the ADA have been applied to the Rehabilitation Act as well. Therefore, these court rulings apply and have modified the rights of federal employees.

ESTABLISHING A PRIMA FACIE CASE OF DISCRIMINATION AND SEXUAL HARASSMENT

The initial burden is on the complainant to establish a prima facie case of discrimination. The complainant must show that he or she is a victim of disparate treatment and that they would not have been treated differently if it had not been for their minority status.

When the agency or corporation receives your complaint, they will articulate some reason for the action taken against you was not discriminatory. The best thing for you to know is where the defense is headed so that you can counter it. You will have to show that the reasons articulated were false. What is meant by a prima facie case? The answer is that you should have evidence as by itself would establish a complaint of discrimination or stand against the defense of the agency or corporation if the evidence is fact.

One of the most significant cases of racial discrimination that should be cited is the case of McDonnell-Douglas v. Green. This case set forth an example for which other similar cases can follow. The specifics of this case was in the hiring policy of McDonnell Douglas. Green, a black male who had previously worked for the company, was laid off. While he was laid off, he participated in an illegal demonstration against the company with other workers. When the company called back the workers who were laid off, the white workers who also participated in the illegal demonstration were re-hired. Green was subsequently not re-hired with the company.

The Supreme Court described the case as that the complainant in a Title VII case of discrimination must carry the initial burden of establishing a prima facie case of racial discrimination under this statue. The complainant must show that he is in a minority status and that the complainant applied for and was qualified for the job the employer was continually seeking applicants. Although, despite his qualifications, he was not re-hired and the position remained opened by the employer seeking other applicants from persons of complainant's qualifications.

The Supreme Court further stated that Green had established his case. He was a black mechanic at McDonnell-Douglas who had performed his job satisfactorily. The job remained open after the company refused to re-hire him. In this case, the complainant did not have to show that the company deliberately discriminated against him but that the adverse re-employment decision demonstrated an irrational basis. Green also showed that there were other whites who demonstrated against the company and were re-hired. The Supreme Court ruled that the decision to not re-hire Green was discriminatory.

If you are trying to prove that your employer discriminated against you in not promoting you, the case of <u>Petit v. U.S.</u> makes a prima facie case by showing that he belongs to a racial minority and that he was qualified for a promotion. Petit was not promoted and the supervisory employees responsible for decision making discriminated against members of the minority status. In the case of <u>Abrams v. Johnson</u> make a prima facie case for failure of the company to promote in that she was a black female employee and that she was passed over twice in favor of a lower rated white employee and in favor of a less experienced white employee. Abrams proved her case by using a subjective evaluation method.

In the case of Taylor v. Safeway Stores, Inc. the complainant makes a prima facie case by showing that he was discharged because he was a black male. Taylor also proved that the person who discharged him had a history of discriminating against blacks.

Class complaints involving discrimination can be in some ways very similar to individual cases of discrimination but also may be very different in other ways. If you as a group are pursuing a class action complaint it would be to your advantage to contact the Equal Employment Opportunity Commission on laws governing these types of complaints.

Some of these cases involving class complaints are cited for prior knowledge in pursuing these complaints.

In Griggs v. Duke Power Company, the company segregated all black employees in one of five departments. After the Title VII civil rights law was passed, the blacks were permitted to transfer to other departments but only if they had high school diplomas or had passed two standardized tests. The white employees were not held to these qualifications. The Supreme Court ruled that all employees must receive the same treatment and not disparate treatment.

In Quarles v. Philip Morris, Inc., the theory of present effects of past discrimination was challenged. Up until six months after the passing of the civil rights law, Philip Morris had maintained a segregated job environment. The blacks maintained that all black departments were made up of all low paying jobs. The white departments were made up of all high paying jobs. The whites were also promoted on the basis of a seniority system. The court found that the company's present system of departmental seniority violated the Title VII civil rights law.

In the case of Phillip v. Martin Marietta Corporation, the company had a history of not hiring women with pre-school age children. The lower courts had previously upheld the company's decision citing that the law did not intend for a broad view of sex discrimination. The Supreme Court rejected the narrow view and stated that gender cases hold the same view as race discrimination cases.

The case of McDonald v. Santa Fe Railroad Transportation Company involved a claim by white employees of equal treatment. Several white employees had been discharged for stealing materials from a company truck. The white employees contended that a black employee, who was also involved in stealing, was not discharged. The lower courts dismissed the white employees' case citing that they were not entitled to protection under Title VII. The Supreme Court overruled their decision and subsequently ruled that white employees are entitled to the same protection as blacks under Title VII.

In the case of Slack v. Havens, black employees in an assembly department of the company were ordered to clean windows and walls in their department. The only white employee in the assembly department was transferred out to another department until the cleaning had been done. The transferred white employee was replaced with a black employee from a different department to assist in the cleaning. The blacks showed that they had established a prima facie case of racial discrimination because the supervisor only assigned black employees to do the housekeeping duties. The black employees also produced a statement that cemented their case made by the supervisor. The supervisor made a statement prior to the case being filed saying, "Colored folks should stay in their places... Colored folk were hired to clean because they clean better."

In establishing your case of discrimination or sexual harassment you will need to explain a predisposition for management or your employer's behavior. In a discrimination case you might want to find out if your employer has had a history of racist behavior or disparate treatment toward members of your class. In a sexual harassment case you should try to find out if there has been sexist behavior from the alleged discriminator in the past. In cases of reprisal you may have filed a discrimination case in the past or just had contact with an EEO counselor about concerns of yours. Whatever the case, you want to try to find out if there has been any other employee who has had similar problems of your nature.

The three types of illegal sexual harassment have different requirements for establishing a case. To establish a quid pro quo sexual harassment case, an employee must show that:

1. The harasser is someone with authority over the employee.
2. The harasser made unwelcome requests for sexual favors from or unwelcome sexual advances toward the employee.
3. The harasser stated or implied that the employee must submit to receive or keep a job, promotion or other benefits of the job.
4. The employee suffered economic harm or tangible work detriment for refusing sexual advances.

To establish a case of hostile environment sexual harassment, the employee must show that:

1. A supervisor, coworker, or non-employee over whom the employer has or could have control.

2. Subjected the employee to unwelcome sexual conduct based on the employee's sex.
3. The harassment was sufficiently pervasive or severe.
4. So as to create a sexually hostile work environment.

To establish a case of sexual favoritism or sexual harassment, the employee must show that:

1. There is a widespread practice of granting job benefits to employees who engage in consensual sexual activity with supervisors.
2. The supervisors then penalize those employees who do not support, or who are not requested to engage in the sexual conduct.

Both women and men who believe they have been penalized or are presently being penalized because of the pervasive sexual favoritism may establish a case of illegal sexual favoritism.

On June 25, 1993, in St. Mary's Honor Center v. Hicks, 509 U.S. 502, the Supreme Court altered the requirements for establishing a disparate treatment case. Unfortunately, the alteration may make it substantially more difficult for complainants to establish disparate treatment cases. As with most Supreme Court shifts in analysis, the precise definition of this alteration will develop over years of lower courts interpretation. However, it appears that the complainant must still prove a prima facie case and the employer must then produce a legitimate, nondiscriminatory reason to justify rejecting the complainant, just as in McDonnell Douglas v. Green. But now, employer's offered reason was unworthy of belief. Some judges may now require that the complainant show additional evidence that the true reason for the employment decision was discrimination.

Under the Hicks modification, it seems that complainants must now: (1) produce direct statements by the agency of discriminatory reasons for making the employment decision (evidence that is very hard to come by); or (2) disprove all possible reasons (and not simply those the agency offers at trial) for the employment decision other than discrimination; or (3) prove that the agency's defense was not applied alike (such as between the complainant and the male employees and the only difference between the complainant and the male employees (or white employees, for ways for the complainant to prove that the agency's offered reasons for the decision was untrue). This is the standard McDonnell Douglas analysis, without the circumstances, thus federal employees may find greater sympathy in the agency complaint process with its access to EEOC administrative judges about one year after filing a complaint, than the analysis available in the federal courts were Hicks rules.

SEXUAL ORIENTATION

Sexual orientation is currently not protected by Title VII of the 1964 Civil Rights Act or any act which amends Title VII. However, in 1998, an Executive Order No. 11478 be amended to prohibit discrimination in the federal government on the basis of sexual orientation to the extent permitted by law. As a result, discrimination on the basis of sexual orientation is illegal but there is no EEO process by which to enforce one's right. Enforcement of one's right to be free of sexual orientation discrimination is available through your union.

THE SUPREME COURT CHANGED THE RULES FOR SEXUAL HARASSMENT COMPLAINTS IN 1998

Sexual harassment cases skyrocketed in the 1990's against employers in private industry, the local, state and federal governments. Many of these cases came out before the allegations of sexual harassment began to surface around the President of the United States. The allegations directed at him certainly helped open flood gates of complaints from employees to suggest that no employer is too large to sue or above the law.

We all will never forget when we first began to hear the explicit details in the case of Anita Hill's charges against now Chief Justice Clarence Thomas in his infamous senate confirmation hearing. These allegations explained to us how harsh and indecent one can be toward the opposite sex with more power. Many women certainly knew of the pain and stigmas attached to a person being sexually harassed with nor forum to address his or her complaint.

In today's sex choice society, it is not uncommon to hear of cases of sexual harassment by the same sex.

In the summer of 1998, a jury in Ocala, Florida, awarded more than $1 million dollars to a woman who said she was grabbed, prodded, and kissed by her female boss in a department store. The complainant said that her supervisor reduced her hours after she refused her advances. The complaint also states that the department store management did nothing to stop the supervisor's advances for three years prior to filing her suit in January 1997.

The Supreme Court established new rules for sexual harassment in the summer of 1998. These new rules clearly make it easier for a person who has been sexually harassed win a lawsuit. The Supreme Court also allowed for employers to have a better defense against complaints if they have effective programs in place educating against sexual harassment in the workplace. Employers must also be aggressive in punishing those found guilty of sexually harassing.

In the July 6, 1998 issue of The U.S. News and World Report, writer Marianne Lavelle did an excellent job in clarifying the new rules for sexual harassment versus the old ones.

Ms. Lavelle states in her article:

What is Harassment?

- Old Rule: To prove harassment, a worker has to show that because she resisted sexual advances she was punished in terms of salary, assignments, or promotions.
- New rule: It can count as harassment even if an employee is otherwise treated well.

The article also gives note to the case of Bullington Industries v. Ellerth in Responsible for the harasser's actions.

- New Rule: The manager can be held responsible for a harasser's actions – unless a company has a strong system of dealing with problems.

The case that changed this rule involved a Boca Raton lifeguard Beth Faragher, now a lawyer, sued the city of Boca Raton for sexual harassment endured by herself and at least seven other female lifeguards. Ms. Faragher stated that she and the other women worked for men who would request sexual favors; grab them by the breast and buttocks, try to break in on their showers, and refer to them regularly by vulgar epithets. Faragher and others spoke to one police lieutenant about the behavior, but he did not believe that is was his place to act on workplace complaints. The city of Boca Raton argued that the city shouldn't be held liable because it had a clear policy against harassment. Kimberly Ellerth alleged she had spent much of her year-long employment as marketing assistant in the mattress-fabric division fending off passes by her supervisor, "Are you wearing shorter skirts yet, Kim, because it would make your job a whole lot easier," he is to have said. But she was never punished and, in fact, had received one promotion. The Supreme Court ruled that sexual harassment is defined by the ugly behavior of the manager, not what happened to the worker later. The article further states that Justice Anthony Kennedy noted that the Ellerth case "involves numerous alleged threats, and we express no opinion as to whether a single unfulfilled threat is sufficient to constitute discrimination."

The second question in the article asks,

Is Ignorance a Defense?

- Old Rule: If a manager isn't informed that one of his employee's is harassing other workers, the supervisor probably isn't the court ruled, though, that it's not enough to have a policy, it must be disseminated and enforced effectively.

The third question asked in the article is,

Whom Do You Inform?

- Old Rule: Tell someone if you have been harassed.
- New Rule: Tell a person with decision making power if you have been harassed.

The courts made it known that the complaint has the responsibility of reporting an incident of harassment to the superior of both the harasser and the complainant or the person responsible for the administering the sexual harassment policy. The complainants have the right to take reasonable care to avoid harm to them.

SUPREME COURT RULING ON TWO LANDMARK CASES IN 1999

On June 14, 1999, the Supreme Court ruled in the case of West V. Gibson that the EEOC does have the right to award compensatory damages. Soon after the 1991 act entitling federal employees to receive compensatory damages at the administrative level of their complaints, EEOC and the Merit Protection Board started award the damages. The case came to the Supreme Court because of opposition.

On June 22, 1999, the Supreme Court ruled in the case of Olmstead v. L.C. that the unnecessary segregation of individuals with disabilities in institutions may constitute discrimination based on disability. The court ruled that the American with Disabilities Act may require states to provide community-based services rather than institutional placements for individuals with disabilities. This historic pronouncement makes attainable a goal being reached with people who have disabilities. The case was brought forth in 1995 by the Atlanta Legal aid Society on behalf of Lois Curtis and Elaine Wilson, women who were in state mental hospital with mental retardation and psychiatric problems. The women were denied community placements in the community because of their conditions.

SEXUAL HARASSMENT IN SCHOOLS FUNDED BY THE FEDERAL GOVERNMENT

On May 24, 1999, the Supreme Court ruled that school officials can be held accountable only when they know about and are deliberately indifferent to sexual harassment "so severe, pervasive and objectively offensive that it can be said to deprive the victims of access to the educational opportunities or benefits provided by the school."

All schools from elementary to college that accepts federal money can be forced to pay victims of such harassment. The court concluded that the legal standard is high enough to keep children and parents from making a case out of every playground taunt.

The case was brought before the Supreme Court by Aurelia Davis and her daughter, LaShonda, against the Monroe County, Georgia, school system when the high court decided that schools receiving federal funds can be sued in some cases in which a student sexually harasses another.

THE TYPES OF EVIDENCE INVESTIGATORS WILL BE LOOKING FOR TO SUPPORT YOUR COMPLAINT

1. Material Evidence

   Evidence is material when it relates to one or more of the issues raised in the complaint or raised by the agency's answer to it. To determine whether evidence is material, one must look to the allegations of discriminatory conduct and resultant harm contained in the complaint and the agency's answers to the allegations if the evidence relates to matters at issue and it is material.

2. Relevant Evidence

   Evidence is relevant if it tends to prove or disprove a material issue raised by a complainant. Relevancy and materiality are often used interchangeably. Generally, relevance is the more important concept in an investigation. If evidence is not relevant, whether it is material is of little consequence. A test of relevance is to ask, "What does this evidence tend to prove?" If the answer is that it tends to prove or disprove a proposition that is related to the complaint, then the evidence is relevant.

3. Reliable Evidence

   Evidence is reliable if it is dependable or trustworthy. Evidence should not be ignored because it is of questionable reliability. Such evidence may lead to evidence that is reliable.

Some factors to consider in determining whether testimony is reliable are: whether the witness' testimony is based on his/her own experience and personal knowledge, or based on rumor, hearsay or innuendo, whether the testimony is a statement of fact or is merely a conclusion, and whether witnesses have an interest in the outcome of the complaint, or are otherwise biased.

Some factors to consider in determining whether documents are reliable are: whether they were prepared in response to the investigation or whether they are maintained in the ordinary course or business; whether they are obtained from the custodian of records or the author of the document; whether they are copies or original documents and whether the documents are signed and/or dated.

The rules of evidence were designed to set limits on the reliability of documents and testimony entered in evidence in court. Such formal rules will not be strictly applied in the collection of evidence for the investigation of federal Equal Employment Opportunity complaints. Such rules may be used, however, as a guide in assessing the evidentiary weight to be given particular items of evidence.

4. <u>Comparative Evidence</u>

Comparative evidence must be sought in every case alleging disparity in treatment on a basis by a law enforced by the EEOC. One of the challenges of developing comparative evidence is gathering sufficient evidence to determine whether the comparators are similarly situated with respect to the complaint.

In general, similar situated means that the persons who are being compared are so situated that it is reasonable to expect that they would receive the same treatment in the context of a particular employment decision. It is important to remember that individuals may be similarly situated for one employment decision, but not for another. For example, a female GS-4 clerk may be similarly situated to a male GS-7 para-legal in a discrimination case involving the approval of annual leave whether the same rules are applied to both the same supervisor or whether both are in the same unit or subject to the same chain of command. The investigator would be obligated to find out whether they were indeed persons, not named by the complaint but similarly situated, whose treatment could be compared to the complaint's treatment.

5. Direct Evidence

Direct evidence of discrimination consists of facts which reveal that intentional discrimination caused an adverse action without the need to resort to inference or circumstantial evidence.

Direct evidence is relevant in cases involving disparate treatment where the question is whether the employer intentionally treated employees differently because of a protected factor. It is also relevant in cases involving the effect of policies where the question is whether the policy disparately treats all employees in the protected class.

Direct evidence is rare. The statement " I would never hire a woman for that job" is direct evidence of discrimination on the basis of sex in hiring.

6. Statistical Evidence

Statistical evidence or a survey of the general environment will be conducted as appropriate. For example, this evidence may be probative when allegations involved comparative treatment of groups, as in an allegation of a pattern of discrimination, or the adverse effect of an agency policy or practice.

7. Documentary Evidence

All relevant documents should be obtained. The complainant, the supervisor, the manager who took the personnel action, or the personnel office of the agency, may be sources to help identify relevant documents. Statistical evidence can usually be obtained through the EEO office or the personnel of the agency.

Equal Employment Opportunity Commission, Resolving Federal EEO Complaints, Spring 1995, pp. 5-6 through 5-11.

PROVING PRETEXT TO DISCRIMINATE IN A PRIMA FACIE CASE OF DISCRIMINATION AND SEXUAL HARASSMENT

In the 1980's during the Reagan years of his presidency the pendulum began to shift more toward conservative views approaching discrimination. The Supreme Court began to be stacked with more conservative judges who were inclined to turn the clock back on discrimination laws.

I have already stated earlier in this manual that discrimination cases are very difficult to prove unless they are prepared well in the informal stage. Discrimination cases must show a distinct pattern of biasness in order to be proven. You must show that your employer used derogatory remarks directed at you because of your race, sex, religion or national origin. Other classes may be used that I have not named. Your employer may have treated you different but it didn't have anything to do with your race, sex, religion, or national origin. He also may not have violated any employment laws when he treated you differently. Your case must show that your employer intentionally meant to discriminate against you. You should also look to see if your employer is following the regulations according to your job and following proper EEO procedures.

The methods of proving pretext to discrimination are;

1. False information given by the discriminatee
2. Similarly situated individuals of a different class were treated differently than the complainant
3. Your employer used derogatory remarks directed at you or indirectly at your class with intent to do harm

4. Evidence of bias

5. Statistical evidence

In 1991, the Civil Rights Act included compensatory damages in cases of bias and sexual harassment.

BURDENS OF PROOF IN DISCRIMINATION CASES

"Discrimination is a subtle fact. It is as difficult to identify as the origin and causes of many odors. . . Those who feel aggrieved, once having brought forward any proof suggestive of discrimination are entitled to require those most cognizable of the relevant employment practices to come forward and disprove the accusation by the clear weight of the evidence." Hackley v. Johnson, 360 F.Supp. 1247, 1252-53 (D.D.C. 1973).

I. Discrimination: Structural or Motivational

A. Structural Discrimination/Effects

Structural discrimination is at issue when the policy, practice or requirement complained of by its very nature operates to exclude or impact on members of a particular group. The policy, practice, requirement has discriminatory effects even though it is facially neutral and not designed or manipulated to have that result.

Examples: Job requirements such as tests, high school diploma, weight and height standards, work experience; zoning.

B. Motivational Discrimination/Intent

Motivational discrimination is at issue when the complained of practice, policy, requirement, or action involves decision-making which is subject to influence by consideration of impermissible factors, such as race, sex, religion, etc. The discrimination whether overt or covert is the result of deliberate, purposeful or intentional acts.

Examples: Discharge or hire of employee in non-structural situation; refusal to rent housing; racial segregation in schools.

II. Constitutional vs. Statutory Standard: Washington v. Davis

A. Constitutional standard: proof of intent required by the Equal Protection clause.

B. Statutory standard: congress has the power to make illegal practices and policies which merely have the effect of disproportionately affecting a protected group.

C. Washington v. Davis, 426 U.S. 229, 48 L.Ed.2d 597 (1976).

In the constitutional context:

"An invidious discriminatory purpose may often be inferred from the totality of relevant facts including (disproportionate impact)."

But purpose may not be inferred solely based on impact.

D. The totality of relevant facts in Washington v. Davis: challenge of test under the Due Process Clause.

Plaintiffs' Facts:

1. Number of black officers not in proportion to the city's population.

2. Higher percentage of blacks failed the test.

3. The test had not been validated.

Defendants' Facts:

1. Proportion of blacks recruited approximated (i) blacks on the force (44%) and (ii) blacks of the relevant age within a 50-mile radius of Washington, D.C.

2. The department had systematically and affirmatively recruited black officers and many who passed the test did not report for duty.

3. The test was not designed or operated to discriminate.

E. Burden of Proving Intent

1. A prima facie case of discriminatory purpose may be proved by statistics combined with other evidence.

2. Upon the establishment of a prima facie case, the burden shifts to defendants to rebut the presumption of unconstitutional action by showing that permissible racially neutral selection criteria and procedures have produced the result.

3. Systematic exclusion may itself be such an unequal application of the law as to show intentional discrimination.

F. Contrast Washington v. Davis with Griggs v. Duke Power Co., 401 U.S. 424 (1971).

Title VII "proscribes not only overt discrimination but also practices that are fair in form but discriminatory in operation. The touchstone is business necessity."

"If an employment practice . . . cannot be shown to be related to job performance, the practice is prohibited."

Congress has placed on the employer the burden of showing that any given requirement must have a manifest relationship to the employment in question.

III. Proof of Discrimination in Public Decision-Making: Arlington Heights.

A. Burden of Proof

1. Plaintiffs may establish that a particular official action or decision was unconstitutionally motivated by "a sensitive inquiry into such circumstantial and direct evidence of intent as may be available." Areas of inquiry and proof might include:

a. the impact of action (disproportionate?);

b. the historical background of the decision;

c. the specific sequence of events leading up to the challenged decision;

d. departures from the normal procedural sequence;

e. substantive departures;

f. the legislative or administrative history.

2. The burden then shifts to the defendants to establish "that the same decision would have resulted even had the impermissible purpose not been considered." [footnote 21] Arlington Heights v. Metropolitan Housing Development Corp. 429 U.S. 252, 50 L. Ed. 2d 450 (1977).

B. See U.S. and Overton v. Texas Education Agency (Austin) 564 F. 2d 162 (5th Cir. 1977).

The court borrows the tort law test for intent that one may be presumed to intend the natural and foreseeable consequences of one's acts.

C. See also cases applying Arlington Heights to teacher employment decisions: Harkless v. Sweeny Independent School District, 554 F. 2d 1353, 14 EPD ¶ 7669 (5th Cir. 1977); Clark v. Mann, 562 F. 2d 1104, 14 EPD ¶ 7811 (8th Cir. 1977); Williams v. Anderson, 562 F. 2d 1081, 14 EPD ¶ 7812 (8th Cir. 1977).

IV. Role of Statistics.

A. In general,

1. "Figures speak and when they do, courts listen." Brooks v. Beto, 366 F. 2d 1, 9 (5th Cir. 1966).

2. Statistics "come in infinite variety and, like any other kind of evidence, they may be rebutted. In short, their usefulness depends on all of the surrounding facts and circumstances." Teamsters v. U.S., 431 U.S. 324, 52 L. Ed. 2d 450, 14 EPD ¶ 7579 (1977).

3. Statistics showing racial or ethnic imbalance are probative because such imbalance is often a telltale sign of purposeful discrimination; absent explanation, it is ordinarily expected that nondiscriminatory practices will result in more representative balance. See Teamsters n.20.

B. Statistics in Structural Cases.

1. A prima facie case of discriminatory purpose may be proved by a showing of disproportionate adverse impact combined with other evidence.

Washington v. Davis, supra;
Teamsters v. U.S., supra;
Williams v. Anderson, supra.

2. Statistical disparities may be so great that a discriminatory purpose can be inferred. Washington v. Davis, Teamsters, Williams v. Anderson.

Hazelwood School District v. U.S., ___ U.S. ___, 53 L.Ed.2d 768, 14 EPD ¶ 7633 (1977).

3. Statistics may be used to rebut statistics by showing that they are inappropriate, inaccurate, or not the best evidence.

See, Hazelwood School District v. U.S., supra.

4. Compare Clark v. Mann, supra, with Williams v. Anderson, supra.

V. Proof In Individual Employment Cases

A. In general

The weight of the evidence must show disparate treatment, i.e., that the plaintiff would have been treated differently if it were not for his or her particular group characteristics.

Caveat: While the analysis of evidence in terms of shifting burdens may appear neat, the actual presentation of evidence is not as straightforward.

B. Allocating the Burden of Proof

1. Initial burden is on plaintiff to establish a prima facie case of racial discrimination.

2. The burden then shifts to the employer to articulate some legitimate, nondiscriminatory reason for the decision.

3. The burden then shifts to the plaintiff to show that the reasons articulated were pretextual.

   See McDonnell-Douglas v. Green, 411 U.S. 792, 36 L.Ed.2d 668, 5 EPD ¶ 8607 (1973).

C. Making the Prima Facie Case

McDonnell-Douglas v. Green set forth a paradigm for proving discrimination. The court, however, cautions that the establishment of the prima facie case will vary according to the fact situation. See footnote 13; see also, Teamsters, text and footnote 44.

In general, the plaintiff must show:

1. he or she is part of a protected group;

2. an employment decision was taken which adversely affected the employee;

3. evidence exists which indicates that the reason for the adverse decision had to do with the plaintiff's protected group characteristics.

D. Paradigms of Prima Facie Cases

1. Hiring: <u>McDonnell-Douglas v. Green</u>

Plaintiff makes a prima facie case by showing that:

a. he belongs to a protected group;

b. he applied and was qualified for a job for which the employer was seeking applicants;

c. despite his qualifications he was rejected;

d. the position remained open after his rejection and the employer continued to seek applicants.

2. Failure to Promote: (2 examples)

a. <u>Petit v. U.S.</u>, 488 F.2d 1033, 6 EPD ¶ 9036 (Ct. of Claims 1973)

Plaintiff makes a prima facie case by showing that:

(1) he belongs to a racial minority;

(2) he was qualified and might have reasonably expected selection for promotion;

(3) he was not promoted;

(4) the supervisory employees responsible for decision making betrayed in other matters a predisposition towards discrimination against members of the involved minority.

b. <u>Abrams v. Johnson</u>, 534 F.2d 1266, 11 EPD ¶ 10877 (6th Cir. 1976).

Plaintiff makes a prima facie case by showing that:

(1) she was a black employee;

(2) she was passed over twice in favor of a lower-rated white and in favor of a less-experienced white;

(3) subjective evaluation methods were used.

c. Discharge: Taylor v. Safeway Stores, Inc., 6 EPD ¶ 8928 (D. Colo. 1973).

Plaintiff makes a prima facie case by showing that:

(1) he is black;

(2) he was discharged;

(3) the person who discharged him was predisposed to discriminate against blacks.

VI. Burden of Proof in Title VII Class Actions.

A. Baxter v. Savannah Sugar-Refining Corp.

Two-Stage Proceeding.

1. Class Liability Stage

a. Initial burden is on the class to show:

(1) defendants utilize a practice or policy which affects decision-making; and

(2) the practice has a disproportionate impact on the members of the class;

b. The burden then shifts to the employer to show that the practice or policy is a "business necessity" or, in the case of a job requirement, "job-related."

c. If the employer fails to meet its burden, discrimination should be found and the case moved to the second stage.

2. Individual Entitlement Stage

a. Burden is on the individual class member to show:

(1) he or she was available for promotion;

(2) he or she possessed the general characteristics and qualifications (possessed by whites and job-related).

b. The burden then shifts to the employer to show by clear and convincing evidence that the employee would never have advanced because of:

(1) lack of qualifications;

(2) other good and sufficient reasons.

Baxter v. Savannah Sugar Refining Corp. 459 F.2d 437, 7 EPD ¶ 9426 (5th Cir. 1974).

B. Teamsters v. U.S./Pattern and Practice Suit.

1. Liability Stage:

a. Government proved a prima facie case of systematic and purposeful discrimination. A preponderance of the evidence showed that racial discrimination was the company's standard operating procedure rather than the unusual practice. Evidence consisted of:

(1) statistics showing exclusion of minorities;

(2) testimony of individuals about their personal experiences with the company which "brought the cold numbers convincingly to life."

b. Defendants failed to rebut the conclusion. See text and footnotes 23 and 24.

2. Testing:

Employment tests in order to e proved to be "job-related" must be validated. See Albemarle Paper Co. v. Moody, 422 U.S. 405, 9 EPD ¶ 10,230 (1975) for methods of test validation.

VII. Burden of Proof in School Desegregation

A. Historically Dual School System: Swann.

Prima facie case shown by:

1. history of segregation;

2. racially identifiable schools in terms of (a) teachers; (b) quality of school buildings and equipment; (c) organization of sports activities.

   Swann v. Charlotte-Mecklenberg, 402 U.S. 1, 28 L.Ed 2d 554 (1971).

B. Unitary Systems: Keyes.

1. Plaintiffs showed that racially segregated schools in one area of Denver were the result of the Board's deliberate policy by evidence that showed:

   a. a new elementary school was built in the middle of an all-Negro neighborhood;

   b. student attendance zones were gerrymandered;

   c. mobile classrooms were excessively used.

2. This policy of deliberate segregation in a substantial portion of the system created presumptions of deliberateness for the entire system:

   a. presumption that a dual school system existed;

   b. presumption that other segregated schooling is not adventitious.

3. The burden shifts to the school board to rebut this presumption by "clear and convincing" evidence. The Board's burden is to adduce proof sufficient to support a finding that (a) segregative intent was not among the factors that motivated their action; or (b) that past segregative acts did not create or contribute to current segregative conditions.

   It is not enough to rely upon some allegedly logical, racially neutral explanation.

PREPARING YOURSELF TO UNDERTAKE A CASE OF DISCRIMINATION OR SEXUAL HARASSMENT

Taking on a case of discrimination or sexual harassment means that you will be actually going to war against your employer. It won't be easy and it will put you under a great deal of stress emotionally, physically, and financially.

When you notice that you will probably become a victim of discrimination or sexual harassment, you must begin to start saving some of your money to find an attorney to take your case. Most attorneys will not take your case because there is very little monetary award available and for other reasons stated in my introduction.

You will also have to develop thick skin in order to endure the pain that you will experience. When you begin to experience discrimination or harassment you will have to endure many instances of abuse to establish a case against your employer. Simply put, you should not file a case until you have obtained enough evidence.

Most of your acquaintances or so-called friends will abandon you when you undertake this challenge. There will be very few of your coworkers or former coworkers who will stand with you and be a credible witness when you ask them.

Your health should be your number one priority to complete the mission that you are undertaking. If you are not on an exercise routine, consult your doctor to start one. It is very important to keep yourself in good physical condition because your mission will be very painful and emotionally draining for you. You should limit the intake of sweets into your diet because they help to magnify the stress that you will already have. Drink a lot of water to keep your body and mind fresh and active. Your diet should consist of a lot of fruits and unseasoned vegetables. Many of us take our health for granted until it is too late.

Your spiritual health is also important to you. If you are not in a good spiritual environment and you know it is not providing good emotional food, simply say to yourself, "Why am I staying in here?" If you are honest with yourself the answer will help you change your environment. You do not need to be around people who will want to pull you down like the crabs in the bucket syndrome. This syndrome is every time one crab wants to get out of the bucket another crab will reach out and pull the other back in. Human behavior is just like this because of fear, envy, and jealousy. Sometimes you think the very person who should inspire you and give you encouragement will try to do their best to defeat you.

CONSULTING AN ATTORNEY

We all will need to consult an attorney on advice for lifetime purchases, wills and business investments. A regular or occasional visit to an attorney will establish a relationship between the two of you over a period of years. People who want to protect their financial security consult attorneys frequently. When you begin to visit an attorney who you feel comfortable with, you will have also established a friendship that will be helpful when you need an attorney in a crisis.

The problem you will have when you come to an unfamiliar attorney's office on a discrimination case or sexual harassment case is the attorney having the understanding and have compassion for your case. I have already stated earlier that finding a good attorney will be a very difficult task. But you cannot let this stop you because an attorney is supposed to be your greatest asset.

When you visit an attorney's office for consul, always take a friend with you to witness what the attorney says he or she will do for you. If an attorney mishandles your case you will at least have someone to witness for you if you have to sue the attorney. You cannot ever trust everyone totally because many attorneys just want your money.

If you are lucky enough to obtain an attorney be sure to have the person put in writing what they will do for every dollar you give them.

If you are not able to readily obtain counsel your employer will view this as an asset to them. But if you know all of your rights you will not jeopardize your case by acting as your own counsel during the early stages of your complaint.

Never give an attorney or anyone else who acts as a representative original copies of your documents. Always give them copies of your material. People will never have as much care for your documents as you will.

Always go to an attorney's office with extreme confidence that you are a winner. Never give an attorney the impression that you want him or her to feel sorry for you. Your confidence in yourself will make an attorney more willing to take your case.

Simply put, obtain a legal contract for his or her services provided to you. You cannot put all of your trust and faith in your attorney. Your case belongs to you and it is your responsibility to nurture and maintain. I would personally suggest that you file your appeals yourself to insure that your case will not be dismissed at any stage for untimeliness.

I would also suggest that you try to retain an attorney outside of the city where you are employed. Many attorneys in the city where you work will be intimidated by the corporation or federal government and will not effectively prepare a case against your employer. Most attorneys are very greedy and only want your money. Many attorneys will take your money and do nothing to prepare a case for you.

When you go to an attorney's office try to be very professional and take notice of the attorney's willingness to work for you. After all, you have hired him. It would be great if you can find a lawyer who will take your case on a contingency basis. This way you will not have to pay for services until your case is won.

The more you know about your rights from you employer and the Equal Employment Opportunity Commission will impress an attorney who may be familiar with the administrative procedure. Certainly you want an attorney who knows the laws to litigate your case outside of the EEO arena.

Before you contact any EEO personnel, you should exhaust all efforts to obtain an attorney. The Equal Employment Opportunity personnel at your job, if you have them, will only try to prevent you from filing a case. EEO personnel will sometimes give you false information and harass you if you do not have an attorney.

MAKING FORMAL CHARGES OF DISCRIMINATION AND SEXUAL HARASSMENT COMPLAINTS

It is very important to not initiate a complaint against your employer until you have gained a sufficient amount of evidence against them to win.

To establish a credible complaint against your employer you must have your complaint in the best articulated legal form possible to win. You want your allegations to include the abuses you have suffered to provide support to your complaint.

If you have a discrimination case or a sexual harassment case it would be best to go to your federal court house in your state and request cases that have prevailed similar to your complaint.

Listed on the next page are two examples of how to articulate cases of discrimination and sexual harassment.

RACE DISCRIMINATION

Scenario:

You are working for a company who employs about one hundred people and you have been passed over for a promotion several times. The branch office where you work has six white males, three white females and one black male (you).

After five years on the job with outstanding performance appraisals you have noticed the company promote white males and white females with less time and lower rated performance appraisals than yours. The last white male they promoted had only been with the company one year. Filing a complaint on this information may seem to you to be enough for a case of discrimination to be proven. Well, it is not enough because as soon as you file a charge of discrimination on this the company may say that the other employees know how to deal with people better than you. But then you remember that they were given advanced training in public relations and you were not.

Now to cover all your bases you will have to make sure you put in a request for advanced training in public relations. If your superiors refuse your request then you will have a good case of prima facie discrimination. You will also need to look to see if their actions are intentionally against you and look for trustworthy witnesses.

Formal Charges:

1. Denial of promotional opportunities
2. Denial of advanced training
3. Denial of promotion (on the date the personnel action occurred)

SEXUAL HARASSMENT

Scenario:

The company you work for has had a history of males being in management positions. You are the first female to move up in a management position after years of hard work. Everything seems to be going well until your male supervisor begins asking you out for a date. You have refused him at all times and this has deflated his ego.

Now you have noticed that he has been spreading rumors around to other managers that you are a lesbian. What can you do? File a complaint? The answer is no. You will have to wait to find out for sure and if his negative rumors are intentionally directed toward you. On several occasions you have noticed that his boldness and authority has enabled him to pass out lesbian paraphernalia depicting you as a lesbian. You have also received a letter from him directed to you that he knows you are a lesbian. You have some witnesses to testify for you that they have witnessed the harassment against you.

Formal Charges

1. Fostering a pattern of sexual harassment in the work place
2. My supervisor has prejudged my sexual preference which has caused harm and undue stress on my job.
3. The most recent negative action against you. (The letter you received)

I have tried to show you that a complainant has to wait until there is enough evidence to support your claim before you make formal charges against your employer. If you do not have enough against the company or agency they will explain their actions to substantiate their action. Winning a complaint may not mean that you have made the defendant admit to their actions but their actions were corrected and your case was settled to your best interest.

FILING COMPLAINTS THROUGH THE MERIT SYSTEMS PROTECTION BOARD (MSPB)

The U.S. Merit Systems Protection Board is an independent agency in the executive branch of the federal government that serves as the guarding of federal merit systems. The MSPB hears cases on removals, suspensions of more than 14 days, reductions in grade or pay and furloughs of 30 days or less. Other types of actions that may be appealed are: performance-based removals, reductions in force and denials of within-grade salary increases.

The MSPB has limited jurisdiction for persons in excepted service and appointed positions. The MSPB primarily hears cases from employees in competitive service. Employees who are in federal competitive service have a greater advantage to receive rulings in their favor through the MSPB. The MSPB hears cases that may or may not be discrimination. The employer may not have followed the proper procedures or they may not have jurisdiction. Contact the Washington headquarters at U.S. Merit Systems Protection Board, 1120 Vermont Avenue, NW, Washington, DC 20419. You may also call the board's 800 number where you can leave a message, 1-800-209-8960. You can send e-mail to the board at MSPB@MSPB.GOV.

THE WHISTLEBLOWER ALLEGATION

The Whistleblower Protection Act became effective on July 9, 1989 (Public Law 101-102). Congress enacted this law to strengthen protections for federal employees, former employees and applicants for employment who claim that they have been subject to personnel actions because of whistleblowing activities.

The 103rd Congress further expanded whistleblower protections by enacting Public Law 103-424, which became effective October 29, 1994. This law made additional personnel actions subject to Whistleblower Protection Act coverage to employees of government corporations and to Title 38 employees in the Veterans Administration.

What is whistleblowing? Whistleblowing means disclosing information that you reasonably believe is evidence of a violation of any law, rule, or regulation, or gross mismanagement, a gross waste of funds, an abuse of authority, or a substantial and specific danger to public safety or health. What are your appeal rights as a whistleblower? The Civil Service Reform Act of 1978 (CSRA) established both the Merit System Protection Board and the Office of Special Counsel. As a federal employee and former employee, you have the right to appeal certain personnel actions taken against you to the board. If you are subject to a personnel action that you believe is the result of a prohibited personnel practice, you have the right to file a complaint with the Office of Special Counsel and to ask the Special Counsel to seek corrective action from the board. The Merit Systems Protection Board's regulations governing appeals generally are contained in Title 5 of the Code of Federal Regulations (CFR), Chapter II, Part 1201.

Additional regulations that apply only to whistleblower appeals are contained in 5 CFR Part 1209. Because the Part 1209 regulations contain only the special provisions applying to whistleblower appeals, they must be used in conjunction with Part 1201.

When an employee is alleging discrimination in connection with a whistleblower allegation to MSPB or the Office of Special Counsel, he or she may appeal the adverse decision to the Equal Employment Opportunity Commission.

The board also hears complaints of alleged violations of the Uniformed Services Employment and Reemployment Rights Act (USERRA). Beginning in October 1998 (unless the President issues regulations earlier) the board will hear complaints from White House employees of alleged violations of several work place laws under the Presidential and Executive Accountability Act.

The majority of the cases brought to the board are appeals of agency adverse actions – that is, removals, suspensions of more than 14 days, reductions in grade or pay, and furloughs of 30 days or less. The next largest number of cases involve appeals of the Office of Personnel Management.

For the Merit Systems Protection Board to have jurisdiction over any appeal of a personnel action, it must possess jurisdiction over both the action and the employee filing the appeal. Approximately 2 million federal employees, or about two-thirds of the full-time civilian work force, currently have appeal rights to the board. Employees eligible to appeal specific actions vary in accordance with the law and regulations governing those actions. In some cases, classes of employees, such as political appointees, are excluded. Employees of specific agencies such as intelligence agencies, the Federal Aviation

Administration, and the General Accounting Office are excluded with respect to certain actions.

The Special Counsel has jurisdiction over prohibited personnel practice complaints with respect to a broader range of personnel actions, including appointments, promotions details, transfers, reassignments, and decisions concerning pay, benefits, awards, education or training. Therefore, a whistleblower could file a complaint with the Special Counsel with respect to most personnel actions allegedly based on whistleblowing. If a whistleblower filed a complaint with the Special Counsel and the Special Counsel did not seek corrective action from the board, no further recourse is available unless the action was directly appealable to the board.

Under the Whistleblower Protection Act, a whistle lower gained the right to appeal directly to the board if he or she first complains to the Special Counsel and the Special Counsel does not seek corrective action on his or her behalf. This right exists with the respect to any personnel action that can be subject of a prohibited personnel practice complaint to the Special Counsel, even though the actions may not be directly appealable to the board.

The Whistleblower Protection Act does not affect the right of a whistleblower to appeal directly to the board if he or she is subject to a personnel action that is appealable to the board under any other law, rule or regulation.

You must file your case of whistleblowing within 45 days of alleged violation of wrongdoing by an agency subjected to an adverse personnel action.

Your case may be filed with the Merit Systems Protection Board or the Office of Special Counsel.

The Office of Special Counsel investigates allegations of certain activities prohibited by civil service law, rules, or regulations and litigation before the Merit Systems Protection Board.

The Office of Special Counsel's address is:

Office of Special Counsel
1730 M Street NW
Washington, DC 20036-4505
Phone Number (202) 653-7188
Toll Free 1-800-872-9855

Their field offices are located at:

Dallas Field Office
525 Griffin Street, Room 824, Box # 103
Dallas, TX 75202
(214) 747-1519

San Francisco Bay Area Field Office
1301 Clay Street (Suite 36 5 S)
Oakland, CA 94612-5217
(510) 637-3460

Detroit Field Office
477 Michigan Avenue
(Suite 495)
Detroit, MI 48226
(313) 226-4496

THE REPRISAL ALLEGATION

The Equal Employment Opportunity Commission states that it is unlawful to restrain, interfere, coerce or discriminate against complainants, their representatives, witnesses, directors of Equal Employment Opportunity, Equal Employment Opportunity officers, investigators, counselors and other agency officials with responsibility for processing discrimination complaints because of involvement with a discrimination charge during any stage in the presentation and processing of a complaint, including the counseling stage or because an individual filed a charge of discrimination, testified, assisted or participated in any manner with an investigation, proceeding or hearing or because of any opposition to an unlawful employment practice.

In the federal government where you have Equal Employment Opportunity offices, many EEO officials will work closely with management to bring reprisals against you. When you meet with someone who you suspect to not be properly informing you of your rights, record the proceeding. Many people will be intimidated with the presence of a tape recorder and ultimately treat you with respect. Also, it would be to your advantage to have someone present with you to witness the proceedings.

In 1987, the Equal Employment Opportunity Commission made it possible for a complaint to sue a federal agency that may violate you in connection with your complaint. When violations occur in the processing of your complaint and you win your case against those violations, the decision rendered by the Equal Employment Opportunity Commission is final in federal cases and does not need to be heard by a federal judge.

Once you have filed your original charge against your employer you will have to try to remain squeaky clean and perform to the best of your ability at all times. Your employer will try to find anything to pin against you to terminate your employment once you have filed a complaint. This allegation can be another easy charge to prove providing that you can show documents that you were not at fault for being dismissed. The reprisal allegation will be considered separate from the protected class or group that you are in. A person may lose their case on discrimination or sexual harassment but win a case on reprisal if they have had contact with an EEO official in a previous complaint.

RETALIATION AS A BASIS TO YOUR COMPLAINT

Many people are afraid of filing complaints against their employers because they feel that they may be retaliated against. The Equal Employment Opportunity procedure provides a way that a complainant may prove that he or she is receiving adverse actions against them because they have filed a complaint.

The reason that you may want to add retaliation as a basis to your complaint is because your employer may take action against you that is a first time action for anyone who has committed the offense. For this reason you may not be able to show how they discriminated against you by not having a similar comparison to show a difference.

The difference between the reprisal allegation and using retaliation to base your complaint is simply that your allegations against your employer will enable you to show a pattern of behavior that is directly solely against you.

Many complainants do not know that their complaints can be based on retaliation. They may not be informed that they may use their race, sex and retaliation to base their complaint. This additional basis makes it easier to prove your case of discrimination.

FEDERAL AGENCIES INVESTIGATING DISCRIMINATION COMPLAINTS AND COMPLAINTS OF SEXUAL HARASSMENT

When you go formal with your complaint you will want to believe that your complaint will be investigated fairly and objectively. Unfortunately many investigations by federal agencies will be bias and only serve to defend the agency against your complaint.

The investigator is supposed to be unbiased and objective in investigating your complaint. However, in many cases the investigator is partial to the agency because he or she is hired as a contractor by the agency to investigate discrimination complaints.

I would suggest that you approach the investigator very cautiously with your evidence until you can receive a fair hearing before an administrative judge. During this stage of your complaint before EEOC, you the complainant and the agency will both receive a fair hearing. You and the agency will receive equal time to present and challenge information being presented.

If you have a mountain of evidence against your employer and you know they cannot defend their actions you should go full steam ahead to win as soon as possible. No one wants to lose a discrimination or sexual harassment complaint and the agency will do anything possible to make you lose your complaint.

TIMELY FILING ALL OFFICIAL FORMS

In all stages of your complaint you must be sure to file all forms within the time frame specified by officials. This will insure that your complaint is not dismissed. When you appeal to the Equal Employment Opportunity Commission, be sure to file everything within their guidelines. Send all materials certified with a return receipt. You will have to show that you have sent your information and appeals on time. Your return receipt copies will be evidence to support your claim. Do not hand deliver anything that is very important to your case, especially not to the defendant. Many officials will conveniently lose the information you give them.

When you start receiving documents for or against your case, it is important to never throw anything away. Some information may seem pointless at the time you received it but it may be important to you later on. My method was to post the dates you receive and send out information on a current calendar to have a visual view of how many days you have to respond to appeals. You also may want to keep records on file in your home computer.

If you work for private industry and have no Equal Employment Opportunity office within your company to be familiar with what will be asked during an investigation, I am providing a form to assist you.

When you file your case in court you must be sure that you or your attorney states the head of the agency in a federal complaint. In the case of a company complaint name the defendants who directed the action against along with the president or CEO of the company. In sexually harassment cases you will have to name the person who actually sexually harassed you as the codefendant in your case.

Remember that many personnel officials in government will try to talk you out of filing a formal complaint against the agency. Some of them will even harass you when you try to file in person. If you experience this simply send a request to file a complaint to their office certified with a return receipt.

SAMPLE

FORMAL COMPLAINT OF DISCRIMINATION BECAUSE OF RACE, COLOR, RELIGION, SEX, OR NATIONAL ORIGIN

1. Complainant's Name (Last, First, Middle)	2. Complainant's Work Telephone No. ( ) ______ Home Telephone No. ( ) ______
3. Complainant's Address (Include City, State, and ZIP Code)	4. Is complainant being represented? Yes ____ No ____ If yes, name of representative.
5a. Name of Agency organization you believe discriminated against you.	5b. Address of alleged discriminating organization (Include City, State, and ZIP Code)
6a. Are you now working for the Federal Government? ☐ Yes (Answer 6b, c, and d below) ☐ No (Do not answer 6b, c, and d below)	6b. Name of agency where you are currently employed
6c. Address of your current employer (Include City, State, and ZIP Code)	6d. Title and grade of your current job

7. Date on which most recent alleged discrimination took place (Month, Day, and Year)

8. Check below why you believe you were discriminated against. Because of your:

☐ Race. If so, state your race ______.
☐ Color. If so, state your color ______.
☐ Religion. If so, state your religion ______.
☐ Sex. If so, state your sex ______
☐ National origin. If so, state your national origin ______

9a. I have discussed my complaint with an Equal Employment Opportunity counselor (see instructions) ☐ Yes ☐ No	9b. Name of counselor

10. Explain specifically how you were discriminated against (treated differently from other employees or applicants) because of your race, color, religion, sex, or national origin. If your complaint involves more than one basis for your dissatisfaction, list and number each such allegation separately and furnish specific, factual information in support of each. (You may continue your answer on another sheet of paper if you need more space.)

ALLEGATION #1:

11. List below the names of your witnesses and what factual information each will be expected to contribute through his testimony to the investigation of your complaint.

12. What specific corrective action do you want taken on your complaint? (If more than one allegation is being made, state overall corrective action desired and the specific corrective action desired for each separate allegation.)

13. Who specifically should take this corrective action, with respect to each allegation?

14. Date this complaint form was signed by complainant (Month, Day, and Year)	15. Signature of Complainant

131

NEGOTIATED GRIEVANCE PROCEDURES (LOCAL UNIONS)

The title above may have a name that you might not readily recognize when you first hear it. The title refers to nothing but a union. It also may be referred to as a collective bargaining agent.

Unions have had a history of being the greatest asset and protector of your rights on the job. However, lately, this may not always be true. Many unions today will sell out its members at the bargaining table and be friends with management. You may not learn this until it is too late when you have been fired from your job.

If you are in a union with private industry or the government, I would suggest that you watch them closely when they are representing you. I would not tell them that you plan to file a charge of discrimination or enter district court about your complaint until they have exhausted all means to settle your case. If you tell them your plans, you may be surprised that management already knows what you are planning and have an effective defense against you. By whose decision the parties agree to be bound.

It would be best to not risk your plan being exposed until the last minute.

Sometimes unions may try to seduce you to join them if you are facing a serious charge against you. I would say to you not to join unless you know they will honestly fight for you. If you know they have no clout, simply do not join. If you join a union be sure to read the front and back of all forms before you sign them. Many union agreement forms may have enclosed in fine print or on the back of a form that you will only let the union arbitrate your case. If the union is the only one to arbitrate your case, you may not be able to sue your employer in court. Many people have lost their cases or settled for too little because they agreed to not arbitrate their case beyond the union agreement. Simply put, they signed away their right to sue. If you join a union, do not agree to sole arbitration by the union. The legal definition of arbitration is the settlement of disputed questions, whether of law or fact.

If you belong to a union and they discriminate against you, then you must file a case with the Equal Employment Opportunity Commission against them.

Unions can be very effective with some issues if you are a blue collar worker. If you are a blue collar worker it would be to your advantage to join. If you are a professional worker, I would do a great deal of research about the union before you join.

CLASS COMPLAINTS

A class is a group of employees, former employees or applicants for employment who, it is alleged, have been or are being adversely affected by an agency personnel management policy or practice that discriminates against the group on the basis of their race, color, religion, sex, national origin, age or handicap defined by the Equal Employment Opportunity Commission.

The Commission defines a class complaint as a written complaint of discrimination filed on behalf of a class by the agent of the class (the representative). The agent and a legal representative protect the interest of the class.

Class complaints are usually processed in the same manner as individual complaints but some of the time limits for filing may be extended because of the size of the class. They are most of the times easier to prove than individual complaints. Because a group of people are complaining about the same issues will bring the strength to any case. Most lawyers prefer class complaints over individual complaints. There are some drawbacks to class complaints. The originator of the class complaint may have more interest in the class than other members. Some of the other class members may not be able to endure the hardship of the case and may want to quit the case. The employer or the company will offer a settlement to the class that is far beneath the resolution that has been agreed on by all class members. Some members will bail out to take the settlement.

Many meetings with all class members will be required to sustain the class complaint. These meetings will serve as pep rallies for all class members.

Your attorney or law firm representing the class must be qualified with experience in handling class complaint. If your legal counsel is not qualified to handle class complaints a judge may dismiss the case on the grounds of inadequate counsel.

In complaints alleging a class action or systemic discrimination, the complainants must prove that the agency has a regular practice of discrimination against a protected group. Although complainants in class actions usually offer evidence of individual discriminatory acts, they are not required to show at the outset that each person for whom they will ultimately seek relief was a victim of discrimination. Once a case is established, the judge will determine which members of the class were actually victimized by the employer's actions and thus are entitled to relief. Class members may then process their individual claims for relief. Statistics may be used to prove any type of discrimination, but are particularly useful in class action suits. No minimum sample size is prescribed in federal law or statistical theory for determining when an inference of discrimination may be drawn. The adequacy of numerical comparison with small sets of data depends on the degree of certainty required by the fact-finder as well as on the type of inference that the statistics are meant to demonstrate. As courts become increasingly sophisticated in their treatment of statistical analysis, expert testimony from consultants specializing in statistics is now essential for the presentation of most class actions.

Among the basic requirement of the class action determination are: numerosity (is the affected class so numerous that joinder of claims would be impractical – usually more than 50 people): commonality (are there common questions of fact and law): typicality (are the claims and defenses of the named complainant typical of the absent class members claims and defenses); and adequacy of representation (can the class representative fairly and appropriately represent absent class members).

FILING COMPLAINTS AGAINST BUSINESSES WHO DISCRIMINATE IN HIRING, SERVICE AND BENEFITS

I have devoted most of the course to instructions on employment discrimination. However, discrimination of any form is a terrible experience for anyone to endure. My personal experiences have been primarily employment discrimination but I have had experiences from business who discriminate in their hiring practices, service to customer and benefits. Many African-Americans thought that years approaching the next century would bring prosperity to all Americans. But it seems that the horrible experiences of the 1960's seem to be coming back. The reason it seems that discrimination is resurfacing is because it has never been dead. Lately, many blacks and other minorities are experiencing overt discrimination from businesses at an alarming rate. A person may not know that he or she is being discriminated against by a business unless they know of an identical situation like theirs was handled differently because of their race.

Most cases of business discrimination may be hard to prove without the assistance of whites who may receive preferential treatment. It is sad that many businesses are discriminating against anyone who has money to purchase their products.

Let's talk about hiring first, for example, many blacks may know the reason why they were not hired on a particular job. You may know it, but can you prove it? The businesses and companies have all the resources to defend themselves against your complaint. They are not going to admit to you personally that you were not hired because they do not want a certain race there. If they did and admitted it, your case would be very easy to prove. In the 1980's, a major employment personnel firm based in

New York City had a policy of excluding placing blacks to major companies who were seeking qualified applicants. Many blacks had suspected that the personnel firm was using discriminatory practices but they couldn't prove it. So they contact a major television network news magazine to assist them in investigating the practices of the employment agency. The news magazine show used several actors in the New York City area to pose as potential employment applicants. The black actors were instructed to go to the agency and apply to jobs with very impressive educations and employment experiences. The employment agency would never return phone calls to the black applicants nor would they refer them out to prospective employers. White actors were sent to the same agency by the news magazine show to apply for the same jobs with their education and experience to qualify. In order for the news magazine show to prove that the employment agency was discriminating against blacks, the black applicants had more education and experience than the white applicants. Even though this was the case, no blacks were sent out on prospective professional jobs and the whites were begged to accept the jobs. There was also a memo sent around from top management officials instructing job counselors to code applications and use buzz words to discriminate against blacks. After a thorough investigation was completed by the news magazine show it was later discovered that their offices in Atlanta, Georgia, was the location for the Vice President for Recruitment and Placement. The person who held this position was responsible for carrying out the orders from the top. The person carrying out these orders and head of the Atlanta office was a black female. When she was confronted about their practices she vehemently denied that they did not occur in their agency. So the news magazine showed her a tape of how the blacks were treated and how the whites were treated. She was also shown a copy of the memo from top management instructed how to code and use buzz words to discriminate against black applicants. There was no way she could dispute the taped recording of the practices. Many blacks are used as pawns by companies to cover up their discriminatory practices.

In the late 1970's, I attended a jobs fair in Atlanta, Georgia, that was open to the public. The advertisement for the jobs fair instructed applicants to bring a resume with you to the jobs fair. It wasn't long before I noticed I had become invisible to the job recruiters. When I would present my resume to the recruiters, they would act as if I had a terrible disease and ignore me. Obviously, I was offended and my self-esteem was being crushed. I later noticed when whites would walk up to the recruiter they were welcomed with open arms. The whites were very warmly accepted and told in great detail about the company and benefits. I said to myself, "I wish I had a video camera to record this." The video cameras were not as popular as they are now and very expensive. But if I had a camera I would have sued them for discriminating in their hiring practices. I walked away hurt and feeling not wanted. I still remember that jobs fair and the practices of the company recruiters to this day. I later found out that the reason the recruiters were so eager to hire the whites and not blacks was because the company official only wanted whites in the professional jobs. They were also paid bonuses for each white they could bring into the company. I also noticed that the recruiter would be offended when whites were not interested in their company. All of the company recruiters were white.

Many employers who discriminate against minorities use codes to eliminate them and the only way to detect this is to have someone on the inside inform you. They may not want to testify to this but they can certainly give you documents that prove discrimination anonymously.

This practice by employers is not exclusively done by white companies. It would be unjust if I did not mention that some black companies mistreat white applicants the same way white companies mistreat black applicants. I worked for a big insurance company owned by a black multi-millionaire and witnessed discrimination. One morning a white female came into the company looking for a job as an insurance saleswoman and filled out an application. She waited for almost an hour and did not get an interview with the manager. All of the employees at the company were black. There were no other applicants waiting for an interview before or after her. I began to notice the woman's solemn face and she eventually left feeling very hurt. I empathized with her pain because I had experienced many similar situations. The manager came in where we were having a meeting smiling and said, "We make them feel like we do when we apply for their jobs." My heart sank to the floor and I realized I could no longer work for the company. I quit the next day and this was my first job out of college. What I had seen and heard was wrong.

Some businesses desperately want to return to the days of blacks being served at the back door or not at all. When I heard of the discriminatory practices of the Denny's Restaurant in the Washington, D.C. area in the late 1980's, I could not believe it. But when so many blacks made the same complaints I knew something was wrong. Later, the blacks who were denied service at Denny's won a case of discrimination against them. Since the Denny's incident there have been numerous other cases of discrimination in service to African-Americans and other minorities. The most recent case that I have heard of businesses discriminating involved a black family wanted to purchase an expensive lap top computer from the Office Depot company. After deciding on the computer they wanted to purchase, they wanted to write a personal check for the amount of the purchase. Even though the family had all of the necessary identification to submit with the check the manager refused their check. The family would not take this lying down and hired a detective to investigate the practice to see if they were being discriminated against. The detective used a white family with identical resources to go in Office Depot and purchase a similar computer. The management warmly accepted the white family's personal check for their means to purchase the computer. The detective instructed the black family to go back to Office Depot to see if they could purchase another lap top computer similar to the one purchased by the white family. Their purchase by personal check was again denied so the family sued because they believed they had been discriminated against. The convincing evidence they had was all scenes by both families were videotaped.

There are many incidents where minorities are victims of discrimination after they have purchased something. There are also many incidents where minorities are charged more for products. Some examples are in buying homes and cars. If you suspect this has happened to you, you should not ignore it but challenge the practice. The only remedy for ignorance is education. Employ the measures taken by the family at Office Depot.

The hidden video camera has become an effective way to prove these complaints. The most popular case of violating the rights of a citizen was the Rodney King incident. If the incident had not been videotaped, Rodney King would have never won a four million dollar judgment against the city of Los Angeles.

Lawyers probably will gladly accept your case if you have a videotape of the incident or have your homework done otherwise. If you do not own a video tape recorder, you can rent one for your use and return it when you are finished.

Many blacks and whites are in denial about discrimination and do not want you to complain. The ultra-conservative movement has produced many black thinkers like Supreme Court Justice Clarence Thomas. I think of the days of Dr. Martin Luther King, Jr. and wonder where would America be if he and others chose to close their eyes. No race of people will voluntarily relinquish its power. It is unthinkable that many people think that is what will happen one day. If Dr. King and others had turned their heads like so many of black Americans are doing, the mere existence of black people in America would be very minimal. Dr. King could have easily turned his head in those days of the Montgomery bus boycotts because he did not come from a poverty-stricken background. But he chose to take a stand because it was the right thing to do. If a person doesn't stand for something, they will fall for anything.

COURT PROCEDURE IN A LAWSUIT

In a lawsuit, the person suing is the plaintiff, and the person who you bring forth the lawsuit against is called the defendant.

A. Commencement of Action

1. Filing a Complaint With the Court

(a) Payment of a Filing Fee

(1) Cost – App. $150-$300

B. Service of Process

1. The defendant must be served with a writ, notice or summons. In federal cases, the complaint filed by you may be enough to serve the defendant.

C. Pleadings

1. Once the defendant has been served, he will have generally about 15 or 20 days to reply. If the defendant does not respond in this time frame, the case is won by the plaintiff on default.

D. Motion to Dismiss

1. The defendant may ask the court to dismiss the case if the complaint has been brought in the wrong court, haven't been properly served or the proper defendant is not named on the complaint.

E. Motion for Judgment on the Pleadings.

1. When this motion is made, either party may ask for a judgment on the merits of the case as shown by the record.

F. Discovery

1. At this stage of the court complaint, each party has to supply the opposing party with a list of all witnesses, documents to produce, and what they intend to state about the case.

G. Depositions

1. Testimonies are taken from witnesses to record statements for the record during the discovery phase. Testimonies are taken from witnesses who are out of the state or country and from persons who have a physical condition that would permit them from coming to court.

H. Motion for Summary Judgment

1. In most courts, either party may bring to the court's attention that a complaint or defense is false and ask for a summary judgment. A large majority of discrimination cases do not survive this stage. This is the reason you need to have your case thoroughly proven when you come to court.

I. Pretrial Conference

1. A pretrial conference may be requested by either party to have a round table discussion with the judge to eliminate matters that are not in dispute and to determine what issues remain for litigation. The pretrial conference is not intended to compel both parties to settle the case. Witnesses who refuse to testify are served with a subpoena.

J. The Trier of Facts

1. In many federal civil cases a judge usually renders a decision in a case. But if a decision is opinion-based, either party may request that the case be heard by a jury.

K. Basis for a Decision

1. A judge or jury can only decide on the evidence presented before the court.

L. Trial Procedure

1. Opening statements to the judge or jury.
2. Direct examinations of witnesses called by the plaintiff or defendant.
3. Cross-examinations are done by the opposing party to witnesses.
4. Redirect examinations may be asked by the attorney to overcome the cross-examinations asked.
5. Re-cross-examinations may be asked to further examination by the defendant's attorney.

M. Charge to the Jury and the Verdict

1. The judge will give instruction to the jury and ask for a verdict

N. Decision From the Judge

1. The judge will render a decision when he is the only person to decide the case.

O. Mistrial

1. The court may render a mistrial when a juror has been found guilty of misconduct.

P. Judgment and Costs

1. When a judgment is rendered, the losing party may be required to pay all court cost.

Q. Appeal

1. After a judgment, the losing party appeal to the next court.

R. Execution

1. After an appeal has been exhausted, the losing party will comply with the lower court's decision.

(Some court's procedure may differ slightly from this procedure)

THE UNITED STATES DISTRICT COURTS

The most important thing to do when entering District Court is to file your case in the appropriate time frame.

Most federal judges in Federal Courts are conservative appointed and are insensitive to discrimination complaints. They will try to find every reason to get your case dismissed.

If you are entering Federal Court without an attorney, you can request your District Court to appoint an attorney and have the filing fee waived. If the court does not appoint you an attorney and you want to proceed on your own, ask the court for a filing pro se package to simplify the process. Many courts will not ell you about the filing pro se forms unless you ask.

When you start the discovery process, be sure to answer everything truthfully and to the best of your knowledge. Do not lie about anything because the defendant will try to catch you in a lie when they request a deposition from you.

When you request discovery from the defendant, be sure to ask questions (interrogatives) that will reveal how much they actually know to defend your case. This will be an asset to you and make you more confident when it is time for your hearing in court.

During the deposition stage, do not try to rehearse what you want to say. Be yourself and be composed the best you can be. This will be the first time you can possibly get the defendant to settle with you. When you go to the deposition, be as well dressed as you can be. Wear professional navy blue or gray attire to the deposition and hearing. Don't wear flashy bright colors that are easily found in today's shops. Stay away from flashy jewelry unless it is something that will boasts your confidence. You do not want them to perceive you are shallow and have no confidence in yourself.

The next step in District Court will be the defendant seeking summary judgment to get your case dismissed. If you have presented affidavits and have witnesses to substantiate what you have stated in your case, you can survive this hearing. If not, the judge may dismiss your case and not send it to trial. This depends on what type of judge you may have, especially if he or she is not biased.

Before you have your summary judgment hearing, request that the proceeding be audio-taped. Many judges will edit credible information out of your case to support their dismissal. Be sure that the court reporter or the person who has been hired by the court signs the transcript that the information is true and correct.

My experience in my District Court was one of the most troubling experiences I have ever had in my life. It was most troubling for me not because of the extreme biasness I experienced but because bias federal judges have the power to practice biasness with no accountability.

On March 21, 2003, I was in my District Court in open court to have a decision from the Equal Employment Opportunity Commission adjudicated, Corbett vs. West, Jr., appeal no. 01934622, June 24, 1994. A federal judge and an assistant United States attorney conspired to not render a judgment in open court that was mandatory and binding in Federal Court because it was against a federal agency. The assistant United States attorney told the judge in a pleading, "You are the judge, you don't have to do this," after knowing there was no defense and a judgment was supposed to be enacted in the case. The judge rendered the bench decision, "I am not giving this to you because I don't believe you completed the requirement for a judgment." The judge simply was telling me that on this day I am your God because I have the power to give you justice or not to do so.

I had my immediate family, wife, son and myself in open court to minimize what I already knew, I was going to be viewed as a Black criminal and not a citizen of the United States who deserved due process under the United States Constitution. My brother-in-law was standing in as a witness to the proceeding.

The appeal no. 01934622 from the Equal Employment Opportunity Commission will be viewed later in this manual.

That experience was another reason for writing this manual although I started writing it eight years before the experience. I have personally witnessed the extreme racism practiced daily in America.

UNITED STATES APPELLATE COURTS

If you were not successful in the District Court in your case and you know that you should have received a judgment in your favor, then you should appeal your case to your appropriate court of appeals. But if you know that your case has been dismissed for a good reason and it does not have merit, then you may consider dropping your case. The courts will order that you pay the defendant's expenses for defending your case if they feel your case is frivolous, but if you know that the court is biased and a decision was erroneous and not based on the truth, then you owe it to yourself to continue on.

The most important reason for appealing your case is believing in yourself and knowledge of any grave error that may have been committed in the lower court. At this point you should research cases and laws to prove your case.

If you have not done any research at this point, you should not panic because you will still have time. The most complete source of information on cases and codes available to you is an employment discrimination law book. This book may be found in your community library, but if the library does not have it then you may have to purchase it yourself. It will be the greatest thing that you can do for your case. The book can be bought on www.Amazon.com. Some of them are expensive but you may be able to buy one cheaper or a used one on EBay. The book will be valuable because you can pass it on to other family members or friends.

You can also research cases and codes on the internet. The best way to research cases is to use www.Findlaw.com. Their web site is the easiest to find cases and codes of all the internet law guides.

When you appeal to your appeals court, be sure to ask for a sample brief to follow the court procedure on line. I found that having a sample brief to follow is the best was to correctly file your brief.

UNITED STATES SUPREME COURT

The Supreme Court only hears a limited number of cases each year arising out of Federal or State Courts. They involve important questions about the constitution or federal law.

If you believe grave error has been committed in a lower court or a court decision is not based on federal law then you must appeal to this court. This is the highest court in America and the last stop for you to receive justice.

If you do not know how to correctly file our case in the Supreme Court, you can request a sample copy of a correct filing to assist you.

The Supreme Court states as its jurisdiction according to the constitution is:

"The judicial Power shall extend to all Cases, in Law and Equity, arising under this Constitution, the Laws of the United States, and Treaties made, or which shall be made, under their Authority; - to all Cases affecting Ambassadors, other public Ministers and Consuls; - to all Cases of admiralty and maritime jurisdiction; - to Controversies to which the United States shall be a Party; - to Controversies between two or more States between a State and Citizens of another State; - between Citizens of different States; - between Citizens of the same State claiming Lands under Grants of different States, and between a State , or the Citizens thereof, and foreign States, Citizens or Subjects."

THE NO FEAR ACT

The No Fear Act became law on April 30, 2002. The bill is called HR 169 (Notification of Federal Employees Anti-Discrimination and Retaliation Act 2001).

The No Fear Act requires that government agencies found liable for discrimination (race, sex, color, religion or national origin) and whistleblowing will be held directly accountable for breaking the law.

No longer will agencies be able to abdicate their culpability by sending judgment tabs to the Department of Justice.

Whistleblowers will receive additional protection for exposing abuse, fraud and mismanagement.

Agencies will regularly report to congress on discrimination judgments and status of managers found liable for discrimination.

The United States government is the largest employer in the nation. It should provide leadership in ensuring that the workplace is free from bias and injustice.

GLOSSARY OF EEO TERMS

1. Administrative Judge

   An official assigned by the EEOC to hold hearings on formal complaints of discrimination and to otherwise process individual and class complaints for EEOC.

2. Age Discrimination

   A claim of discrimination based on age by an individual who is at least 40 years of age at the time of the alleged discriminatory act.

3. Agent of the Class

   A member of a class who files the complaint and acts for the class during the processing of the complaint. This person alleges that an agency personnel practice or policy discriminates against members of the class on the basis of race, color, religion, sex, national origin, age, physical or mental disability, equal pay, and/or reprisal.

4. Allegation of Reprisal

   A claim of restraint, interference, coercion, discrimination, or retaliation in connection with presenting a complaint or because of any opposition to an employment practice unlawful under Title 29 C.F.R. Part 1614. Reprisal claims can be brought by complainants, their representatives, witnesses, and personnel involved in the complaint process.

5. Arbitration

The final resolution or decision of a grievance filed under a negotiated grievance procedure by an impartial person (an arbitrator) selected by labor and management. If allegations of discrimination are not excluded from a negotiated grievance procedure, they may be filed under such procedure and eventually be decided through arbitration. Only labor and management may invoke arbitration to resolve a grievance.

6. Civilian Personnel Officer

The individual who is designated by an agency to administer the civilian personnel program for federal civilian employees.

7. Class

A group of employees, former employees, or applicants for federal employment, who allege that they have been, are being, or may be adversely affected by an agency personnel management policy or practice. The policy or practice must allegedly discriminate against the group based on their common race, color, religion, sex, national origin, age, physical or mental disability, equal pay and/or reprisal.

8. Class Complaint

A written discrimination complaint filed on behalf of a class by the agent of class alleging that an agency personnel policy or practice discriminates against the class, and fulfills all of the following element:

A. The class is so numerous that a consolidated complaint of the class is impractical.

B. There are questions of fact common to the class.

C. The agent's individual claim is typical of the claims of the class.

D. The agent of the class, and his or her representative, if any, will fairly and adequately protect the interests of the class.

9. Compensatory Damages

Compensation for loss or suffering caused by unlawful intentional discrimination.

10. Complainant

A federal employee, private company employee, a former federal employee or an applicant for federal employment who files a formal complaint of discrimination based on his or her race, color, religion, sex, national origin, age, physical or mental disability, equal pay, and/or reprisal.

11. Director of Equal Employment Opportunity

The official designated by the head of a federal agency to administer the agency's EEO program in accordance with 29 C.F.R. 1614. 102(b)(3).

12. Discrimination

Any act or failure to act based in whole or in part on a person's race, color, religion, sex, national origin, age, physical or mental disability, equal pay, and/or reprisal, that adversely affect privileges, benefits, working conditions, results in disparate impact on employees or applicants.

13. Disparate Treatment

Disparate treatment are the most common of all EEO cases. The definition of disparate means different or unequal. Disparate treatment occurs when an employee from a protected class is treated differently for various reasons from the majority population.

Disparate treatment cases are often referred to as "intentional discrimination" because the employer intended to discriminate against you because of your race, sex, age, etc. One example of disparate treatment is an employer who will repeatedly not select a black applicant or a female applicant because the employer did not want a black or female in that job. Another example of disparate treatment is when an employer treats one employee differently than another employer due to the difference in race, sex, age, etc.

14. Disparate Impact

The disparate impact analysis challenges a facially neutral rule or policy that has an adverse impact against an EEO status and is not job related. The classic impact cases were high school diploma or so-called general intelligence written test requirements which tended to screen out a disproportionate number of black applicants, and the minimum height requirement which tended to screen out a high proportion of female and Asian applicants. Disparate impact cases not only include objective employment practices, but also include subjective employment practices such as interviews or performance appraisals.

15. EEO Counselor

An agency employee working under the direction of the EEO officer, who makes informal inquiries and seeks resolution of informal complaints. EEO counselors may be assigned to full-time or part-time EEO counselor positions or be given collateral duties and responsibilities.

16. EEO Management Directive (MD) – 110

EEO MD – 110 (Federal Sector Complaint Processing Manual) is issued by the EEOC and provides federal agencies with EEOC's policies, procedures and guidance relating to the processing of discrimination complaints governed by the EEOC's regulations in Title 29 C.F.R. Part 1614.

17. EEO Officer

The individual designated by the agency to manage the day-to-day operation of an agency's EEO program. This includes managing and operating the complaint processing system, supervising and training EEO counselors, and advising the appropriate agency officials on the proposed disposition of complaints.

18. Equal Employment Opportunity Commission (EEOC)

The federal agency responsible for enforcing laws which prohibit discrimination based on race, color, religion, sex, national origin, age (40 and over), physical or mental disability, equal pay and/or reprisal. In federal sector complaints of discrimination, the EEOC hold hearings and issues recommended findings of fact and conclusions of law. The EEOC Office of Federal Operations makes decisions on discrimination complaints that have been appealed. It also reviews, upon request, decision on negotiated grievances and Merit Systems Protection Board Appeals if they include issues of discrimination.

19. Equal Pay Act Complaint

The Equal Pay Act (EPA) of 1963, 29 U.S.C. Section 206 (d), amended the Fair Labor Standards Act, 29 U.S.C. Section 201, ET Seq., to prohibit discrimination on account of sex in the payment of wages. Administration and enforcement of the EPA is the responsibility of the EEOC. Federal sector EPA complaints are processed under Title 29 C.F.R. Section 1614. 202. Processing federal sector EPA complaints is governed by Section V, Chapter 3 of EEO MD – 110.

20. <u>Failure to Reasonably Accommodate</u>

Failure to reasonably accommodate a qualified individual with a disability or religious obligation after the individual request such an accommodation is a form of discrimination.

21. <u>Federal Labor Relations Authority (FLRA)</u>

The federal agency responsible for deciding appeals on arbitration awards filed by a union or an agency regarding grievances filed under negotiated grievance procedure.

22. <u>Final Decision</u>

The decision, with or without a hearing, or an agency on a complaint of employment.

23. <u>Harassment</u>

Harassment is unwelcome conduct (including speech) that is sexual in nature or references one's protected status in an offensive, insulting, and annoying manner. Harassment is often repetitive or persistent.

24. <u>Formal Complaint</u>

A written complaint (ordinarily on an agency complaint form) filed under 29 C.F.R. Part 1614, alleging that a specific act of discrimination or reprisal has taken place that is personal to the individual.

25. Individual With Disability

A. A person who - -

1. Has a physical or mental impairment which substantially limits one or more of such person's major life activities.

2. Has a record of such an impairment.

3. Is regarded as having such an impairment.

B. Physical or mental impairment.

1. Any physiological disorder or condition, cosmetic disfigurement, or anatomical loss affecting one or more of the following body systems:

(a) Neurological

(b) Musculoskeletal

(c) Special Sense Organs

(d) Cardiovascular

(e) Reproductive

(f) Digestive

(g) Genitourinary

(h) Hemic and Lymphatic

(i) Skin

(j) Endocrine

2. Any mental or psychological disorder, such as mental retardation, organic brain syndrome, emotional or mental illness, and specific learning disabilities.

C. Major life activities

Functions such as: caring for one's self, performing manual tasks, walking, seeing, hearing, speaking, breathing, learning and working.

D. Has a record of such an impairment.

Has a history of, or has been classified (or misclassified) as having, a mental or physical impairment that substantially limits one or more major life activities.

E. Is regarded as having such an impairment.

This term is defined as one of the following:

1. A physical or mental impairment that does not substantially limit major life activities but is treated by an employer as constituting such a limitation.
2. A physical or mental impairment that substantially limits major life activities only as a result of the attitude of an employer toward such impairment.
3. None of the impairments defined in (2) above but is treated by an employer as having such an impairment.

26. <u>Informal Complaint</u>

A matter of alleged discrimination which an aggrieved person brings to the attention of an EEO counselor before a formal discrimination complaint is filed.

27. <u>Investigative Report</u>

The Report of Investigation (ROI) prepared by an investigator after a formal discrimination complaint is filed and accepted for processing.

28. Merit Systems Protection Board (MSPB)

The federal agency responsible for deciding appealable personnel actions and mixed case complaints.

25. Mixed Case Complaint

A complaint involving an action appealable to MSPB which alleges that the action was taken because of discrimination. Actions appealable to the MSPB include but are not limited to removals, demotions, suspensions for more than 14 days, reductions-in-force, and furloughs for less than 30 days.

26. Negotiated Grievance Procedure

A grievance procedure contained in a collective bargaining agreement negotiated between an agency and a recognized labor organization. An allegation of discrimination may be processed under a negotiated grievance procedure as provided for by Title 5 United States Code, Section 7121 (d). Unless specifically excluded by agreement between labor and management, and employee may file an allegation of discrimination to be processed under a negotiated grievance procedure or under 29 C.F.R. Part 1614, but not both.

27. Negotiated Settlement Agreement

A written settlement agreement knowingly and voluntarily signed by the complainant or agent and the agency during the pre-complaint or formal complaint process which resolves a counseling matter or discrimination complaint. The terms of the agreement are binding on both parties.

28. <u>Notice of Intent to File a Civil Action</u>

Under Section 15 (D) of the Age of Discrimination in Employment Act (ADEA), 29 U.S.C. Section 633 (a), an aggrieved age discrimination claimant may bypass the administrative complaint process in Title 29 C.F.R. Part 1614, and file a civil action directly in an appropriate federal district court. When a federal age discrimination claimant has not filed an administrative age discrimination complaint, and has provided the EEOC with not less than thirty (30) days of notice of intent to sue, filed within one hundred eighty (180) days after the alleged unlawful practiced occurred, the claimant may file a civil action any time thereafter within the applicable limitations period. Complainants need not notify the EEOC when filing civil actions under the Civil Rights Act of 1964, as amended, or under the Rehabilitation Act.

29. <u>Official Time</u>

Time officially authorized for a complaint, class agent or representative to prepare a complaint.

30. <u>Qualified Person With a Disability</u>

With respect to employment, a person with a disability who, with or without reasonable accommodation, can perform the essential functions of the position in question without endangering the health and safety or himself, herself or others and who, depending upon the type of appointing authority being used, either - -

A. Meets the experience or education requirements (which may include passing a written test) of the position in question.

B. Meets the criteria for appointment under one of the special appointing authorities for disabled persons.

31. Reasonable Accommodation

A change or adjustment to a job or work site that makes it possible for an otherwise qualified employee with a disability to perform the essential function of a position. This may include, but shall not be limited to: (1) making facilities readily accessible to and usable by disabled persons, and (2) job restructuring, part-time or modified work schedules, acquisition or modification of equipment or devices, appropriate or modification of examinations, the provision of readers and interpreters, and other similar actions.

32. Remedial Action

Full relief provided to an applicant or employee when there has been a finding that such individual has been discriminated against. This may include, but is not limited to, retroactive appointment or promotion, back pay, compensatory damages, attorney fees and/or costs, cancellation of an unwarranted personnel action, or expunction from the agency's records of any reference to, or any record of, an unwarranted disciplinary action that is not a personnel action.

33. Reportable Contact

A reportable contact is any contact with an EEO counselor by an aggrieved person who alleges discrimination on the basis of race, color, religion, sex, age, national origin, physical or mental disability, equal pay and/or reprisal.

34. Representative

A person selected and designated by an aggrieved person or a complainant, the class agent, or a witness in the matter. The representative may accompany, represent, and advise the complainant, the agent, or the witness at any stage of the complaint process.

35. Reprisal

Unlawful restraint, coercion or discrimination against complainants, their representatives, witnesses, directors of EEO, EEO officers, investigators, counselors, and other agency officials with responsibility for processing EEO discrimination complaints during any stage in the presentation and processing of the complaint, including the pre-complaint process, or because of opposition to any unlawful EEO employment discrimination.

36. Sexual Harassment

Unwelcome sexual advances, requests for sexual favors, and/or other verbal or physical conduct of a sexual nature based on one or more of the following conditions:

A. Submission to conduct is made either explicitly or implicitly a term or condition of an individual's employment.

B. Submission to or rejection of such conduct by an individual is used as the basis for employment decisions affecting such individual.

C. Such conduct has the purpose or effect of unreasonably interfering with an individual's work performance or creating an intimidating, hostile, or offensive work environment.

37. Target Disabilities

Disabilities targeted for emphasis in affirmative action program planning. The disabilities are as follows: deafness; blindness; missing extremities; partial paralysis; complete paralysis; convulsive disorders; mental retardation; mental illness; and distortion of limbs and/or spine.

WHY I MADE A DECISION TO FILE A DISCRIMINATION COMPLAINT

The reason I made a decision to file a discrimination complaint is based on religious principles. I believe that your body is a temple made by God and your personal responsibility is to not let anyone destroy it. When you are discriminated against or made to feel inhuman, you will begin to develop self-hatred that will ultimately be a threat to your health and welfare. But if you file a complaint or take other legal action to guard against discrimination, you will begin to feel a sense of dignity and pride in your self.

I saved about a hundred articles, but the ones I have included in this manual are most inspiring. One article I read in the newspaper in 2004 was very troubling to read. The article was titled, Study Finds More US Blacks Attempt Suicide. Many African-Americans in previous years have rarely thought of suicide because of their religious and cultural beliefs. In present-day society evidence has shown that this is no longer true. The American Medical Association did a study from 2001 and 2003 in suicide attempts in the general population in the United States. The study has found evidence that Blacks are committing suicides at an alarming increase. Although, it is still believed that Whites commit suicides significantly more than Black Americans. The study suggests that Blacks entering the United States from the Caribbean and other countries where racism is not the dominant social disease cannot handle the overt discrimination they experience in America. The article states specifically in the last paragraph, "It is likely many recent arrivals of African decent other than African-American are more vulnerable to discrimination and other societal pressures.

Many African-Americans in my peer groups who tried to ignore discrimination and do nothing succumb to heart-attacks and strokes. I paraphrase their fears as being scared to death.

I would be totally dishonest if I did not say I also did it because I wanted to advance my career and be rewarded of the monetary privileges of employment like everyone else.

But if you notice, this is the last reason that I decided to file a complaint. If your reason is solely based on money, you may not survive your complaint. My family sacrificed a lot of comforts in society for me to achieve success. There are many more reasons why I filed my complaint but these are paramount.

Your spiritual faith will be tested many times so you will need deep inner strength. Surround yourself with only positive thinking people who want you to be successful.

NEWSPAPER AND MAGAZINE ARTICLES ON DISCRIMINATION, SEXUAL HARASSMENT AND WHISTLEBLOWING COMPLAINTS

I have taken hundreds of newspaper and magazine articles that I have found related to discrimination complaints and saved them over the years. Before winning my complaint, many of the articles gave me inspiration; uplifted me when I felt down and ultimately gave me the desire to continue on. The people who won their cases and now are in print are no different than you but they had a desire to succeed. The articles will provide you with information that will be helpful to you in forming your complaint. Some of the articles may be very similar to what you are experiencing or your already existing complaint. The articles should show you that you can win your complaint and build you with confidence. The rare vital ingredient is courage. I wished that I could have displayed all of the articles that I have but it would be impossible because of permission to reprint costs and copyrights.

The Internet is also a valuable tool in learning about other cases whether they are articles or actual court cases. Just keyword Discrimination and you will find many articles and cases on discrimination. Of all the articles that I have read, I found three articles that really got my attention. One article was titled Workplace Discrimination—You Don't Have To Take It describes that when companies like Avis, Denney's and Texaco are exposed for discriminating against African American employees they leap over backwards to inform the public of top-level appointments of them. That is really how anti-discrimination laws should work but however, the biggest impediment to fair employment is the lack of awareness among the people who most need the knowledge—the victims.

African-Americans being the most discriminated group of people in the history of planet earth, most of them do not know what to do when it happens. That is the biggest reason it continues to happen, lack of knowledge. The laws and statues are so cumbersome that protect our civil rights. They are filled with loopholes, standards of proof and arbitrary deadlines that one must know to win your case.

The article further states that most lawyers will not take a discrimination case on "contingency"—meaning they want their money up front. If people have just lost their job and have no income, it would be virtually impossible to come up with thousands of dollars to pay an attorney. Many times attorneys you pay will not have the expertise in civil rights laws to litigate your case. They may say things to you like "You can't win unless you can prove they called you a name." Discrimination is cultural, systematic, and rarely is clear-cut.

The second article, Private Job Discrimination Lawsuits Tripled in 1990's described the Justice Department's statistics on private complainant alleging discrimination. The article states the reason for the increase is "The growth in civil rights cases has been due largely to the increase employment cases between private parties."

The third article, Whistleblowers Can Get Rich Helping Feds states that one billion dollars was paid out in these cases since the inception of the law in the 1980s. It further states you risk your whole livelihood by blowing the whistle but you can become very rich by taking a stand against fraud and corruption. One man received twenty million dollars in one settlement and split one hundred million in another case in

Medicare fraud cases. Two other men received seventeen million dollars each after they blew the whistle on Tap Pharmaceutical in its pricing and marketing the cancer drug "Lupron."

On the following pages, I am displaying three articles from *The Huntsville Times*, Huntsville, Alabama of people who courageously took a stand against racism. By displaying these articles in no way minimizes the efforts of others who have also taken a stand against racism in the Huntsville, Alabama area and throughout the continental United States. I graciously appreciate *The Huntsville Times* for giving me permission to reprint their articles.

Madison worker files suit alleging discrimination

Black employee alleges he was unjustly fired

MADISON - A black former employee of the Madison Department of Public Works has filed a federal lawsuit alleging racial discrimination by the city.

The federal Equal Employment Opportunity Commission investigated the former employee's claim and concluded in February 2007 that the agency could state that the law was violated.

Birmingham lawyer Kimberly Dodson filed the lawsuit Tuesday on behalf of William Summerour Jr. Summerour had been employed with the city for five years when he was fired Aug. 9, 2007, without oral or written warnings, according to the suit.

Dodson would not comment about the lawsuit Wednesday.

Summerour says in his lawsuit that his work was scrutinized more severely than that of white employees, and that he was passed over for promotions, denied other opportunities to advance on the job and fired because he protested his treatment.

Mayor Sandy Kirkindall said he could not comment on pending litigation.

"One thing I can say is that his allegations are without merit," said Kirkindall.

Summerour filed a discrimination claim against the city in 2003, the lawsuit says, but he did not follow up on it.

The lawsuit gives this account of Summerour's case:

The situation began to unravel when the city bought a Freightliner truck in 2006. Despite receiving his commercial driver's license in 2004, he was not allowed to operate the truck. But white employees in the department who either had less seniority or training or received their commercial licenses later than Summerour were allowed to operate the Freightliner.

On July 24, 2007, an EEOC investigator conducted a field investigation of Summerour's allegations of racial discrimination. On July 31, Summerour's supervisor called a meeting that included all his crew members. The meeting did not comply with the city's policy and procedures. An altercation of an unspecified nature broke out between many of the employees.

Summerour went to the Personnel Department office immediately after the meeting. He became ill and had to go home. He was absent from work the next day.

When Summerour returned to work Aug. 2, three police officers and the department director, Skip Adkins, who was not named as a party in the lawsuit, met him at the entrance to his work place. Adkins told Summerour that he was on administrative leave until Aug. 8.

When Summerour returned to work Aug. 9, Adkins, again accompanied by three police officers, told him he was fired.

The lawsuit seeks Summerour's reinstatement, back pay, promotion, compensatory damages and fees for his lawyer.

City ends race bias suit, pays $225K

Guntersville's only black firefighter will stay on job

GUNTERSVILLE - A racial discrimination lawsuit filed by Guntersville's only black firefighter has been settled for a reported $225,000, and the city has agreed to several personnel changes.

Anthony Berry, the firefighter who filed the suit in U.S. District Court in Birmingham, was not available for comment Monday.

Berry has been a firefighter for the city since 1993 and filed the suit last year after the Equal Employment Opportunity Commission took no action on a complaint he filed against the city.

According to Berry's suit, Mayor James Townson did not take steps to prevent Berry from working in a "racially hostile" environment inside the department. He said he was treated differently from white firefighters and was subjected to racial epithets.

Besides the cash settlement, the city agreed to allow Berry to continue at his job on the condition that he release the city and officials from further liability.

The settlement also requires the city to employ a personnel coordinator or director whose job includes receiving and investigating discrimination complaints.

The city also agreed to provide training to its employees and their supervisors in the areas of anti-harassment and diversity, with the EEOC providing the training at no cost to [illegible]ty.

Prosecutor wins suit over office racial bias

Local lawyer, boss demoted for supporting her to get jobs back

[illegible]

The U.S. Justice Department has been ordered to reinstate a Huntsville woman to her former job as a federal prosecutor nearly five years after she alleged racial and sexual discrimination.

In its ruling favoring Assistant U.S. Attorney Deirdra Brown-Fleming, the Equal Employment Opportunity Commission also ordered the reinstatement of Brown-Fleming's former supervisor, Victor Conrad, who claimed he was demoted for reporting the situation to his superiors and supporting Brown-Fleming.

In addition to reinstatement, Brown-Fleming is to receive back pay.

The EEOC ruled in December that U.S. Attorney Alice Martin fired Brown-Fleming in 2002 as a reprisal for filing a racial discrimination complaint.

The EEOC, based in Washington, D.C., ordered compensation that will likely total more than $4.4 million in taxpayers' money, Brown-Fleming said.

LAWSUITS THAT HAVE BEEN WON

1. Article
   Age-bias suit settled for a record $250 Million
   The Associated Press

   Who initially filed the complaint
   The U.S. Equal Employment Opportunity Commission filed the case in California on behalf of seven disabled retirees who worked as police and firefighters.

   Nature of the Complaint
   The police and firefighters who were hired after they turned 30 years old and given reduced benefits because they were older.

   Outcome of the case
   The age-discrimination case would require the California Public Employees Retirement System to pay $50 million in retroactive benefits to public safety workers who retired because of injury but didn't get full benefits. The average individual would receive $30,000 in back benefits and around $110,000 extra in future benefits. $200,000,000 was set-aside for future benefits.

   Who represented the complainant(s) or plaintiff(s) in the case
   The plaintiff(s) were represented by EEOC.

2. Article
   Texaco will pay $176 M in bias suit
   The Associated Press

   Who initially filed the complaint
   The class-action lawsuit was filed on behalf of 1500 current and former Black workers.

   Nature of the complaint
   The lawsuit was filed in 1994 on behalf of Blacks who were denied promotions and raises due to the "good old boy" system reserved for whites.

   Outcome of the case
   Texaco will pay 115,000,000 in cash and $26.1 million in pay raises over five years. $35 million was reserved for sensitivity and diversity training programs.

   Who represented the complainant(s) or plaintiff(s) in the case
   Attorneys represented the plaintiffs.

3. Article
Breaking Labor Laws Cost Wal-Mart $78 M
The Associated Press

Who initially filed the complaint
The class-action lawsuit was filed by Dolores Hummel, the lead plaintiff in the case involving 187,000 current and former employees.

Nature of the case
The employees were forced to work off the clock during their breaks.

Outcome of the case
A jury awarded $78.5 million and the plaintiffs seek another $62 million in damages because the jury found that Wal-Mart acted in bad faith.

Who represented the complainant(s) or plaintiff(s) in the case
An attorney represented the plaintiffs.

4. Article
Wal-Mart workers win more than meal
The Associated Press

Who initially filed the complaint
The class-action lawsuit was filed in California on behalf of thousands of employees who worked at Wal-Mart stores.

Nature of the complaint
The Wal-Mart employees were denied lunch breaks.

Outcome of the case
A California jury awarded $172 million in the case.

Who represented the complainant(s) or plaintiff(s) in the case
An attorney represented the plaintiffs

5. Article
Winn-Dixie Grocery Chain settles Discrimination Suit for $33 million

Who initially filed the complaint
The class-action lawsuit was filed in Federal Court by 13 current and former employees.

Nature of the complaint
The race and sex discrimination claims were filed because the black and female employees were denied advancement to management positions.

Outcome of the Case
The settlement agreement would pay $120,000 among the 13 plaintiffs and $13 million to other employees who filed verified discrimination claims. An additional $11 million to be paid as incentive bonuses, $1 million in diversity awards and $4 million for training and administrative expenses.

Who represented the complainant(s) or plaintiff(s) in the case
A law firm based in Jacksonville, Florida represented the plaintiffs who received $3.9 million in fees.

6. Article
Coca-Cola settle suit with Black Employees
National Newspapers Publishers Association

Who initially filed the complaint
The class-action lawsuit was filed by thousands of Black workers who worked for the company from April 1995-2000.

Nature of the complaint
In the lawsuit, Black employees accused Coca-Cola of discriminating in pay, promotion and evaluations.

Outcome of the case
Coca-Cola Company agreed to pay a record $192.5 million to settle the race discrimination case.

Who represented the complainant(s) or plaintiff(s) in the case
The plaintiffs were represented by Mehri, Malkin and Ross, a Washington, D.C. law firm.

7. Article
U.S. settles sex bias suit for record $508 million
Jet Magazine

Who initially filed the complaint
Women filed the lawsuit that applied for jobs with the U.S. Information Agency.

Nature of the Complaint
Woman complained about being denied jobs with the agency in its broadcast arm because of their gender.

Outcome of the case
Each woman, about 1,100 would receive $450,000 before taxes.

Who represented the complainants(s) or plaintiff(s) in the case
Attorneys represented the women.

8. Article
DOT Bias Suit Nears its Costly End
The Associated Press

Who initially filed the Complaint
Johnny Reynolds, the lead plaintiff filed the class-action lawsuit on behalf of Black employees being denied hiring.

Nature of the complaint
The Department of Transportation had a long history of denying Blacks into the department.

Outcome of the case
The lawsuit was won and the state agreed to mass recruitment of blacks in the department. Johnny Reynolds, the lead plaintiff died two years before the case started the resolution stage.

Who represented the complainant(s) and plaintiff(s) in the case
A law firm represented the class-action lawsuit.

9. Article
Home Depot Settles Bias Suit for $5.5 million
The Associated Press

Who initially filed the complaint
Home Depot workers in Colorado filed the complaint.

Nature of the complaint
Current and former workers alleged that Home Depot discriminated against them based on gender, race and nationality. Some workers also alleged that they were retaliated against for claiming discrimination.

Outcome of the case
The settlement includes $3 million that will be divided among 38 plaintiffs and $2.5 million for other individuals who were harmed by the same actions.

Who represented the complainant(s) or plaintiff(s) in the case
The plaintiffs were represented by the Equal Employment Opportunity Commission.

10. Article
American General Life and Accident Insurance Company pays $206 million settling claims it overcharged Blacks
Jet Magazine

Who initially filed the complaint
The Federal class-action was filed in Tennessee and Tennessee Insurance commissioners threatened sanctions.

Nature of the complaint
The insurance commissioners in Tennessee filed the complaint along with the NAACP over unfair practices, mainly collecting for more money in premiums than the policies was worth.

Outcome of the case
Some 9.1 million-policy holders would receive part of the settlement.

Who represented the complainant(s) or plaintiff(s) in the case
Insurance commissioners in Florida and Tennessee along with the National Association for Advancement of Colored People (NAACP)

11. Article
Women ex-newscaster wins $8.3 million in gender discrimination lawsuit
The Associated Press

Who initially filed the complaint
Janet Peckinpaugh, a newscaster claimed her gender and age was the reason she lost her job.

Nature of the complaint
Her lawyer, David Golub, argued that she was replaced on the newscast with a younger woman and demoted. She also complained of being retaliated against by one of her coworkers.

Outcome of the case
A jury in U.S. District Court decided that the former anchor was discriminated against because of her gender but dismissed her age discrimination claim.

Who represented the complainant(s) or plaintiff(s) in the case
An attorney represented the plaintiff

12. Article
Boeing to Settle Race – Bias Suits for $15M
The Associated Press

Who initially filed the complaint
Two complaints were initially filed in a class-action lawsuit in Boeing's Seattle and Philadelphia areas by 70 plaintiffs and 194 others were named during the course of the complaint.

Nature of the complaint
The complaints were filed by the plaintiffs because of denials of promotional opportunities.

Outcome of the case
The 264 named plaintiffs received $3.8 million shared between them, $3.5 will go to other class members, and $3.7 million for equal opportunity and diversity training at Boeing.

Who represented the complainant(s) or plaintiff(s) in the case
Attorneys who received $4 million represented the plaintiffs.

13. Article
UPS to pay $12.1 M in Discrimination Suit
The Associated Press

Who initially filed the complaint
Atlanta-based employees initially filed the class action lawsuit

Nature of the complaint
The complaint by black part-time workers alleges that UPS did not adequately inform them of the procedures and opportunities for advancement.

Outcome of the case
The major part of the settlement will go to 12,000 current and former part-time hourly black workers in the company's Northwest and Pacific regions.

Who represented the complainant(s) or plaintiff(s) in the case
Attorneys represented the plaintiffs

14. Article
Boeing pays $61.5M in Lawsuit
The Associated Press

Who initially filed the complaint
The lawsuit was filed by Brett Roby in a whistleblower case accusing Boeing of installing faulty gears in two Army helicopters that crashed.

Nature of the complaint
Roby was fired from Speco Corporation, Springfield, Ohio as a quality control engineer after he alleges that the company supplied quality transmission gears to Boeing Corporation who also knew the gears were bad. The lawsuit was taken over by the federal government.

Outcome of the case
Speco settled with the government for $7.2M in 1996 and was no longer a defendant. Roby received $1.7 million from Speco Corporation. Roby will also be paid $10.5 million by Boeing Corporation. The federal Government received $43.5 million.

Who represented the complainant(s) or plaintiff(s) in the case
The plaintiff (Brett Roby) was represented by attorneys who received $7.5 million in legal fees.

15. Article
Johnson & Johnson Employee gets 11.7 million in bias case
The Associated Press

Who initially filed the complaint
Jennifer Passatino, 43, a 17 year employee filed the complaint.

Nature of the complaint
Passatino alleged that the company retaliated against her after she and a coworker went to personnel to complain about demeaning and sexist comments from male coworkers. They also complained for being passed over for promotions.

Outcome of the case
A federal jury awarded Passatino $8.6 million in punitive damages. $2.1 million in economic losses and $1 million for emotional distress.

Who represented the complainant(s) or plaintiff(s) in the case
The plaintiff was represented by an attorney.

16. Article
Jury awards $6M In Age-Bias Lawsuit
The Associated Press

Who initially filed the complaint
Carl Morse filed the lawsuit pertaining to an age-discrimination claim.

Nature of the complaint
Morse claimed he was terminated because the preferred younger employees. The company, Southern Union, made several comments hinting toward a preference for younger workers.

Outcome of the case
A federal jury awarded 6 million for intentional discrimination and $450,000 for mental anguish, emotional pain and suffering in the judgment.

Who represented the complaint(s) or plaintiff(s) in the case
An attorney represented the plaintiff.

17. Article
Mitsubishi will pay $9.5 million to Settle Lawsuit
The Associated Press

Who initially filed the complaint
Twenty-nine original plaintiffs filed the class-action lawsuit.

Nature of the complaint
The women accused the automaker of being subjected to obscene remarks, groping and sexual discrimination.

Outcome of the case
The $9.5 million will be divided among 27 of the original 29 plaintiffs receiving as much as $500,000 depending on their experience. Two of the plaintiff's had different attorneys.

Who represented the complainant(s) or plaintiff(s) in the case
Patricia Benassi was the attorney for the 27 plaintiffs.

18. Article
Black Woman Executive Wins $7.6 Mil in Boston Transit Agency Bias Suit
Jet Magazine

Who initially filed the complaint
Roberta Edwards, chief administration officer, filed the complaint.

Nature of the complaint
In her lawsuit, Edwards charged that she was "ostracized and harassed" by senior officials after she appeared to be sympathetic to a female who filed a discrimination complaint.

Outcome of the case
Roberta Edwards received nearly $7 million.

Who represented the complainant(s) or plaintiff(s) in the case
The plaintiff was represented by attorneys who received $1.4 million in legal fees.

19. Article
Man awarded $18 M in Harassment case
The Huntsville Times

Who initially filed the complaint
James Stevens, an employee of Vons Companies Inc. filed the complaint

Nature of the complaint
Stevens claimed he was fired after he accused a female of sexual harassment. Stevens testified that he was also subject to other various forms of sexual harassment, offensive sexual remarks and a simulated sex act with a feather duster.

Outcome of the case
The case taking place in Simi Valley, California awarded the plaintiff in a jury award more than $16 million in punitive damages and $1.7 million for economic loss and emotional distress.

Who represented the complaint(s) or plaintiff(s) in the case
The plaintiff was represented by an attorney.

20. Article
Amtrak Worker Wins $500,000 In Bias Lawsuit
Jet Magazine

Who initially filed the complaint
Abner Morgan, who worked in Amtrak's maintenance yard in Oakland, California from 1990 until 1995.

Nature of the complaint
Morgan claimed that he and other black workers in the rail yard endured racial slurs and discriminatory discipline. They were denied training and work assignments for advancement. He also said that the managers, mostly white, allowed another white manager to perform a racially stereotypical "shuffle" dance for their amusement. Morgan's complaint was supported by a parade of witnesses in District Court. Morgan also had been terminated.

Outcome of the case
Morgan was awarded $250,000 for lost wages and $250,000 for emotional distress.

Who represented the complainant(s) or plaintiff(s) in the case
The plaintiff was represented by an attorney.

21. Article
Pizza Hut To Pay $160,000 In Racial Discrimination Settlement
Jet Magazine

Who initially filed the complaint
The suit was filed by a black family, Jacqueline and Curtis Randle El.

Nature of the complaint
The plaintiffs claimed that Pizza Hut discriminated against them by not allowing their son to celebrate his 10th birthday at the restaurant.

Outcome of the case
The case became a class-action case and was settled for $160,000 among 20 plaintiffs before the trial began.

Who represented the complainant(s) or plaintiff(s) in the case
Fay Clayton, an attorney, represented the plaintiffs.

22. Article
$7.6 Million Award In Bias Lawsuit
The Huntsville Times

Who initially filed the complaint
Rayford Hudson filed the discrimination charge.

Nature of the complaint
Hudson sued Brand Services, a subsidiary of waste management systems alleged that he was fired from the company after being told he was the " wrong color."

Outcome of the case
The $7.6 million award was one of the largest awards in California's history

Who represented the complainant(s) or Plaintiff(s) in the case
The article did not state who represented the plaintiff

23. Article
Wal-Mart Loses $7.5M Discrimination Case
The Huntsville Times

Who initially filed the complaint
Patrick Brady, 21, filed the complaint in U.S. District Court in New York.

Nature of the complaint
Brady stated in his complaint that he was discriminated against because of his handicap, cerebral palsy. Brady was initially hired in the pharmacy department at Wal-Mart, but after one day on the job he was reassigned to low level duties such as garbage collecting and retrieving shopping carts from the parking lot.

Outcome of the case
A federal jury returned the $7.5 million judgment after one day.

Who represented the complainant(s) or the plaintiff(s) in the case
The article did not state who represented the plaintiff

24. Article
Harassment Case Award: $8 Million
The Associated Press

Who initially filed the complaint
Janice M. Dumas employee of Tyson foods, Inc initially filed the complaint.

Nature of the complaint
Dumas claimed she was forced out of her job by a hostile work environment caused by routine sexual harassment. The complaint further states that her supervisor often engaged in vulgar language, sexually offensive jokes and lewd actions in a room where women employees took their breaks. Ms. Haynes complained to upper level management, who were men, condoned the actions of her supervisor.

Outcome of the case
A federal jury awarded $8 million to Ms. Dumas but Tyson's attorney asked the judge to reduce the award to $300,000 in punitive awards and $23,000 in back pay.

- Note:

  Knowledge of the law would reveal that the Tyson attorney does not know the law. $300,000 in punitive awards is limited to federal government employees in civilian capacity. Employees in private industry do not have the $300,000 cap on punitive awards. Private employee punitive awards have no cap. In this case, Janice M. Dumas is an employee in private industry with no punitive damages cap.

Who represented the complainant(s) or plaintiff(s) in the case
Alicia Haynes, the plaintiff's attorney stated that the size of the verdict get the company to pay attention to the in her representation.

25. Article
$5 Million Awarded In Gender Bias Suit
The Associated Press

Who initially filed the complaint
Mary Ann Luciano, an assistant vice president filed the complaint against Olsten Corporation.

Nature of the complaint
Ms. Luciano alleged that she was a victim of the "glass ceiling" also stating that she was fired from her job and the company reneged on a promise to promote her to vice president.

Outcome of the case
Ms. Luciano was awarded $5.18 million by a jury which found that Olsten Corporation discriminated against women.

Who represented the complainant(s) or plaintiff(s)
The article did not state who represented the plaintiff.

26. Article
Pizza Worker Wins $237,000 For Harassment By Female Boss
The Associated Press

Who initially filed the complaint
The U. S. Equal Employment Opportunity Commission filed the case against Domino's Pizza on behalf of David Papa, an employee of the pizza chain.

Nature of the complaint
David Papa accused his female boss of sexual harassment involving sexual comments about his body, touching him, and stating she loved him. After he told her to stop, she fired him.

Outcome of the case
The Equal Employment Opportunity Commission received a $237,000 judgment in the case which became the first case ever filed by the commission against a woman sexually harassing a man.

Who represented the complainant(s) or plaintiff(s) in the case
The EEOC represented the plaintiff in the case.

27. Article
Female Professor Wins $12.6M In Tenure Suit
The Associated Press

Who initially filed the complaint
Leslie Craine filed the sex discrimination suit against Trinity College in Hartford, Connecticut.

Outcome of case
The award included $671,304 for lost of past and future wages, $2 million for sex discrimination, $4 million for emotional distress and $6 million in punitive damages was the largest ever won in a tenure related lawsuit in 1994

Who represented the complainant(s) or plaintiff(s) in the case
The plaintiff was represented by attorneys.

28. Article
White IRS Employee Wins Discrimination Suit
The Associated Press

Who initially filed the complaint
Gary Hoeffken filed the complaint against the Internal Revenue Service.

Nature of the complaint
Hoeffken accused a black supervisor at IRS of retaliation when he was demoted from his supervisor job after he claimed that there were to many minorities being promoted.

Outcome of the case
Hoeffken received a judgment in U.S. District Court totaling $200,000.

Who represented the complainant(s) or plaintiff(s) in the case
The article did not state if the plaintiff was represented by an attorney.

29. Article
Sexual Harassment Lawsuit Reportedly Settled For $1M
The Associated Press

Who initially filed the complaint
Fifteen women filed the class-action lawsuit against Del Laboratories, a cosmetic and pharmaceutical company.

Nature of the complaint
The women accused the chief executive Dan K. Wasong of indulging in lewd abusive behavior for years, grabbing the breast of one employee, conducting business with his pant zipper open, routinely using vulgar abusive language and using his executive bathroom with the door open.

Outcome of the case
At the time of the lawsuit, the $1 million settlement was the largest reported by EEOC. Del laboratories denied all of the allegations as part of the settlement.

30. Article
Interstate Bakeries Corp. Ordered To Pay $131 Million Judgment In Racial Discrimination Suit.
Jet Magazine

Who initially filed the complaint
Twenty-one black workers filed the complaint against a Wonder Bread Plant.

Nature of the complaint
The workers claimed they suffered racial discrimination which consisted of blacks being called racial slurs, being called the racial epithet "boy' and being denied equal access to holidays which whites were given.

Outcome of the case
The jury found that the company acted with malice and oppression toward 17 of the 21 plaintiffs in the lawsuit. The 17 plaintiffs will share the punitive award. All 21 plaintiffs will share the actual damages.

Who represented the complainant(s) or plaintiff(s) in the case
All of the plaintiffs were represented by attorneys.

31. Article
Drug Agent Wins DEA Bias Case
The Huntsville Times

Who initially filed the complaint
Peter Probst, a white DEA agent filed the case against the Drug Enforcement Agency.

Nature of the complaint
Probst was discriminated against after he supported a black colleagues claim of racial discrimination. He was suspended for 10 days for misconduct and insubordination. He was also subjected to harassing late night calls and low job ratings.

Outcome of the case
Probst won a$180,000 compensatory award and 10 days backpay after it was rescinded in the judgment.

Who represented the complainant(s) or plaintiff(s) in the case
The article did not state if the plaintiff was represented by an attorney.

32. Article
Woman Wins Age Discrimination Suit
The Huntsville Times

Who initially filed the complaint
Martha Nance, 61, filed the complaint against Max Federal Credit Union.

Outcome of the case
A jury agreed that the plaintiff is entitled to $140,000 in backpay, reinstatement to her job or the amount she would have made on the job if she decided not to return.

<u>Who represented the complainant(s) or Plaintiff(s) in the case</u>
The plaintiff was represented by attorneys.

33. <u>Article</u>
Former Employees Win Against TVA In Discrimination Lawsuit
<u>The Huntsville Times</u>

<u>Who initially filed the complaint</u>
Twenty-one workers of Tennessee Valley Authority filed the case.

<u>Nature of the complaint</u>
The employees were dismissed in a disability downsizing case, reducing the amount of lifetime compensation to the group and rehiring other disable workers in a cost-saving scheme.

<u>Outcome of the case</u>
The disabled employees would receive checks ranging from $400,000 to more than $1 million in a $12.2 million verdict in a U.S. District Court.

<u>Who represented the complainant(s) or plaintiff(s) in the case</u>
The plaintiffs were represented by attorneys in the class-action case.

34. <u>Article</u>
Woman Wins Same-Sex Harassment Lawsuit
<u>The Associated Press</u>

<u>Who initially filed the complaint</u>
Peggy Moore, filed the complaint against Belk Department Store

<u>Nature of the complaint</u>
Moore filed the complaint against her supervisor for same-sex harassment consisting of grabbing, prodding and kissing her. In another incident, the supervisor disrobed in front of her and asked Moore if she liked her body. Moore said she quit after she could no longer take the harassment.

<u>Outcome of the case</u>
A jury awarded more than $1 million to the plaintiff totaling $33,400 for lost wages and benefits, $30,000 for future losses, $100,000 for pain and suffering, and $850,000 in punitive damages.

<u>Who represented the complainant(s) or plaintiff(s) in the case</u>
The article did not state if the plaintiff was represented by an attorney.

35. <u>Article</u>
Jury Awards $2M To Ex- Shelton State Official
<u>The Associated Press</u>

Who initially filed the complaint
Ted Spring, a former vice president filed the complaint against the president of Shelton State Community College in Alabama.

Nature of the Complaint
Spring was fired in a whistleblowing case after he reported allegations of fraud and unethical conduct at the college.

Outcome of the case
Spring's $2 million award included backpay, punitive damages and compensation for emotional damages.

Who represented the complainant(s) or plaintiff(s) in the case
The plaintiff was represented by an attorney.

36. Article
Jury Awards $990k To 12 Female Prison Nurses
The Huntsville Times

Who initially filed the complaint
Twelve female nurses filed the complaint against Washington Correctional Institution in Florida.

Nature of complaint
The nurses complained that they had been harassed on their daily rounds by male inmates. The Florida corrections officials condoned the sexual harassment.

Outcome of the case
A jury awarded the 12 female nurses nearly $1 million.

Who represented the complainant(s) or plaintiff(s) in the case
The article did not state who represented the plaintiffs.

37. Article
EEOC Settled Race Lawsuit Against Ford
National Newspaper publisher Association

Who initially filed the complaint
Twenty-three black workers at Ford Motor Company in Detroit, Michigan filed the complaint.

Nature of the complaint
The black workers claimed they were racially insulting them, mocking their style of speech and placing a hangman's noose on a forklift.

Outcome of the case
The workers will receive $300,000 as part of the settlement agreement.

Who represented the complainant(s) or plaintiff(s) in the case
The plaintiffs were represented by the Equal Employment Opportunity Commission.

38. Article
Wal-Mart Settles Lawsuit With Federal Government
The Huntsville Times

Who initially filed the complaint
The Equal Employment Opportunity Commission filed the complaint against Wal-Mart.

Nature of the complaint
EEOC accused Wal- Mart of using a pre-employment questionnaire prospective employees which violated the Americans with Disabilities Act between Jan. 1, 1994 through Dec. 31, 1998. The questions asked for to much information about the type of disability an applicant had.

Outcome of the case
The settlement totaled $6,8 million to the prospective applicant who could be identified

Who represented the complainant(s) or plaintiff(s) in the case
EEOC was the plaintiff in this case representing the chairwoman, Cari M. Dominguez, at the time of the lawsuit.

39. Article
Homeless Man Who Sued Former Employer For Bias Is Awarded $1.25 Million
Jet Magazine

Who initially filed the complaint
Niles A. DeGrate filed the complaint against Eaton Corporation.

Nature of the complaint
DeGrate claimed he was subject to racial slurs, intimidation and being fired from his job. He stated that he was a frequent target of racial abuse in front of customers, food being dumped on his desk, and given fictitious application for buying cars or other items requesting insulting stereotypical information. The information requested would ask if his car was a Lincoln or Cadillac, stolen or financed. Also asked place of birth—free clinic, alley, zoo, car, Colonel Sanders, or Popeye's. He stated he was often called nigger. DeGrate's resume stated that he had a law degree and Biochemistry degree but was told the reason for being fired was because of his performance.

Outcome of the case

DeGrate, who received the $1.25 million judgment said he was going to use some of the money to help the homeless.

Who represented the complainant(s) or plaintiff(s) in the case

The article states that he slipped into homelessness two years prior to the court's decision, living in public buildings and on city streets while he doggedly pursued his legal battle against his former employer.

40. Article

5 Women, 1 Man From D.C. Area Share $1.4 Million Awarded In Harassment Suit

Jet Magazine

Who initially filed the complaint

Six Black plaintiffs filed the complaint against the D.C. Department of Corrections.

Nature of the complaint

The plaintiffs stated that some of the high ranking employees harassed them sexually and punished them for complaining. The female employees testified about being grabbed, kissed and pressured for dates and sex. When the complained about sexual harassment, they were to undesirable job and written up on disciplinary charges. The only man in the case, worked as a shop steward and helped the women file the complaints of sexual harassment. He stated that he was retaliated against for helping the women.

Outcome of the case

A jury awarded a total of $1,425,000 to the victims of sexual harassment and retaliation. Barbara Carter stated " To all those people who told me ... you're just one person, you can't make a difference, I say there is justice. It just takes perseverance and faith in God." Carter was awarded $200,000. The other plaintiffs were Bessye Neal, who received $500,000, Shivan Newsome received $75,000 and Teresa Washington received $75,000. Tyrone Posey, the only male, was awarded $75,000.

Who represented the complainant(s) or plaintiff(s) in the case

The article did not state if the woman had any other representation other than Tyrone Posey, shop steward.

41. Article

Jury Awards Disabled Federal Workers $3 Million

Internet Article

Who initially filed the complaint

Lisa Bremer, a U.S. department of Commerce filed the complaint.

Nature of the complaint
Bremer, a disabled federal employee who was diagnosed with multiple sclerosis in 1991 worked successfully from home for eight years, two days a week. Bremer was rated outstanding and received numerous performance awards. A jury decided for the plaintiff on her claim that she was denied reasonable accommodations by law. The department had revoked he accommodation.

Outcome of the case
The $3 million that was awarded to Lisa Bremer on August 10, 2005 was reduced to $303,881 on July 10 2007 because of the cap of $300,000 in compensatory damages to federal employees.

Who represented the complainant(s) or plaintiff(s) in the case
The plaintiff was represented by a Washington, D. C. law firm.

42. Article
U.S. to pay $3.8M in Compensation to Black Diplomats
The Associated Press

Who initially filed the complaint
Seventeen Black foreign service workers filed the complaint against the State Department of the United States Government.

Nature of the complaint
The Black worker claimed they were denied advancement and career opportunities because of their race.

Outcome of the case
In addition to compensation which was a settlement agreement, the State Department agreed to reinstate four black junior officers who were dismissed after failing to receive permanent position. They also agreed to pay $2.1 million in legal fees. More than 300 diplomats service people will share $3.8M settlement beginning in 1984.

Who represented the complainant(s) or plaintiff(s) in the case
The group had different law firms to represent them because they felt that the entire group was not informed of the settlement agreement beginning in 1984.

43. Article
Student Wins $500,000 In Harassment Case
The Associated Press

Who initially filed the complaint
A 14-year old girl at Antioch Unified School District near San Francisco filed the complaint.

Nature of the complaint
The case involved sexual harassment among school children and the official who ignored her claims. The girl stated that she was barraged daily with insults and threats from a sixth grade boy. His lewd insults included grabbing his crotch in front of her and asking why her breast weren't larger. He also told her he would beat her up and even kill her, which terrified her daily.

Outcome of the case
The jury ordered the school district to pay 93.4% of the $500,000, the boys parents pay $27,000 and the former principal pay $6,000.

Who represented the complainant(s) or plaintiff(s) in the case
The article did not state who represented the plaintiff.

44. Article
Lockheed Martin settles Age Bias Suit
The Associated Press

Who initially filed the complaint
Two thousand former employees of Martin Marietta Corporation, A part of Lockheed Martin Corporation.

Nature of the complaint
The former employees were forced out in a series of job cutbacks based on their age. The complaint alleged Martin targeted employees age 40 years and older in a series of major layoffs and forced retirements over a five year period.

Outcome of the case
The $13 million settlement was reported to be the largest age-bias in the nation. The company agreed to pay for retraining courses provided by the company.

Who represented the complainant(s) or plaintiff(s) in the case
The Equal Employment Opportunity Commission filed the complaint for the plaintiffs and represented them.

45. Article
Knicks's Isiah, MSG Lose Suit
The Associated Press

Who initially filed the complaint
Anucha Brown Sanders file the complaint of sexual harassment against New York Knicks coach Isiah Thomas and Madison Square Garden.
Nature of the complaint
In the sexual harassment complaint, Browne Sanders alleged Coach Isiah Thomas verbally insulted her continually and made unwanted sexual advances. Madison Square Garden allowed the hostile environment to persist.

Outcome of the case
Browne Sanders won a $11.6 million judgment in a U.S. District Court. Cablevision Systems Corporation who owns the Madison Square Garden shares fell 35 cents in stock trading the same afternoon of the judgment.

Who represented the complainant(s) or plaintiff(s) in the case
The plaintiff was represented by an attorney.

46. Article
NASA Awards Black Workers $3.75M To Settle Suit Over Job Promotions
The Associated Press

Who initially filed the complaint
More than 100 workers filed complaint with the Equal Employment Opportunity Commission against NASA's Goddard Space Flight Center in Greenbelt, Md., and Wallops Island Flight Facility in Virginia.

Nature of the complaint
The Black employees said they were discriminated against in promotions.

Outcome of the case
In addition to the $3.75 million settlement, independent experts will also review NASA's system for determining promotions and handling employee appraisals, as well as it process for mediating complaints through Equal Employment Opportunity.

Who represented the complainant(s) or plaintiff(s) in the case
The NASA workers were represented by an attorney.

47. Article
Porn in cockpit costs Continental $875,000 in suit
The Associated Press

Who initially filed the complaint
Captain Tammy Blakely, a 13-year employee with Continental filed the complaint against the airline.

Nature of the complaint
Blakely, the first female captain at the airline and possibly in the nation claim the other pilots left pornographic pictures in flight manuals, behind equipment panels and pasted in drawers to surprise the next crew flying the airline. Blakely said the naked pictures of the women created a hostile environment.

Outcome of the case
A Federal jury awarded the $875,000 to Blakely who said she was apprehensive about returning to her job.

Who represented the complainant(s) or plaintiff(s) in the case
The article did not state if the plaintiff was represented by an attorney.

48. Article
Holiday Inn Pays to Settle Discrimination Suit
The Associated Press

Who initially filed the complaint
The Equal Employment Opportunity Commission filed the complaint on behalf of 1,000 black prospective job applicants.

Nature of the complaint
The black workers claimed they were turned down for jobs between 1990-1995 after applying. EEOC investigator found the motel coded job applications from black people with the number "8," after the black-eight ball in pool. The investigators also found that desk clerks were told to place black people on the first floor so police could be able to remove them quickly from the hotel after an arrest.

Outcome of the case
The case was settled for $1 million and the hotel attorney admitted the bias job application coding.

Who represented the complainant(s) or plaintiff(s) in the case
EEOC represented the plaintiffs in the class-action settlement.

49. Article
U.S. Will Pay Female CIA Officer $410,000 in Sex Discrimination Suit
The Associated Press

Who initially filed the complaint
Janine Brookner, a senior female CIA officer filed the complaint against the Central Intelligence Agency

Nature of the complaint
The complaint alleged that the CIA officer was discriminated against by superiors after reporting a colleague for beating his wife. Brookner states that she was falsely portrayed as a "drunk and a sexual provocateur." She was also accused of uttering a racial epithet, drinking too much and wearing "brief shorts and a thin T-shirt" with no underwear while at her home.

Outcome of the case
The CIA agreed to pay the $410,000 settlement after a CIA spokesman said the settlement was not put into writing to be settled.

Who represented the complainant(s) or plaintiff(s) on the case
The CIA officer was represented by an attorney in the case.

50. Article
Publix Will Pay $81.5 million to women in Bias Lawsuit
The Associated Press

Who initially filed the complaint
Eight women accused the grocery chain of putting them in dead-end low paying jobs.

Nature of complaint
The lawsuit was filed in 1985 by eight women who accused Publix of passing over them for raises and repeatedly being denied for management jobs. The eight women along with four others who joined the lawsuit early on said they watched men with less experience and seniority receive promotions. Some of the women said their requests for promotions were met with unwanted sexual advances from managers.

Outcome of the case
Over 150,000 women will receive compensation from the $81.5 million settlement. The 12 original plaintiffs will receive $90,000 a piece.

Who represented the complainant(s) or plaintiff(s) in the case
The article did not state if the women were represented by an attorney but did have representation and support from the United Food and Commercial Workers union. The Equal Employment Opportunity Commission later joined the lawsuit, expanding it to cover current and past employees in Florida, Georgia, South Carolina and Alabama.

One of the last two articles I found in the newspaper before publication was written by the Associated Press on September 19, 2008 titled Transsexual Wins Federal Bias Lawsuit. The case was brought forth by Diane Schroer who was formerly David Schroer. She changed sex from male to female after being promised a job with the Library of Congress. After she announced her sex change, she was denied the job. No details were reported of the monetary award in the judgment. Diane was represented by the American Civil Liberties Union (ACLU).

The last article I found before publication was presented to me by a friend who received a court case in the mail on September 24, 2008 informing him that he is part of a class-action lawsuit. The case is Roe Wade vs. The Kroger Company involving African Americans who worked for Kroger, a giant grocery store chain, claiming they were paid less than Caucasians performing the same work. They also claimed that salaried Africans-Americans were subject to racial harassment.

The proposed monetary settlement was set at $16 million pending approval by a United States District Court Judge in the Western District of Kentucky.

The African-American class is being presented by law firms in Washington, D. C. and Birmingham, Alabama.

I hope you can see the significance of tracking newspaper articles after these recent discoveries to inspire, uplift you and give you confidence to win or settle your complaint.

EEOC reported discrimination cases are on the rise and won by more complainants since 1993. The period from 1993 – 2001, EEOC reported that cases won by plaintiffs rose 84%.

THE HISTORY OF THE TITLE VII CIVIL RIGHTS ACT OF 1964

In the late 1950's, many Blacks were side tracked into low paying jobs despite their education and qualifications. The best paying jobs and the most secure jobs for Blacks were school teachers and ministers. The income disparity was far less for Blacks than Whites who had similar educational backgrounds and other qualifications. The Industrial Revolution in America made it possible for most Americans to cash in on the wealth and prosperity of the country. But, despite the prosperity in America, Black Americans were locked out.

Many Blacks, especially in the South, began to speak out and say, "Enough is Enough." They began to hold meetings in churches, funeral homes, and residences to devise strategies to put an end to segregation and discrimination in America. Dr. Martin Luther King, Jr. now had appeared on the forefront of the Civil Rights movement and began to teach people to non-violently march to protest against segregation and discrimination. Dr. King began to meet with President John F. Kennedy and later President Lyndon Johnson to discuss the passing of a Civil Rights Bill. The presidents were sympathetic to the plight of Black Americans but the bill had to pass through the Senate.

Finally, in 1964, the bill made its way through the Senate and was passed. On July 2, 1965, the bill became effective and made into law. The bill had other issues besides employment discrimination that were addressed. The bill covered any employer who had 25 or more persons who worked at least 20 weeks of the preceding year. The employers had six months to correct their bias practices of employment.

The Civil Rights Act of 1964 established a five man commission appointed by the president with the consent of the Senate to regulate the commission. The commission was established to investigate the complaints and not to enforce the law. If the employer had been found to be in violation of the law, he or she was given a timeframe to settle the complaint. If no settlement was reached, the Equal Employment Opportunity Commission advised the complainant of his or her right to file a civil action in an appropriate US District Court. The court may appoint an attorney free of charge to the complainant. The court may permit the Attorney General to intervene.

TITLE VII OF THE CIVIL RIGHTS ACT OF 1964

EDITOR'S NOTE: The following is the text of Title VII of the Civil Rights Act of 1964 (Pub. L. 88-352) (Title VII), as amended, as it appears in volume 42 of the United States Code, beginning at section 2000e. Title VII prohibits employment discrimination based on race, color, religion, sex and national origin. The Civil Rights Act of 1991 (Pub. L. 102-166) (CRA) amends several sections of Title VII. These amendments appear in boldface type. In addition, section 102 of the CRA (which is printed elsewhere in this publication) amends the Revised Statutes by adding a new section following section 1977 (42 U.S.C. 1981), to provide for the recovery of compensatory and punitive damages in cases of intentional violations of Title VII, the Americans with Disabilities Act of 1990, and section 501 of the Rehabilitation Act of 1973. Cross references to Title VII as enacted appear in italics following each section heading. Editor's notes also appear in italics.

An Act

To enforce the constitutional right to vote, to confer jurisdiction upon the district courts of the United States to provide injunctive relief against discrimination in public accommodations, to authorize the attorney General to institute suits to protect constitutional rights in public facilities and public education, to extend the Commission on Civil Rights, to prevent discrimination in federally assisted programs, to establish a Commission on Equal Employment Opportunity, and for other purposes.

Be it enacted by the Senate and House of Representatives of the United States of America in Congress assembled, That this Act may be cited as the "Civil Rights Act of 1964."

Definitions

SEC. 2000e. *[Section 701]*

For the purposes of this subchapter-

(a) The term "person" includes one or more individuals, governments, governmental agencies, political subdivisions, labor unions, partnerships, associations, corporations, legal representatives, mutual companies, joint-stock companies, trusts, unincorporated organizations, trustees, trustees in cases under title 11 *[bankruptcy],* or receivers.

(b) The term "employer" means a person engaged in an industry affecting commerce who has fifteen or more employees for each working day in each of twenty or more calendar weeks in the current or preceding calendar year, and any agent of such a person, but such term does not include (1) the United States, a corporation wholly owned by the Government of the United States, an Indian tribe, or any department or agency of the District of Columbia subject by statute to procedures of the competitive service (as defined in section 2102 of title 5 *[of the United States Code]*), or (2) a bona fide private membership club (other than a labor organization) which is exempt from taxation under section 501(c) of title 26 *[the Internal Revenue Code of 1954]*, except that during the first year after March 24, 1972 *[the date of enactment of the Equal Employment Opportunity Act of 1972]*, persons having fewer than twenty-five employees (and their agents) shall not be considered employers.

(c) The term "employment agency" means any person regularly undertaking with or without compensation to procure employees for an employer or to procure for employees opportunities to work for an employer and includes an agent of such a person.

(d) The term "labor organization" means a labor organization engaged in an industry affecting commerce, and any agent of such an organization, and includes any organization of any kind, any agency, or employee representation committcc, group, association, or plan so engaged in which employees participate and which exists for the purpose, in whole or in part, of dealing with employers concerning grievances, labor disputes, wages, rates of pay, hours, or other terms or conditions of employment, and any conference, general committee, joint or system board, or joint council so engaged which is subordinate to a national or international labor organization.

(e) A labor organization shall be deemed to be engaged in an industry affecting commerce if (1) it maintains or operates a hiring hall or hiring office which procures employees for an employer or procures for employees opportunities to work for an employer, or (2) the number of its members (or, where it is a labor organization composed of other labor organizations or their representatives, if the aggregate number of the members of such other labor organization) is (A) twenty-five or more during the first year after March 24, 1972 *[the date of enactment of the Equal Employment Opportunity Act of 1972]*, or (B) fifteen or more thereafter, and such labor organization-

(1) is the certified representative of employees under the provisions of the National Labor Relations Act, as amended *[29 U.S.C. 151 et seq.]*, or the Railway Labor Act, as amended *[45 U.S.C. 151 et seq.]*;

(2) although not certified, is a national or international labor organization or a local labor organization recognized or acting as the representative of employees of an employer or employers engaged in an industry affecting commerce; or

(3) has chartered a local labor organization or subsidiary body which is representing or actively seeking to represent employees of employers within the meaning of paragraph (1) or (2); or

(4) has been chartered by a labor organization representing or actively seeking to represent employees within the meaning of paragraph (1) or (2) as the local or subordinate body through which such employees may enjoy membership or become affiliated with such labor organization; or

(5) is a conference, general committee, joint or system board, or joint council subordinate to a national or international labor organization, which includes a labor organization engaged in an industry affecting commerce within the meaning of any of the preceding paragraphs of this subsection.

(f) The term “employee” means an individual employed by an employer, except that the term “employee” shall not include any person elected to public office in any State or political subdivision of any State by the qualified voters thereof, or any person chosen by such officer to be on such officer's personal staff, or an appointee on the policy making level or an immediate adviser with respect to the exercise of the constitutional or legal powers of the office. The exemption set forth in the preceding sentence shall not include employees subject to the civil service laws of a State government, governmental agency or political subdivision. **With respect to employment in a**

foreign country, such term includes an individual who is a citizen of the United States.

(g) The term “commerce” means trade, traffic, commerce, transportation, transmission, or communication among the several States; or between a State and any place outside thereof; or within the District of Columbia, or a possession of the United States; or between points in the same State but through a point outside thereof.

(h) The term “industry affecting commerce” means any activity, business, or industry in commerce or in which a labor dispute would hinder or obstruct commerce or the free flow of commerce and includes any activity or industry ``affecting commerce'' within the meaning of the Labor Management Reporting and Disclosure Act of 1959 *[29 U.S.C. 401 et seq.]*, and further includes any governmental industry, business, or activity.

(i) The term “State” includes a State of the United States, the District of Columbia, Puerto Rico, the Virgin Islands, American Samoa, Guam, Wake Island, the Canal Zone, and Outer Continental Shelf lands defined in the Outer Continental Shelf Lands Act *[43 U.S.C. 1331 et seq.]*.

(j) The term “religion” includes all aspects of religious observance and practice, as well as belief, unless an employer demonstrates that he is unable to reasonably accommodate to an employee's or prospective employee's religious observance or practice without undue hardship on the conduct of the employer's business.

(k) The terms “because of sex” or “on the basis of sex'” include, but are not limited to, because of or on the basis of pregnancy, childbirth, or related medical conditions; and women affected by pregnancy, childbirth, or related medical conditions shall be treated the same for all employment-related purposes, including receipt of benefits under fringe benefit programs, as other persons not so affected but similar in their ability or inability to work, and nothing in section 2000e-2(h) of this title *[section 703(h)]* shall be interpreted to permit otherwise. This subsection shall not require an employer to pay for health insurance benefits for abortion, except where the life of the mother would be endangered if the fetus were carried to term, or except where medical complications have arisen from an abortion: Provided, That nothing herein shall preclude an employer from providing abortion benefits or otherwise affect bargaining agreements in regard to abortion.

(l) The term "complaining party" means the Commission, the Attorney General, or a person who may bring an action or proceeding under this subchapter.

(m)The term "demonstrates" means meets the burdens of production and persuasion.

(n) The term "respondent"' means an employer, employment agency, labor organization, joint labor management committee controlling apprenticeship or other training or retraining program, including an on-the-job training program, or Federal entity subject to section 2000e-16 of this title .

Exemption

SEC. 2000e-1. *[Section 702]*

(a) This subchapter shall not apply to an employer with respect to the employment of aliens outside any State, or to a religious corporation, association, educational institution, or society with respect to the employment of individuals of a particular religion to perform work connected with the carrying on by such corporation, association, educational institution, or society of its activities.

(b) It shall not be unlawful under section 2000e-2 or 2000e-3 of this title *[section 703 or 704]* for an employer (or a corporation controlled by an employer), labor organization, employment agency, or joint labor management committee controlling apprenticeship or other training or retraining (including on-the-job training programs) to take any action otherwise prohibited by such section, with respect to an employee in a workplace in a foreign country if compliance with such section would cause such employer (or such corporation), such organization, such agency, or such committee to violate the law of the foreign country in which such workplace is located.

(c) (1) If an employer controls a corporation whose place of incorporation is a foreign country, any practice prohibited by section 2000e-2 or 2000e-3 of this title *[section 703 or 704]* engaged in by such corporation shall be presumed to be engaged in by such employer.

(2) Sections 2000e-2 and 2000e-3 of this title *[sections 703 and 704]* shall not apply with respect to the foreign operations of an employer that is a foreign person not controlled by an American employer.

(3) For purposes of this subsection, the determination of whether an employer controls a corporation shall be based on-

(A) the interrelation of operations;

(B) the common management;

(C) the centralized control of labor relations; and

(D) the common ownership or financial control, of the employer and the corporation.

Unlawful Employment Practices

SEC. 2000e-2. *[Section 703]*

(a) It shall be an unlawful employment practice for an employer -

(1) to fail or refuse to hire or to discharge any individual, or otherwise to discriminate against any individual with respect to his compensation, terms, conditions, or privileges of employment, because of such individual's race, color, religion, sex, or national origin; or

(2) to limit, segregate, or classify his employees or applicants for employment in any way which would deprive or tend to deprive any individual of employment opportunities or otherwise adversely affect his status as an employee, because of such individual's race, color, religion, sex, or national origin.

(b) It shall be an unlawful employment practice for an employment agency to fail or refuse to refer for employment, or otherwise to discriminate against, any individual because of his race, color, religion, sex, or national origin, or to classify or refer for employment any individual on the basis of his race, color, religion, sex, or national origin.

(c) It shall be an unlawful employment practice for a labor organization-

(1) to exclude or to expel from its membership, or otherwise to discriminate against, any individual because of his race, color, religion, sex, or national origin;

(2) to limit, segregate, or classify its membership or applicants for membership, or to classify or fail or refuse to refer for employment any individual, in any way which would deprive or tend to deprive any individual of employment opportunities, or would limit such employment opportunities or otherwise adversely affect his status as an employee or as an applicant for employment, because of such individual's race, color, religion, sex, or national origin; or

(3) to cause or attempt to cause an employer to discriminate against an individual in violation of this section.

(d) It shall be an unlawful employment practice for any employer, labor organization, or joint labor management committee controlling apprenticeship or other training or retraining, including on-the-job training programs to discriminate against any individual because of his race, color, religion, sex, or national origin in admission to, or employment in, any program established to provide apprenticeship or other training.

(e) Notwithstanding any other provision of this subchapter, (1) it shall not be an unlawful employment practice for an employer to hire and employ employees, for an employment agency to classify, or refer for employment any individual, for a labor organization to classify its membership or to classify or refer for employment any individual, or for an employer, labor organization, or joint labor management committee controlling apprenticeship or other training or retraining programs to admit or employ any individual in any such program, on the basis of his religion, sex, or national origin in those certain instances where religion, sex, or national origin is a bona fide occupational qualification reasonably necessary to the normal operation of that particular business or enterprise, and (2) it shall not be an unlawful employment practice for a school, college, university, or other educational institution or institution of learning to hire and employ employees of a particular religion if such school, college, university, or other educational institution or institution of learning is, in whole or in substantial part, owned, supported, controlled, or managed by a particular religion or by a particular religious corporation, association, or society, or if the curriculum of such school, college, university, or other educational institution or institution of learning is directed toward the propagation of a particular religion.

(f) As used in this subchapter, the phrase "unlawful employment practice" shall not be deemed to include any action or measure taken by an employer, labor organization, joint labor management committee, or employment agency with respect to an individual who is a member of the Communist Party of the United States or of any other organization required to register as a Communist-action or Communist-front organization by final order of the Subversive Activities Control Board pursuant to the Subversive Activities Control Act of 1950 *[50 U.S.C. 781 et seq.]*.

(g) Notwithstanding any other provision of this subchapter, it shall not be an unlawful employment practice for an employer to fail or refuse to hire and employ any individual for any position, for an employer to discharge any individual from any position, or for an employment agency to fail or refuse to refer any individual for employment in any position, or for a labor organization to fail or refuse to refer any individual for employment in any position, if-

(1) the occupancy of such position, or access to the premises in or upon which any part of the duties of such position is performed or is to be performed, is subject

to any requirement imposed in the interest of the national security of the United States under any security program in effect pursuant to or administered under any statute of the United States or any Executive order of the President; and

(2) such individual has not fulfilled or has ceased to fulfill that requirement.

(h) Notwithstanding any other provision of this subchapter, it shall not be an unlawful employment practice for an employer to apply different standards of compensation, or different terms, conditions, or privileges of employment pursuant to a bona fide seniority or merit system, or a system which measures earnings by quantity or quality of production or to employees who work in different locations, provided that such differences are not the result of an intention to discriminate because of race, color, religion, sex, or national origin, nor shall it be an unlawful employment practice for an employer to give and to act upon the results of any professionally developed ability test provided that such test, its administration or action upon the results is not designed, intended or used to discriminate because of race, color, religion, sex or national origin. It shall not be an unlawful employment practice under this subchapter for any employer to differentiate upon the basis of sex in determining the amount of the wages or compensation paid or to be paid to employees of such employer if such differentiation is authorized by the provisions of section 206(d) of title 29 *[section 6(d) of the Fair Labor Standards Act of 1938, as amended]*.

(i) Nothing contained in this subchapter shall apply to any business or enterprise on or near an Indian reservation with respect to any publicly announced employment practice of such business or enterprise under which a preferential treatment is given to any individual because he is an Indian living on or near a reservation.

(j) Nothing contained in this subchapter shall be interpreted to require any employer, employment agency, labor organization, or joint labor management committee subject to this subchapter to grant preferential treatment to any individual or to any group because of the race, color, religion, sex, or national origin of such individual or group on account of an imbalance which may exist with respect to the total number or percentage of persons of any race, color, religion, sex, or national origin employed by any employer, referred or classified for employment by any employment agency or labor organization, admitted to membership or classified by any labor organization, or admitted to, or employed in, any apprenticeship or other training program, in comparison with the total number or percentage of persons of such race, color, religion, sex, or national origin in any community, State, section, or other area, or in the available work force in any community, State, section, or other area.

(k) (1) (A) An unlawful employment practice based on disparate impact is established under this title only if-

(i) a complaining party demonstrates that a respondent uses a particular employment practice that causes a disparate impact on the basis of race, color, religion, sex, or national origin and the respondent fails to demonstrate that the challenged practice is job related for the position in question and consistent with business necessity; or

(ii) the complaining party makes the demonstration described is subparagraph (C) with respect to an alternative employment

practice and the respondent refuses to adopt such alternative employment practice.

(B) (i) With respect to demonstrating that a particular employment practice causes a disparate impact as described in subparagraph (A)(i), the complaining party shall demonstrate that each particular challenged employment practice causes a disparate impact, except that if the complaining party can demonstrate to the court that the elements of a respondent's decisionmaking process are not capable of separation for analysis, the decisionmaking process may be analyzed as one employment practice.

(ii) If the respondent demonstrates that a specific employment practice does not cause the disparate impact, the respondent shall not be required to demonstrate that such practice is required by business necessity.

(C) The demonstration referred to by subparagraph (A)(ii) shall be in accordance with the law as it existed on June 4, 1989, with respect to the concept o "alternative employment practice."

(2) A demonstration that an employment practice is required by business necessity may not be used as a defense against a claim of intentional discrimination under this title.

(3) Notwithstanding any other provision of this title, a rule barring the employment of an individual who currently and knowingly uses or

possesses a controlled substance, as defined in schedules I and II of section 102(6) of the Controlled Substances Act (21 U.S.C. 802(6)), other than the use or possession of a drug taken under the supervision of a licensed health care professional, or any other use or possession authorized by the Controlled Substances Act *[21 U.S.C. 801 et seq.]* **or any other provision of Federal law, shall be considered an unlawful employment practice under this title only if such rule is adopted or applied with an intent to discriminate because of race, color, religion, sex, or national origin.**

(l) It shall be an unlawful employment practice for a respondent, in connection with the selection or referral of applicants or candidates for employment or promotion, to adjust the scores of, use different cutoff scores for, or otherwise alter the results of, employment related tests on the basis of race, color, religion, sex, or national origin.

(m) Except as otherwise provided in this title, an unlawful employment practice is established when the complaining party demonstrates that race, color, religion, sex, or national origin was a motivating factor for any employment practice, even though other factors also motivated the practice.

(n) (1) (A) Notwithstanding any other provision of law, and except as provided in paragraph (2), an employment practice that implements and is within the scope of a litigated or consent judgment or order that resolves a claim of employment discrimination under the Constitution or Federal civil rights laws may not be challenged under the circumstances described in subparagraph (B).

(B) A practice described in subparagraph (A) may not be challenged in a claim under the Constitution or Federal civil rights laws-

(i) by a person who, prior to the entry of the judgment or order described in subparagraph (A), had-

(I) actual notice of the proposed judgment or order sufficient to apprise such person that such judgment or order might adversely affect the interests and legal rights of such person and that an opportunity was available to present objections to such judgment or order by a future date certain; and

(II) a reasonable opportunity to present objections to such judgment or order; or

(ii) by a person whose interests were adequately represented by another person who had previously challenged the judgment or order on the same legal grounds and with a similar factual situation, unless there has been an intervening change in law or fact.

(2) Nothing in this subsection shall be construed to-

(A) alter the standards for intervention under rule 24 of the Federal Rules of Civil Procedure or apply to the rights of parties who have successfully intervened pursuant to such rule in the proceeding in which the parties intervened;

(B) apply to the rights of parties to the action in which a litigated or consent judgment or order was entered, or of members of a class

represented or sought to be represented in such action, or of members of a group on whose behalf relief was sought in such action by the Federal Government;

(C) prevent challenges to a litigated or consent judgment or order on the ground that such judgment or order was obtained through collusion or fraud, or is transparently invalid or was entered by a court lacking subject matter jurisdiction; or

(D) authorize or permit the denial to any person of the due process of law required by the Constitution.

(2) Any action not precluded under this subsection that challenges an employment consent judgment or order described in paragraph (1) shall be brought in the court, and if possible before the judge, that entered such judgment or order. Nothing in this subsection shall preclude a transfer of such action pursuant to section 1404 of title 28, United States Code.

Other Unlawful Employment Practices

SEC. 2000e-3. *[Section 704]*

(a) It shall be an unlawful employment practice for an employer to discriminate against any of his employees or applicants for employment, for an employment agency, or joint labor-management committee controlling apprenticeship or other training or retraining, including on-the-job training programs, to discriminate against any individual, or for a labor organization to discriminate against any member thereof or applicant for membership, because he has opposed any practice made an unlawful employment practice by this subchapter, or because he has made a charge, testified, assisted, or participated in any manner in an investigation, proceeding, or hearing under this subchapter.

(b) It shall be an unlawful employment practice for an employer, labor organization, employment agency, or joint labor-management committee controlling apprenticeship or other training or retraining, including on-the-job training programs, to print or publish or cause to be printed or published any notice or advertisement relating to employment by such an employer or membership in or any classification or referral for employment by such a labor organization, or relating to any classification or referral for employment by such an employment agency, or relating to admission to, or employment in, any program established to provide apprenticeship or other training by such a joint labor management committee, indicating any preference, limitation, specification, or discrimination, based on race, color, religion, sex, or national origin, except that such a notice or advertisement may indicate a preference, limitation, specification, or discrimination based on religion, sex, or national origin when religion, sex, or national origin is a bona fide occupational qualification for employment.

Equal Employment Opportunity Commission

SEC. 2000e-4. *[Section 705]*

(a) There is hereby created a Commission to be known as the Equal Employment Opportunity Commission, which shall be composed of five members, not more than three of whom shall be members of the same political party. Members of the Commission shall be appointed by the President by and with the advice and consent of the Senate for a term of five years. Any individual chosen to fill a vacancy shall be appointed only for the unexpired term of the member whom he shall succeed, and all members of the Commission shall continue to serve until their successors are appointed and qualified, except that no such member of the Commission shall continue to serve (1) for more than sixty days when the Congress is in session unless a nomination to fill such vacancy shall have been submitted to the Senate, or (2) after the adjournment sine die of the session of the Senate in which such nomination was submitted. The President shall designate one member to serve as Chairman of the Commission, and one member to serve as Vice Chairman. The Chairman shall be responsible on behalf of the Commission for the administrative operations of the Commission, and, except as provided in subsection (b) of this section, shall appoint, in accordance with the provisions of title 5 *[United States Code]* governing appointments in the competitive service, such officers, agents, attorneys, administrative law judges *[hearing examiners]*, and employees as he deems necessary to assist it in the performance of its functions and to fix their compensation in accordance with the provisions of chapter 51 and subchapter III of chapter 53 of title 5 *[United States Code]*, relating to classification and General Schedule pay rates: Provided, That assignment, removal, and compensation of administrative law judges *[hearing examiners]* shall be in accordance with sections 3105, 3344, 5372, and 7521 of title 5 *[United States Code]*.

(b) (1) There shall be a General Counsel of the Commission appointed by the President, by and with the advice and consent of the Senate, for a term of four years. The General Counsel shall have responsibility for the conduct of litigation as provided in sections 2000e-5 and 2000e-6 of this title *[sections 706 and 707].* The General Counsel shall have such other duties as the Commission may prescribe or as may be provided by law and shall concur with the Chairman of the Commission on the appointment and supervision of regional attorneys. The General Counsel of the Commission on the effective date of this Act shall continue in such position and perform the functions specified in this subsection until a successor is appointed and qualified.

(2) Attorneys appointed under this section may, at the direction of the Commission, appear for and represent the Commission in any case in court, provided that the Attorney General shall conduct all litigation to which the Commission is a party in the Supreme Court pursuant to this subchapter.

(c) A vacancy in the Commission shall not impair the right of the remaining members to exercise all the powers of the Commission and three members thereof shall constitute a quorum.

(d) The Commission shall have an official seal which shall be judicially noticed.

(e) The Commission shall at the close of each fiscal year report to the Congress and to the President concerning the action it has taken *[the names, salaries, and duties of all individuals in its employ]* and the moneys it has disbursed. It shall make such further reports on the cause of and means of eliminating discrimination and such recommendations for further legislation as may appear desirable.

(f) The principal office of the Commission shall be in or near the District of Columbia, but it may meet or exercise any or all its powers at any other place. The Commission may establish such regional or State offices as it deems necessary to accomplish the purpose of this subchapter.

(g) The Commission shall have power-

(1) to cooperate with and, with their consent, utilize regional, State, local, and other agencies, both public and private, and individuals;

(2) to pay to witnesses whose depositions are taken or who are summoned before the Commission or any of its agents the same witness and mileage fees as are paid to witnesses in the courts of the United States;

(3) to furnish to persons subject to this subchapter such technical assistance as they may request to further their compliance with this subchapter or an order issued thereunder;

(4) upon the request of (i) any employer, whose employees or some of them, or (ii) any labor organization, whose members or some of them, refuse or threaten to refuse to cooperate in effectuating the provisions of this subchapter, to assist in such effectuation by conciliation or such other remedial action as is provided by this subchapter;

(5) to make such technical studies as are appropriate to effectuate the purposes and policies of this subchapter and to make the results of such studies available to the public;

(6) to intervene in a civil action brought under section 2000e-5 of this title *[section 706]* by an aggrieved party against a respondent other than a government, governmental agency or political subdivision.

(h) **(1)** The Commission shall, in any of its educational or promotional activities, cooperate with other departments and agencies in the performance of such educational and promotional activities.

(2) In exercising its powers under this title, the Commission shall carry out educational and outreach activities (including dissemination of information in languages other than English) targeted to-

(A) individuals who historically have been victims of employment discrimination and have not been equitably served by the Commission; and

(B) individuals on whose behalf the Commission has authority to enforce any other law prohibiting employment discrimination, concerning rights and obligations under this title or such law, as the case may be.

(i) All officers, agents, attorneys, and employees of the Commission shall be subject to the provisions of section 7324 of title 5 *[section 9 of the Act of August 2, 1939, as amended (the Hatch Act)]*, notwithstanding any exemption contained in such section.

(j) (1) The Commission shall establish a Technical Assistance Training Institute, through which the Commission shall provide technical assistance and training regarding the laws and regulations enforced by the Commission.

(2) An employer or other entity covered under this title shall not be excused from compliance with the requirements of this title because of any failure to receive technical assistance under this subsection.

(3) There are authorized to be appropriated to carry out this subsection such sums as may be necessary for fiscal year 1992.

Enforcement Provisions

SEC. 2000e-5. *[Section 706]*

(a) The Commission is empowered, as hereinafter provided, to prevent any person from engaging in any unlawful employment practice as set forth in section 2000e-2 or 2000e 3 of this title *[section 703 or 704]*.

(b) Whenever a charge is filed by or on behalf of a person claiming to be aggrieved, or by a member of the Commission, alleging that an employer, employment agency, labor organization, or joint labor-management committee controlling apprenticeship or other training or retraining, including on-the-job training programs, has engaged in an unlawful employment practice, the Commission shall serve a notice of the charge (including the date, place and circumstances of the alleged unlawful employment practice) on such employer, employment agency, labor organization, or joint labor-management committee (hereinafter referred to as the "respondent") within ten days, and shall make an investigation thereof. Charges shall be in writing under oath or affirmation and shall contain such information and be in such form as the Commission requires. Charges shall not be made public by the Commission. If the Commission determines after such investigation that there is not reasonable cause to believe that the charge is true, it shall dismiss the charge and promptly notify the person claiming to be aggrieved and the respondent of its action. In determining whether reasonable cause exists, the Commission shall accord substantial weight to final findings and orders made by State or local authorities in proceedings commenced under State or local law pursuant to the requirements of subsections (c) and (d) of this section. If the Commission determines after such investigation that there is reasonable cause to believe that the charge is true, the Commission shall endeavor to eliminate any such alleged unlawful employment practice by informal methods of conference, conciliation, and persuasion. Nothing said or done during and as a part of such informal endeavors may be made public by the Commission, its officers or employees, or used as evidence in a subsequent proceeding without the written consent of the persons concerned. Any person who makes public information in violation of this subsection shall be fined not more than $1,000 or imprisoned for not more than one year, or both. The Commission shall make its determination on reasonable cause as promptly as possible and, so far as practicable, not later than one hundred and twenty days from the filing of the charge or, where applicable under subsection (c) or (d) of this section, from the date upon which the Commission is authorized to take action with respect to the charge.

(c) In the case of an alleged unlawful employment practice occurring in a State, or political subdivision of a State, which has a State or local law prohibiting the unlawful employment practice alleged and establishing or authorizing a State or local authority to grant or seek relief from such practice or to institute criminal proceedings with respect thereto upon receiving notice thereof, no charge may be filed under subsection (a) of this section by the person aggrieved before the expiration of sixty days after proceedings have been commenced under the State or local law, unless such proceedings have been earlier terminated, provided that such sixty-day period shall be extended to one hundred and twenty days during the first year after the effective date of such State or local law. If any requirement for the commencement of such proceedings is imposed by a State or local authority other than a requirement of the filing of a written and signed statement of the facts upon which the proceeding is based, the proceeding shall be deemed to have been commenced for the purposes of this subsection at the time such statement is sent by registered mail to the appropriate State or local authority.

(d) In the case of any charge filed by a member of the Commission alleging an unlawful employment practice occurring in a State or political subdivision of a State which has a State or local law prohibiting the practice alleged and establishing or authorizing a State or local authority to grant or seek relief from such practice or to institute criminal proceedings with respect thereto upon receiving notice thereof, the Commission shall, before taking any action with respect to such charge, notify the appropriate State or local officials and, upon request, afford them a reasonable time, but not less than sixty days (provided that such sixty-day period shall be extended to one hundred and twenty days during the first year after the effective day of such State or local law), unless a shorter period is requested, to act under such State or local law to remedy the practice alleged.

(e) **(1)** A charge under this section shall be filed within one hundred and eighty days after the alleged unlawful employment practice occurred and notice of the charge (including the date, place and circumstances of the alleged unlawful employment practice) shall be served upon the person against whom such charge is made within ten days thereafter, except that in a case of an unlawful employment practice with respect to which the person aggrieved has initially instituted proceedings with a State or local agency with authority to grant or seek relief from such practice or to institute criminal proceedings with respect thereto upon receiving notice thereof, such charge shall be filed by or on behalf of the person aggrieved within three hundred days after the alleged unlawful employment practice occurred, or within thirty days after receiving notice that the State or local agency has terminated the proceedings under the State or local law, whichever is earlier, and a copy of such charge shall be filed by the Commission with the State or local agency.

(2) For purposes of this section, an unlawful employment practice occurs, with respect to a seniority system that has been adopted for an intentionally discriminatory purpose in violation of this title (whether or not that discriminatory purpose is apparent on the face of the seniority provision), when the seniority system is adopted, when an individual becomes subject to the seniority system, or when a person aggrieved is injured by the application of the seniority system or provision of the system.

(f) (1) If within thirty days after a charge is filed with the Commission or within thirty days after expiration of any period of reference under subsection (c) or (d) of this section, the Commission has been unable to secure from the respondent a conciliation agreement acceptable to the Commission, the Commission may bring a civil action against any respondent not a government, governmental agency, or political subdivision named in the charge. In the case of a respondent which is a government, governmental agency, or political subdivision, if the Commission has been unable to secure from the respondent a conciliation agreement acceptable to the Commission, the Commission shall take no further action and shall refer the case to the Attorney General who may bring a civil action against such respondent in the appropriate United States district court. The person or persons aggrieved shall have the right to intervene in a civil action brought by the Commission or the Attorney General in a case involving a government, governmental agency, or political subdivision. If a charge filed with the Commission pursuant to subsection (b) of this section, is dismissed by the Commission, or if within one hundred and eighty days from the filing of such charge or the expiration of any period of reference under subsection (c) or (d) of this section, whichever is later, the Commission has not filed a civil action under this section or the Attorney General has not filed a civil action in a case involving a government, governmental agency, or political subdivision, or the Commission has not entered into a conciliation agreement to which the person aggrieved is a party, the Commission, or the Attorney General in a case involving a government, governmental agency, or political subdivision, shall so notify the person aggrieved and within ninety days after the giving of such notice a civil action may be brought against the respondent named in the charge (A) by the person claiming to be aggrieved or (B) if such charge was filed by a member of the Commission, by any person whom the charge alleges was aggrieved by the alleged unlawful employment practice. Upon application by the complainant and in such circumstances as the court may deem just, the court may appoint an attorney for such complainant and may authorize the commencement of the action without the payment of fees, costs, or security. Upon timely application, the court may, in its discretion, permit the Commission, or the Attorney General in a case involving a government, governmental agency, or political subdivision, to intervene in such civil action upon certification that the case is of general public importance. Upon request, the court may, in its discretion, stay further proceedings for not more than sixty days pending the termination of State or local proceedings described in subsection (c) or (d) of this section or further efforts of the Commission to obtain voluntary compliance.

(2) Whenever a charge is filed with the Commission and the Commission concludes on the basis of a preliminary investigation that prompt judicial action is necessary to carry out the purposes of this Act, the Commission, or the Attorney General in a case involving a government, governmental agency, or political subdivision, may bring an action for appropriate temporary or preliminary relief pending final disposition of such charge. Any temporary restraining order or other order granting preliminary or temporary relief shall be issued in accordance with rule 65 of the Federal Rules of Civil Procedure. It shall be the duty of a court having jurisdiction over proceedings under this section to assign cases for hearing at the earliest practicable date and to cause such cases to be in every way expedited.

(3) Each United States district court and each United States court of a place subject to the jurisdiction of the United States shall have jurisdiction of actions brought under this subchapter. Such an action may be brought in any judicial district in the State in which the unlawful employment practice is alleged to have been committed, in the judicial district in which the employment records relevant to such practice are maintained and administered, or in the judicial district in

which the aggrieved person would have worked but for the alleged unlawful employment practice, but if the respondent is not found within any such district, such an action may be brought within the judicial district in which the respondent has his principal office. For purposes of sections 1404 and 1406 of title 28 *[of the United States Code]*, the judicial district in which the respondent has his principal office shall in all cases be considered a district in which the action might have been brought.

(4) It shall be the duty of the chief judge of the district (or in his absence, the acting chief judge) in which the case is pending immediately to designate a judge in such district to hear and determine the case. In the event that no judge in the district is available to hear and determine the case, the chief judge of the district, or the acting chief judge, as the case may be, shall certify this fact to the chief judge of the circuit (or in his absence, the acting chief judge) who shall then designate a district or circuit judge of the circuit to hear and determine the case.

(5) It shall be the duty of the judge designated pursuant to this subsection to assign the case for hearing at the earliest practicable date and to cause the case to be in every way expedited. If such judge has not scheduled the case for trial within one hundred and twenty days after issue has been joined, that judge may appoint a master pursuant to rule 53 of the Federal Rules of Civil Procedure.

(g) **(1)** If the court finds that the respondent has intentionally engaged in or is intentionally engaging in an unlawful employment practice charged in the complaint, the court may enjoin the respondent from engaging in such unlawful employment practice, and order such affirmative action as may be appropriate, which may include, but is not limited to, reinstatement or hiring of employees, with or without back pay (payable by the employer, employment agency, or labor organization, as the case may be, responsible for the unlawful employment practice), or any other equitable relief as the court deems appropriate. Back pay liability shall not accrue from a date more than two years prior to the filing of a charge with the Commission. Interim earnings or amounts earnable with reasonable diligence by the person or persons discriminated against shall operate to reduce the back pay otherwise allowable.

(2) **(A)** No order of the court shall require the admission or reinstatement of an individual as a member of a union, or the hiring, reinstatement, or promotion of an individual as an employee, or the payment to him of any back pay, if such individual was refused admission, suspended, or expelled, or was refused employment or advancement or was suspended or discharged for any reason other than discrimination on account of race, color, religion, sex, or national origin or in violation of section 2000e-3(a) of this title *[section 704(a)]*.

(B) **On a claim in which an individual proves a violation under section 2000e2(m) of this title *[section 703(m)]* and a respondent demonstrates that the respondent would have taken the same action in the absence of the impermissible motivating factor, the court-**

(i) **may grant declaratory relief, injunctive relief (except as provided in clause (ii), and attorney's fees and costs**

demonstrated to be directly attributable only to the pursuit of a claim under section 2000e-2(m) of this title *[section 703(m)]*; and

(ii) shall not award damages or issue an order requiring any admission, reinstatement, hiring, promotion, or payment, described in subparagraph (A).

(h) The provisions of chapter 6 of title 29 *[the Act entitled "An Act to amend the Judicial Code and to define and limit the jurisdiction of courts sitting in equity, and for other purposes," approved March 23, 1932 (29 U.S.C. 105-115)]* shall not apply with respect to civil actions brought under this section.

(i) In any case in which an employer, employment agency, or labor organization fails to comply with an order of a court issued in a civil action brought under this section, the Commission may commence proceedings to compel compliance with such order.

(j) Any civil action brought under this section and any proceedings brought under subsection (i) of this section shall be subject to appeal as provided in sections 1291 and 1292, title 28 *[United States Code]*.

(k) In any action or proceeding under this subchapter the court, in its discretion, may allow the prevailing party, other than the Commission or the United States, a reasonable attorney's fee **(including expert fees)** as part of the costs, and the Commission and the United States shall be liable for costs the same as a private person.

Civil Actions by the Attorney General

SEC. 2000e-6. *[Section 707]*

(a) Whenever the Attorney General has reasonable cause to believe that any person or group of persons is engaged in a pattern or practice of resistance to the full enjoyment of any of the rights secured by this subchapter, and that the pattern or practice is of such a nature and is intended to deny the full exercise of the rights herein described, the Attorney General may bring a civil action in the appropriate district court of the United States by filing with it a complaint (1) signed by him (or in his absence the Acting Attorney General), (2) setting forth facts pertaining to such pattern or practice, and (3) requesting such relief, including an application for a permanent or temporary injunction, restraining order or other order against the person or persons responsible for such pattern or practice, as he deems necessary to insure the full enjoyment of the rights herein described.

(b) The district courts of the United States shall have and shall exercise jurisdiction of proceedings instituted pursuant to this section, and in any such proceeding the Attorney General may file with the clerk of such court a request that a court of three judges be convened to hear and determine the case. Such request by the Attorney General shall be accompanied by a certificate that, in his opinion, the case is of general public importance. A copy of the certificate and request for a three-judge court shall be immediately furnished by such clerk to the chief judge of the circuit (or in his absence, the presiding circuit judge of the circuit) in which the case is pending. Upon receipt of such request it shall be the duty of the chief judge of the circuit or the presiding circuit judge, as the case may be, to designate immediately three judges in such circuit, of whom at least one shall be a circuit judge and another of whom shall be a district judge of the court in which the proceeding was instituted, to hear and determine such case, and it shall be the duty of the judges so designated to assign the case for hearing at the earliest practicable date, to participate in the hearing and determination thereof, and to cause the case to be in every way expedited. An appeal from the final judgment of such court will lie to the Supreme Court.

In the event the Attorney General fails to file such a request in any such proceeding, it shall be the duty of the chief judge of the district (or in his absence, the acting chief judge) in which the case is pending immediately to designate a judge in such district to hear and determine the case. In the event that no judge in the district is available to hear and determine the case, the chief judge of the district, or the acting chief judge, as the case may be, shall certify this fact to the chief judge of the circuit (or in his absence, the acting chief judge) who shall then designate a district or circuit judge of the circuit to hear and determine the case.

It shall be the duty of the judge designated pursuant to this section to assign the case for hearing at the earliest practicable date and to cause the case to be in every way expedited.

(c) Effective two years after March 24, 1972 *[the date of enactment of the Equal Employment Opportunity Act of 1972]*, the functions of the Attorney General under this section shall be transferred to the Commission, together with such personnel, property, records, and unexpended balances of appropriations, allocations, and other funds employed, used, held, available, or to be made available in connection with such functions unless the President submits, and neither House of Congress vetoes, a reorganization plan pursuant to chapter 9 of title 5 *[United States Code]*, inconsistent with the provisions of this subsection. The Commission shall carry out such functions in accordance with subsections (d) and (e) of this section.

(d) Upon the transfer of functions provided for in subsection (c) of this section, in all suits commenced pursuant to this section prior to the date of such transfer, proceedings shall continue without abatement, all court orders and decrees shall remain in effect, and the Commission shall be substituted as a party for the United States of America, the Attorney General, or the Acting Attorney General, as appropriate.

(e) Subsequent to March 24, 1972 *[the date of enactment of the Equal Employment Opportunity Act of 1972]*, the Commission shall have authority to investigate and act on a charge of a pattern or practice of discrimination, whether filed by or on behalf of a person claiming to be aggrieved or by a member of the Commission. All such actions shall be conducted in accordance with the procedures set forth in section 2000e-5 of this title *[section 706]*.

Effect on State Laws

SEC. 2000e-7. *[Section 708]*

Nothing in this subchapter shall be deemed to exempt or relieve any person from any liability, duty, penalty, or punishment provided by any present or future law of any State or political subdivision of a State, other than any such law which purports to require or permit the doing of any act which would be an unlawful employment practice under this subchapter.

Investigations, Inspections, Records, State Agencies

SEC. 2000e-8. *[Section 709]*

(a) In connection with any investigation of a charge filed under section 2000e-5 of this title *[section 706]*, the Commission or its designated representative shall at all reasonable times have access to, for the purposes of examination, and the right to copy any evidence of any person being investigated or proceeded against that relates to unlawful employment practices covered by this subchapter and is relevant to the charge under investigation.

(b) The Commission may cooperate with State and local agencies charged with the administration of State fair employment practices laws and, with the consent of such agencies, may, for the purpose of carrying out its functions and duties under this subchapter and within the limitation of funds appropriated specifically for such purpose, engage in and contribute to the cost of research and other projects of mutual interest undertaken by such agencies, and utilize the services of such agencies and their employees, and, notwithstanding any other provision of law, pay by advance or reimbursement such agencies and their employees for services rendered to assist the Commission in carrying out this subchapter. In furtherance of such cooperative efforts, the Commission may enter into written agreements with such State or local agencies and such agreements may include provisions under which the Commission shall refrain from processing a charge in any cases or class of cases specified in such agreements or under which the Commission shall relieve any person or class of persons in such State or locality from requirements imposed under this section. The

Commission shall rescind any such agreement whenever it determines that the agreement no longer serves the interest of effective enforcement of this subchapter.

(c) Every employer, employment agency, and labor organization subject to this subchapter shall (1) make and keep such records relevant to the determinations of whether unlawful employment practices have been or are being committed, (2) preserve such records for such periods, and (3) make such reports therefrom as the Commission shall prescribe by regulation or order, after public hearing, as reasonable, necessary, or appropriate for the enforcement of this subchapter or the regulations or orders thereunder. The Commission shall, by regulation, require each employer, labor organization, and joint labor-management committee subject to this subchapter which controls an apprenticeship or other training program to maintain such records as are reasonably necessary to carry out the purposes of this subchapter, including, but not limited to, a list of applicants who wish to participate in such program, including the chronological order in which applications were received, and to furnish to the Commission upon request, a detailed description of the manner in which persons are selected to participate in the apprenticeship or other training program. Any employer, employment agency, labor organization, or joint labor-management committee which believes that the application to it of any regulation or order issued under this section would result in undue hardship may apply to the Commission for an exemption from the application of such regulation or order, and, if such application for an exemption is denied, bring a civil action in the United States district court for the district where such records are kept. If the Commission or the court, as the case may be, finds that the application of the regulation or order to the employer, employment agency, or labor organization in question would impose an undue hardship, the Commission or the court, as the case may be, may grant appropriate relief. If any person required to comply with the provisions of this subsection fails or refuses to do so, the United States district court for the district in which such person is found, resides, or transacts business, shall, upon application of the Commission, or the Attorney General in a case involving a government, governmental agency or political subdivision, have jurisdiction to issue to such person an order requiring him to comply.

(d) In prescribing requirements pursuant to subsection (c) of this section, the Commission shall consult with other interested State and Federal agencies and shall endeavor to coordinate its requirements with those adopted by such agencies. The Commission shall furnish upon request and without cost to any State or local agency charged with the administration of a fair employment practice law information obtained pursuant to subsection (c) of this section from any employer, employment agency, labor organization, or joint labor-management committee subject to the jurisdiction of such agency. Such information shall be furnished on condition that it not be made public by the recipient agency prior to the institution of a proceeding under State or local law involving such information. If this condition is violated by a recipient agency, the Commission may decline to honor subsequent requests pursuant to this subsection.

(e) It shall be unlawful for any officer or employee of the Commission to make public in any manner whatever any information obtained by the Commission pursuant to its authority under this section prior to the institution of any proceeding under this subchapter involving such information. Any officer or employee of the Commission who shall make public in any manner whatever any information in violation of this subsection shall be guilty, of a misdemeanor and upon conviction thereof, shall be fined not more than $1,000, or imprisoned not more than one year.

Investigatory Powers

SEC. 2000e-9. *[Section 710]*

For the purpose of all hearings and investigations conducted by the Commission or its duly authorized agents or agencies, section 161 of title 29 *[section 11 of the National Labor Relations Act]* shall apply.

Posting of Notices; Penalties

SEC. 2000e-10. *[Section 711]*

(a) Every employer, employment agency, and labor organization, as the case may be, shall post and keep posted in conspicuous places upon its premises where notices to employees, applicants for employment, and members are customarily posted a notice to be prepared or approved by the Commission setting forth excerpts, from or, summaries of, the pertinent provisions of this subchapter and information pertinent to the filing of a complaint.

(b) A willful violation of this section shall be punishable by a fine of not more than $100 for each separate offense.

Veteran's Special Rights or Preference

SEC. 2000e-11. *[Section 712]*

Nothing contained in this subchapter shall be construed to repeal or modify any Federal, State, territorial, or local law creating special rights or preference for veterans.

Rules and Regulations

SEC. 2000e-12. *[Section 713]*

(a) The Commission shall have authority from time to time to issue, amend, or rescind suitable procedural regulations to carry out the provisions of this subchapter. Regulations issued under this section shall be in conformity with the standards and limitations of subchapter II of chapter 5 of title 5 *[the Administrative Procedure Act]*.

(b) In any action or proceeding based on any alleged unlawful employment practice, no person shall be subject to any liability or punishment for or on account of (1) the commission by such person of an unlawful employment practice if he pleads and proves that the act or omission complained of was in good faith, in conformity with, and in reliance on any written interpretation or opinion of the Commission, or (2) the failure of such person to publish and file any information required by any provision of this subchapter if he pleads and proves that he failed to publish and file such information in good faith, in conformity with the instructions of the Commission issued under this subchapter regarding the filing of such information. Such a defense, if established, shall be a bar to the action or proceeding, notwithstanding that (A) after such act or omission, such interpretation or opinion is modified or rescinded or is determined by judicial authority to be invalid or of no legal effect, or (B) after publishing or filing the description and annual reports, such publication or filing is determined by judicial authority not to be in conformity with the requirements of this subchapter.

Forcibly Resisting the Commission or its Representatives

SEC. 2000e-13. *[Section 714]*

The provisions of sections 111 and 1114, title 18 *[United States Code]*, shall apply to officers, agents, and employees of the Commission in the performance of their official duties. Notwithstanding the provisions of sections 111 and 1114 of title 18 *[United States Code]*, whoever in violation of the provisions of section 1114 of such title kills a person while engaged in or on account of the performance of his official functions under this Act shall be punished by imprisonment for any term of years or for life.

Transfer of Authority

[Administration of the duties of the Equal Employment Opportunity Coordinating Council was transferred to the Equal Employment Opportunity Commission effective July 1, 1978, under the President's Reorganization Plan of 1978.]

Equal Employment Opportunity Coordinating Council

SEC. 2000e-14. *[Section 715]*

[There shall be established an Equal Employment Opportunity Coordinating Council (hereinafter referred to in this section as the Council) composed of the Secretary of Labor, the Chairman of the Equal Employment Opportunity Commission, the Attorney General, the Chairman of the United States Civil Service Commission, and the Chairman of the United States Civil Rights Commission, or their respective delegates.]

The Equal Employment Opportunity Commission *[Council]* shall have the responsibility for developing and implementing agreements, policies and practices designed to maximize effort, promote efficiency, and eliminate conflict, competition, duplication and inconsistency among the operations, functions and jurisdictions of the various departments, agencies and branches of the Federal Government responsible for the implementation and enforcement of equal employment opportunity legislation, orders, and policies. On or before October 1 *[July 1]* of each year, the Equal Employment Opportunity Commission *[Council]* shall transmit to the President and to the Congress a report of its activities, together with such recommendations for legislative or administrative changes as it concludes are desirable to further promote the purposes of this section.

Effective Date

SEC. 2000e-15. *[Section 716]*

[(a) This title shall become effective one year after the date of its enactment.

(b) Notwithstanding subsection (a), sections of this title other than sections 703, 704, 706, and 707 shall become effective immediately.

(c)] The President shall, as soon as feasible after July 2, 1964 *[the enactment of this title]*, convene one or more conferences for the purpose of enabling the leaders of groups whose members will be affected by this subchapter to become familiar with the rights afforded and obligations imposed by its provisions, and for the purpose of making plans which will result in the fair and effective administration of this subchapter when all of its provisions become effective. The President shall invite the participation in such conference or conferences of (1) the members of the President's Committee on Equal Employment Opportunity, (2) the members of the Commission on Civil Rights, (3) representatives of State and local agencies engaged in furthering equal employment opportunity, (4) representatives of private agencies engaged in furthering equal employment opportunity, and (5) representatives of employers, labor organizations, and employment agencies who will be subject to this subchapter.

Transfer of Authority

[Enforcement of Section 717 was transferred to the Equal Employment Opportunity Commission from the Civil Service Commission (Office of Personnel Management) effective January 1, 1979 under the President's Reorganization Plan No. 1 of 1978.]

Employment by Federal Government

SEC. 2000e-16. *[Section 717]*

(a) All personnel actions affecting employees or applicants for employment (except with regard to aliens employed outside the limits of the United States) in military departments as defined in section 102 of title 5 *[United States Code]*, in executive agencies *[other than the General Accounting Office]* as defined in section 105 of title 5 *[United States Code]* (including employees and applicants for employment who are paid from non-appropriated funds), in the United States Postal Service and the Postal Rate Commission, in those units of the Government of the District of Columbia having positions in the competitive service, and in those units of the legislative and judicial branches of the Federal Government having positions in the competitive service, and in the Library of Congress shall be made free from any discrimination based on race, color, religion, sex, or national origin.

(b) Except as otherwise provided in this subsection, the Equal Employment Opportunity Commission *[Civil Service Commission]* shall have authority to enforce the provisions of subsection (a) of this section through appropriate remedies, including reinstatement or hiring of employees with or without back pay, as will effectuate the policies of this section, and shall issue such rules, regulations, orders and instructions as it deems necessary and appropriate to carry out its responsibilities under this section. The Equal Employment Opportunity Commission *[Civil Service Commission]* shall-

(1) be responsible for the annual review and approval of a national and regional equal employment opportunity plan which each department and agency and each appropriate unit referred to in subsection (a) of this section shall submit in order to maintain an affirmative program of equal employment opportunity for all such employees and applicants for employment;

(2) be responsible for the review and evaluation of the operation of all agency equal employment opportunity programs, periodically obtaining and publishing (on at least a semiannual basis) progress reports from each such department, agency, or unit; and

(3) consult with and solicit the recommendations of interested individuals, groups, and organizations relating to equal employment opportunity.

The head of each such department, agency, or unit shall comply with such rules, regulations, orders, and instructions which shall include a provision that an employee or applicant for employment shall be notified of any final action taken on any complaint of discrimination filed by him thereunder. The plan submitted by each department, agency, and unit shall include, but not be limited to-

(1) provision for the establishment of training and education programs designed to provide a maximum opportunity for employees to advance so as to perform at their highest potential; and

(2) a description of the qualifications in terms of training and experience relating to equal employment opportunity for the principal and operating officials of each

such department, agency, or unit responsible for carrying out the equal employment opportunity program and of the allocation of personnel and resources proposed by such department, agency, or unit to carry out its equal employment opportunity program.

With respect to employment in the Library of Congress, authorities granted in this subsection to the Equal Employment Opportunity Commission *[Civil Service Commission]* shall be exercised by the Librarian of Congress.

(c) Within **90 days** of receipt of notice of final action taken by a department, agency, or unit referred to in subsection (a) of this section, or by the Equal Employment Opportunity Commission *[Civil Service Commission]* upon an appeal from a decision or order of such department, agency, or unit on a complaint of discrimination based on race, color, religion, sex or national origin, brought pursuant to subsection (a) of this section, Executive Order 11478 or any succeeding Executive orders, or after one hundred and eighty days from the filing of the initial charge with the department, agency, or unit or with the Equal Employment Opportunity Commission *[Civil Service Commission]* on appeal from a decision or order of such department, agency, or unit until such time as final action may be taken by a department, agency, or unit, an employee or applicant for employment, if aggrieved by the final disposition of his complaint, or by the failure to take final action on his complaint, may file a civil action as provided in section 2000e-5 of this title *[section 706]*, in which civil action the head of the department, agency, or unit, as appropriate, shall be the defendant.

(d) The provisions of section 2000e-5(f) through (k) of this title *[section 706(f) through (k)]*, as applicable, shall govern civil actions brought hereunder, **and the same**

interest to compensate for delay in payment shall be available as in cases involving nonpublic parties.

(e) Nothing contained in this Act shall relieve any Government agency or official of its or his primary responsibility to assure nondiscrimination in employment as required by the Constitution and statutes or of its or his responsibilities under Executive Order 11478 relating to equal employment opportunity in the Federal Government.

Special Provisions with Respect to Denial, Termination, and Suspension of Government Contracts

SEC. 2000e-17. *[Section 718]*

No Government contract, or portion thereof, with any employer, shall be denied, withheld, terminated, or suspended, by any agency or officer of the United States under any equal employment opportunity law or order, where such employer has an affirmative action plan which has previously been accepted by the Government for the same facility within the past twelve months without first according such employer full hearing and adjudication under the provisions of section 554 of title 5 *[United States Code]*, and the following pertinent sections: Provided, That if such employer has deviated substantially from such previously agreed to affirmative action plan, this section shall not apply: Provided further, That for the purposes of this section an affirmative action plan shall be deemed to have been accepted by the Government at the time the appropriate compliance agency has accepted such plan unless within forty five days thereafter the Office of Federal Contract Compliance has disapproved such plan.

[1] So in original. Probably should be subsection “(b)”.

EQUAL PAY ACT OF 1963

The Equal Pay Act of 1963 is a United States Federal Law amending the Fair Labor Standards Act, aimed at abolishing wage differentials based on sex.

The EPA prohibits employers from discriminating to employees at a rate less than the rate paid to employees of the opposite sex for equal work on jobs requiring equal skill, effort, and responsibility, and which are performed under similar working conditions.

EQUAL PAY ACT OF 1963

EDITOR'S NOTE: The following is the text of the Equal Pay Act of 1963 (Pub. L. 88-38) (EPA), as amended, as it appears in volume 29 of the United States Code, at section 206(d). The EPA, which is part of the Fair Labor Standards Act of 1938, as amended (FLSA), and which is administered and enforced by the EEOC, prohibits sex-based wage discrimination between men and women in the same establishment who are performing under similar working conditions. Cross references to the EPA as enacted appear in italics following the section heading. Additional provisions of the Equal Pay Act of 1963, as amended, are included as they appear in volume 29 of the United States Code.

Minimum Wage

SEC. 206. *[Section 6]*

(d) (1) No employer having employees subject to any provisions of this section shall discriminate, within any establishment in which such employees are employed, between employees on the basis of sex by paying wages to employees in such establishment at a rate less than the rate at which he pays wages to employees of the opposite sex in such establishment for equal work on jobs the performance of which requires equal skill, effort, and responsibility, and which are performed under similar working conditions, except where such payment is made pursuant to (i) a seniority system; (ii) a merit system; (iii) a system which measures earnings by quantity or quality of production; or (iv) a differential based on any other factor other than sex: *Provided*, That an employer who is paying a wage rate differential in violation of this subsection shall not, in order to comply with the provisions of this subsection, reduce the wage rate of any employee.

(2) No labor organization, or its agents, representing employees of an employer having employees subject to any provisions of this section shall cause or attempt to cause such an employer to discriminate against an employee in violation of paragraph (1) of this subsection.

(3) For purposes of administration and enforcement, any amounts owing to any employee which have been withheld in violation of this subsection shall be deemed to be unpaid minimum wages or unpaid overtime compensation under this chapter.

(4) As used in this subsection, the term "labor organization" means any organization of any kind, or any agency or employee representation committee or plan, in which employees participate and which exists for the purpose, in whole or in part, of dealing with employers concerning grievances, labor disputes, wages, rates of pay, hours of employment, or conditions of work.

Additional Provisions of Equal Pay Act of 1963

An Act

To prohibit discrimination on account of sex in the payment of wages by employers engaged in commerce or in the production of goods for commerce.

Be it enacted by the Senate and House of Representatives of the United States of America in Congress assembled, That this Act may be cited as the "Equal Pay Act of 1963."

***

Declaration of Purpose

Not Reprinted in U.S. Code *[Section 2]*

(a) The Congress hereby finds that the existence in industries engaged in commerce or in the production of goods for commerce of wage differentials based on sex-

(1) depresses wages and living standards for employees necessary for their health and efficiency;

(2) prevents the maximum utilization of the available labor resources;

(3) tends to cause labor disputes, thereby burdening, affecting, and obstructing commerce;

(4) burdens commerce and the free flow of goods in commerce; and

(5) constitutes an unfair method of competition.

(b) It is hereby declared to be the policy of this Act, through exercise by Congress of its power to regulate commerce among the several States and with foreign nations, to correct the conditions above referred to in such industries.

[Section 3 of the Equal Pay Act of 1963 amends section 6 of the Fair Labor Standards Act by adding a new subsection (d). The amendment is incorporated in the revised text of the Fair Labor Standards Act.]

Effective Date

Not Reprinted in U.S. Code *[Section 4]*

The amendments made by this Act shall take effect upon the expiration of one year from the date of its enactment: Provided, That in case of employees covered by a bona fide collective bargaining agreement in effect at least thirty days prior to the date of enactment of this Act, entered into by a labor organization (as defined in section 6(d)(4) of the Fair

Labor Standards Act of 1938, as amended), the amendments made by this Act shall take effect upon the termination of such collective bargaining agreement or upon the expiration of two years from the date of enactment of this Act, whichever shall first occur.

Approved June 10, 1963, 12 m.

[In the following excerpts from the Fair Labor Standards Act of 1938, as amended, authority given to the Secretary of Labor is exercised by the Equal Employment Opportunity Commission for purposes of enforcing the Equal Pay Act of 1963.]

Attendance of Witnesses

SEC. 209 *[Section 9]*

For the purpose of any hearing or investigation provided for in this chapter, the provisions of sections 49 and 50 of title 15 *[sections 9 and 10]* (relating to the attendance of witnesses and the production of books, papers, and documents), of the Federal Trade Commission Act of September 16, 1914, as amended (U.S.C., 1934 edition, title 15, secs. 49 and 50), are made applicable to the jurisdiction, powers, and duties of the Administrator, the Secretary of Labor, and the industry committees.

Investigations, Inspections, Records, and Homework Regulations

SEC. 211 *[Section 11]*

(a) The Administrator or his designated representatives may investigate and gather data regarding the wages, hours, and other conditions and practices of employment in any industry subject to this chapter, and may enter and inspect such places and such records (and make such transcriptions thereof), question such employees, and investigate such facts, conditions, practices, or matters as he may deem necessary or appropriate to determine whether any person has violated any provision of this chapter, or which may aid in the enforcement of the provisions of this chapter. Except as provided in section 212 *[section 12]* of this title and in subsection (b) of this section, the Administrator shall utilize the bureaus and divisions of the Department of Labor for all the investigations and inspections necessary under this section. Except as provided in section 212 *[section 12]*, the Administrator shall bring all actions under section 217 *[section 17]* of this title to restrain violations of this chapter.

(b) With the consent and cooperation of State agencies charged with the administration of State labor laws, the Administrator and the Secretary of Labor may, for the purpose of carrying out their respective functions and duties under this chapter, utilize the services of State and local agencies and their employees and, notwithstanding any other provision of law, may reimburse such State and local agencies and their employees for services rendered for such purposes.

(c) Every employer subject to any provision of this chapter or of any order issued under this chapter shall make, keep, and preserve such records of the persons employed by him and of the wages, hours, and other conditions and practices of employment maintained by him, and shall preserve such records for such periods of time, and shall make such reports therefrom to the Administrator as he shall prescribe by regulation or order as necessary or appropriate for the enforcement of the provisions of this chapter or the regulations or orders thereunder. The employer of an employee who performs substitute work described in section 207(p)(3) *[section 7(p)(3)]* of this title may not be required under this subsection to keep a record of the hours of the substitute work.

(d) The Administrator is authorized to make such regulations and orders regulating, restricting, or prohibiting industrial homework as are necessary or appropriate to prevent the circumvention or evasion of and to safeguard the minimum wage rate prescribed in this chapter, and all existing regulations or orders of the Administrator relating to industrial homework are continued in full force and effect.

Exemptions

SEC. 213 *[Section 13]*

(a) The provisions of sections 206 *[section 6]* (except subsection (d) in the case of paragraph (1) of this subsection) and section 207 *[section 7]* shall not apply with respect to-

(1) any employee employed in a bona fide executive, administrative, or professional capacity (including any employee employed in the capacity of academic administrative personnel or teacher in elementary or secondary schools), or in the capacity of outside salesman (as such terms are defined and delimited from time to time by regulations of the Secretary, subject to the provisions of subchapter II of chapter 5 of title 5 *[the Administrative Procedure Act]*, except that an employee of a retail or service establishment shall not be excluded from the definition of employee employed in a bona fide executive or administrative capacity because of the number of hours in his workweek which he devotes to activities not directly or closely related to the performance of

executive or administrative activities, if less than 40 per centum of his hours worked in the workweek are devoted to such activities); or

(2) *** (Repealed)

[Note: Section 13(a)(2) (relating to employees employed by a retail or service establishment) was repealed by Pub. L. 101-157, section 3(c)(1), November 17, 1989.]

(3) any employee employed by an establishment which is an amusement or recreational establishment, organized camp, or religious or non-profit educational conference center, if (A) it does not operate for more than seven months in any calendar year, or (B) during the preceding calendar year, its average receipts for any six months of such year were not more than 33 1/3 per centum of its average receipts for the other six months of such year, except that the exemption from sections 206 and 207 *[sections 6 and 7]* of this title provided by this paragraph does not apply with respect to any employee of a private entity engaged in providing services or facilities (other than, in the case of the exemption from section 206 *[section 6]*, a private entity engaged in providing services and facilities directly related to skiing) in a national park or a national forest, or on land in the National Wildlife Refuge System, under a contract with the Secretary of the Interior or the Secretary of Agriculture; or

(4) *** (Repealed)

[Note: Section 13(a)(4) (relating to employees employed by an establishment which qualified as an exempt retail establishment) was repealed by Pub. L. 101-157, Section 3(c)(1), November 17, 1989.]

(5) any employee employed in the catching, taking, propagating, harvesting, cultivating, or farming of any kind of fish, shellfish, crustacea, sponges, seaweeds, or other aquatic forms of animal and vegetable life, or in the first processing, canning or packing such marine products at sea as an incident to, or in conjunction with, such fishing operations, including the going to and returning from work and loading and unloading when performed by any such employee; or

(6) any employee employed in agriculture (A) if such employee is employed by an employer who did not, during any calendar quarter during the preceding calendar year, use more than five hundred man-days or agricultural labor, (B) if such employee is the parent, spouse, child, or other member of his employer's immediate family, (C) if such employee (i) is employed as a hand harvest laborer and is paid on a piece rate basis in an operation which has been, and is customarily and generally recognized as having been, paid on a piece rate basis in the region of employment, (ii) commutes daily from his permanent residence to the farm on which he is so employed, and (iii) has been employed in agriculture less than thirteen weeks during the preceding calendar year, (D) if such employee (other than an employee described in clause (C) of this subsection) (i) is sixteen years of age or under and is employed as a hand harvest laborer, is paid on a piece rate basis in an operation which has been, and is customarily and generally recognized as having been, paid on a piece rate basis in the region of employment, (ii) is employed on the same farm as his parent or person standing in the place of his parent, and (iii) is paid at the same

piece rate as employees over age sixteen are paid on the same farm, or (E) if such employee is principally engaged in the range production of livestock; or

(7) any employee to the extent that such employee is exempted by regulations, order, or certificate of the Secretary issued under section 214 *[section 14]* of this title; or

(8) any employee employed in connection with the publication of and weekly, semiweekly, or daily newspaper with a circulation of less than four thousand the major part of which circulation is within the county where published or counties contiguous thereto; or

(9) *** (Repealed)

[Note: Section 13(a)(9) (relating to motion picture theater employees) was repealed by section 23 of the Fair Labor Standards Amendments of 1974. The 1974 amendments created an exemption for such employees from the overtime provisions only in section 13(b)27.]

(10) any switchboard operator employed by an independently owned public telephone company which has not more than seven hundred and fifty stations; or

(11) *** (Repealed)

[Note: Section 13(a)(11) (relating to telegraph agency employees) was repealed by section 10 of the Fair Labor Standards Amendments of 1974. The 1974 amendments created an exemption from the overtime provisions only in section 13(b)(23), which was repealed effective May 1, 1976.]

(12) any employee employed as a seaman on a vessel other than an American vessel; or

(13) *** (Repealed)

[Note: Section 13(a)(13) (relating to small logging crews) was repealed by section 23 of the Fair Labor Standards Amendments of 1974. The 1974 amendments created an exemption for such employees from the overtime provisions only in section 13(b)(28)]

(14) *** (Repealed)

[Note: Section 13(a)(14) (relating to employees employed in growing and harvesting of shade grown tobacco) was repealed by section 9 of the Fair Labor Standards Amendments of 1974. The 1974 amendments created an exemption for certain tobacco producing employees from the overtime provisions only in section 13(b)(22). The section 13(b)(22) exemption was repealed, effective January 1, 1978, by section 5 of the Fair Labor Standards Amendments of 1977.]

(15) any employee employed on a casual basis in domestic service employment to provide baby sitting services or any employee employed in domestic service employment to provide companionship services for individuals who (because of age or infirmity) are unable to care for themselves (as such terms are defined and delimited by regulations of the Secretary).

***

(g) The exemption from section 206 *[section 6]* of this title provided by paragraph (6) of subsection (a) of this section shall not apply with respect to any employee employed by an establishment (1) which controls, is controlled by, or is under common control with, another establishment the activities of which are not related for a common business purpose to, but materially support the activities of the establishment employing such employee; and (2) whose annual gross volume of sales made or business done, when combined with the annual gross volume of sales made or business done by each establishment which controls, is controlled by, or is under common control with, the establishment employing such employee, exceeds $10,000,000 (exclusive of excise taxes at the retail level which are separately stated).

Prohibited Acts

SEC. 215 *[Section 15]*

(a) After the expiration of one hundred and twenty days from June 25, 1938 *[the date of enactment of this Act]*, it shall be unlawful for any person-

(1) to transport, offer for transportation, ship, deliver, or sell in commerce, or to ship, deliver, or sell with knowledge that shipment or delivery or sale thereof in commerce is intended, any goods in the production of which any employee was employed in violation of section 206 *[section 6]* or section 207 *[section 7]* of this title, or in violation of any regulation or order of the Secretary issued under section 214 *[section 14]* of this title, except that no provision of this chapter shall impose any liability upon any common carrier for the transportation in commerce in the regular course of its business of any goods not produced by such common carrier, and no provision of this chapter shall excuse any common carrier from its obligation to accept any goods for transportation; and except that any such transportation, offer, shipment, delivery, or sale of such goods by a purchaser who acquired them in good faith in reliance on written assurance from the producer that the goods were produced in compliance with the

requirements of this chapter, and who acquired such goods for value without notice of any such violation, shall not be deemed unlawful;

(2) to violate any of the provisions of section 206 *[section 6]* or section 207 *[section 7]* of this title, on any of the provisions of any regulation or order of the Secretary issued under section 214 *[section 14]* of this title;

(3) to discharge or in any other manner discriminate against an employee because such employee has filed any complaint or instituted or caused to be instituted any proceeding under or related to this chapter, or has testified or is about to testify in any such proceeding, or has served or is about to serve on an industry committee;

(4) to violate any of the provisions of section 212 *[section 12]* of this title;

(5) to violate any of the provisions of section 211(c) *[section 11(c)]* of this title, or any regulation or order made or continued in effect under the provisions of section 211(d) *[section 11(d)]* of this title, or to make any statement, report, or record filed or kept pursuant to the provisions of such section or of any regulation or order thereunder, knowing such statement, report, or record to be false in a material respect.

(b) For the purpose of subsection (a)(1) of this section proof that an employee was employed in any place of employment where goods shipped or sold in commerce were produced, within ninety days prior to the removal of the goods from such place of employment, shall be prima facie evidence that such employee was engaged in the production of such goods.

Penalties

SEC. 216 *[Section 16]*

(a) Any person who willfully violates any of the provisions of section 215 *[section 15]* of this title shall upon conviction thereof be subject to a fine of not more than $10,000, or to imprisonment for not more than six months, or both. No person shall be imprisoned under this subsection except for an offense committed after the conviction of such person for a prior offense under this subsection.

(b) Any employer who violates the provisions of section 206 *[section 6]* or section 207 *[section 7]* of this title shall be liable to the employee or employees affected in the amount of their unpaid minimum wages, or their unpaid overtime compensation, as the case may be, and in an additional equal amount as liquidated damages. Any employer who violates the provisions of section 215(a)(3) *[section 15(a)(3)]* of this title shall be liable for such legal or equitable relief as may be appropriate to effectuate the purposes of section 215(a)(3) *[section 15(a)(3)]*, including without limitation employment, reinstatement, promotion, and the payment of wages lost and an additional equal amount as liquidated damages. An action to recover the liability prescribed in either of the preceding sentences may be maintained against any employer (including a public agency) in an Federal or State court of competent jurisdiction by any one or more employees for and in behalf of himself or themselves and other employees similarly situated. No employee shall be a party plaintiff to any such action unless he gives his consent in writing to become such a party and such consent is filed in the court in which such action is brought. The court in such action shall, in addition to any judgment awarded to the plaintiff or plaintiffs, allow a reasonable attorney's fee to be paid by the defendant, and costs of the action. The right provided by this subsection to bring an action by or on behalf of any employee, and the right of any employee to become a party plaintiff to any such action, shall terminate upon the filing of a complaint by the Secretary of Labor in an action under section 217 *[section 17]* in which (1) restraint is sought of any further delay in the payment of unpaid minimum wages, or the amount of unpaid overtime compensation as the case may be, owing to such employee under section 206 *[section 6]* or section 207 *[section 7]* of this title by an employer liable therefore under the provisions of this subsection or (2) legal or equitable relief is sought as a result of alleged violations of section 215(a)(3) *[section 15(a)(3)]* of this title.

(c) The Secretary is authorized to supervise the payment of the unpaid minimum wages or the unpaid overtime compensation owing to any employee or employees under section 206 *[section 6]* or section 207 *[section 7]* of this title, and the agreement of any employee to accept such payment shall upon payment in full constitute a waiver by such employee of any right he may have under subsection (b) of this section to such unpaid minimum wages or unpaid overtime compensation and an additional equal amount as liquidated damages. The Secretary may bring an action in any court of competent jurisdiction to recover the amount of the unpaid minimum wages or overtime compensation and an equal amount as liquidated damages. The right provided by subsection (b) to bring an action by or on behalf of any employee to recover the liability specified in the first sentence of such subsection and of any employee to become a party plaintiff to any such action shall terminate upon the filing of a complaint by the Secretary in an action under this subsection in which a recovery is sought of unpaid minimum wages or unpaid overtime compensation under sections 206 and 207 *[sections 6 and 7]* of this title or liquidated or other damages provided by this subsection owing to such employee by an employer liable under the provisions of subsection (b) of this section, unless such action is dismissed without prejudice on motion of the Secretary. Any sums thus recovered by the Secretary of Labor on behalf of an employee pursuant to this subsection shall be held in a special deposit account and shall be paid on order of the Secretary of Labor, directly to the employee or employees affected. Any such sums not paid to an employee because of inability to do so within a period of three years shall be covered into the Treasury of the United States as miscellaneous receipts. In determining when an action is commenced by the Secretary of Labor under this subsection for the purposes of the statutes of limitations provided in section 255(a) of this title *[section 6(a) of the Portal-to-Portal Act of 1947]*, it shall be considered to be commenced in the case of any individual claimant on the date when the complaint is filed if he is specifically named as a party plaintiff in the complaint, or if his name did not so appear, on the subsequent date on which his name is added as a party plaintiff in such action.

(d) In any action or proceeding commenced prior to, on, or after August 8, 1956 *[the date of enactment of this subsection]*, no employer shall be subject to any liability or punishment under this chapter or the Portal-to-Portal Act of 1947 *[29 U.S.C. 251 et seq.]* or on account of his failure to comply with any provision or provisions or such Act (1) with respect to work heretofore or hereafter performed in a work place to which the exemption in section 213(f) *[section 13(f)]* is applicable, (2) with respect to work performed in Guam, the Canal Zone or Wake Island before the effective date of this amendment of subsection (d), or (3) with respect to work performed in a possession named in section 206(a)(3) *[section 6(a)(3)]* of this title at any time prior to the establishment by the Secretary, as provided therein, of a minimum wage rate applicable to such work.

(e) Any person who violates the provisions of section 212 of this title, relating to child labor, or any regulation issued under that section, shall be subject to a civil penalty of not to exceed $10,000 for each employee who was the subject of such a violation. Any person who repeatedly or willfully violates section 206 or 207 of this title shall be subject to a civil penalty of not to exceed $1,000 for each such violation. In determining the amount of any penalty under this subsection, the appropriateness of such penalty to the size of the business of the person charged and the gravity of the violation shall be considered. The amount of any penalty under this subsection, when finally determined, may be-

(1) deducted from any sums owing by the United States to the person charged;

(2) recovered in a civil action brought by the Secretary in any court of competent jurisdiction, in which litigation the Secretary shall be represented by the Solicitor of Labor; or

(3) ordered by the court, in an action brought for a violation of section 215(a)(4) of this title or a repeated or willful violation of section 215(a)(2) of this title, to be paid to the Secretary.

Any administrative determination by the Secretary of the amount of any penalty under this subsection shall be final, unless within fifteen days after receipt of notice thereof by certified mail the person charged with the violation takes exception to the determination that the violations for which the penalty is imposed occurred, in which event final determination of the penalty shall be made in an administrative proceeding after opportunity for hearing in accordance with section 554 of Title 5, and regulations to be promulgated by the Secretary. Except for civil penalties collected for violations of section 212 of this title, sums collected as penalties pursuant to this section shall be applied toward reimbursement of the costs of determining the violations and assessing and collecting such penalties, in accordance with the provisions of section 9a of this title. Civil penalties collected for violations of section 212 of this title shall be deposited in the general fund of the Treasury.

Injunction Proceedings

SEC. 217 *[Section 17]*

The districts courts, together with the United States District Court for the District of the Canal Zone, the District Court of the Virgin Islands, and the District Court of Guam shall have jurisdiction, for cause shown, to restrain violations of section 215 *[section 15]* of this title, including in the case of violations of section 15(a)(2) of this title the restraint of any withholding of payment of minimum wages or overtime compensation found by the court to be due to employees under this chapter (except sums which employees are barred from recovering, at the time of the commencement of the action to restrain the violations, by virtue of the provisions of section 255 of this title *[section 6 of the Portal-to-Portal Act of 1947]*.

Relation to Other Laws

SEC. 218 *[Section 18]*

(a) No provision of this chapter or of any order thereunder shall excuse noncompliance with any Federal or State law or municipal ordinance establishing a minimum wage higher than the minimum wage established under this chapter or a maximum workweek lower than the maximum workweek established under this chapter, and no provision of this chapter relating to the employment of child labor shall justify noncompliance with any Federal or State law or municipal ordinance establishing a higher standard than the standard established under this chapter. No provision of this chapter shall justify any employer in reducing a wage paid by him which is in excess of the applicable minimum wage under this chapter, or justify any employer in increasing hours of employment maintained by him which are shorter than the maximum hours applicable under this chapter.

Separability of Provisions

SEC. 219 *[Section 19]*

If any provision of this chapter or the application of such provision to any person or circumstances is held invalid, the remainder of the chapter and the application of such provision to other persons or circumstances shall not be affected thereby.

Approved June 25, 1938.

[In the following excerpts from the Portal-to-Portal Act of 1947, the authority given to the Secretary of Labor is exercised by the Equal Employment Opportunity Commission for purposes of enforcing the Equal Pay Act of 1963.]

Part IV - Miscellaneous

SEC. 255 *[Section 6]* **Statute of Limitations**

Any action commenced on or after May 14, 1947 *[the date of the enactment of this Act]*, to enforce any cause of action for unpaid minimum wages, unpaid overtime compensation, or liquidated damages, under the Fair Labor Standards Act of 1938, as amended, *[29 U.S.C. 201 et seq.]*, the Walsh-Healey Act *[41 U.S.C. 35 et seq.]*, or the Bacon-Davis Act *[40 U.S.C. 276a et seq.]*-

(a) if the cause of action accrues on or after May 14, 1947 *[the date of the enactment of this Act]*-may be commenced within two years after the cause of action accrued, and every such action shall be forever barred unless commenced within two years after the cause of action accrued, except that a cause of action arising out a willful violation may be commenced within three years after the cause of action accrued;

SEC. 256 *[Section 7]* **Determination of Commencement of Future Actions**

In determining when an action is commenced for the purposes of section 255 *[section 6]* of this title, an action commenced on or after May 14, 1947 *[the date of the enactment of this Act]* under the Fair Labor Standards Act of 1938, as amended, *[29 U.S.C. 201 et seq.]*, the Walsh-Healey Act *[41 U.S.C. 35 et seq.]*, or the Bacon-Davis Act *[40 U.S.C. 276a et seq.]*, shall be considered to be commenced on the date when the complaint is filed; except that in the case of a collective or class action instituted under the Fair Labor Standards Act of 1938, as amended, or the Bacon-Davis Act, it shall be considered to be commenced in the case of any individual claimant-

(a) on the date when the complaint is filed, if he is specifically named as a party plaintiff in the complaint and his written consent to become a party plaintiff is filed on such date in the court in which the action is brought; or

(b) if such written consent was not so filed or if his name did not so appear-on the subsequent date on which such written consent is filed in the court in which the action was commenced.

SEC. 259 *[Section 10]* **Reliance in Future on Administrative Rulings, Etc.**

(a) In any action or proceeding based on any act or omission on or after May 14, 1947*[the date of the enactment of this Act]*, no employer shall be subject to any liability or punishment for or on account of the failure of the employer to pay minimum wages or overtime compensation under the Fair Labor Standards Act of 1938, as amended, *[29 U.S.C. 201 et seq.]*, the Walsh-Healey Act *[41 U.S.C. 35 et seq.]*, or the Bacon-Davis Act *[40 U.S.C. 276a et seq.]*, if he pleads and proves that the act or omission complained of was in good faith in conformity with and in reliance on any written administrative regulation, order, ruling, approval, or interpretation, of the agency of the United States specified in subsection (b) of this section, or any administrative practice or enforcement policy of such agency with respect to the class of employers to which he belonged. Such a defense, if established, shall be a bar to the action or proceeding, notwithstanding that after such act or omission, such administrative regulation, order, ruling, approval, interpretation, practice, or enforcement policy is modified or rescinded or is determined by judicial authority to be invalid or of no legal effect.

(b) The agency referred to in subsection (a) shall be-

(1) in the case of the Fair Labor Standards Act of 1938, as amended *[29 U.S.C. 201 et seq.]*-the Administrator of the Wage and Hour Division of the Department of Labor;

SEC. 260 *[Section 11]* **Liquidated Damages**

In any action commenced prior to or on or after May 14, 1947 *[the date of the enactment of this Act]* to recover unpaid minimum wages, unpaid overtime compensation, or liquidated damages, under the Fair Labor Standards Act of 1938, as amended, *[29 U.S.C. 201 et seq.]* if the employer shows to the satisfaction of the court that the act or omission giving rise to such action was in good faith and that he had reasonable grounds for believing that his act or omission was not a violation of the Fair Labor Standards Act of 1938, as amended, *[29 U.S.C. 201 et seq.]* the court may, in its sound discretion, award no liquidated damages or award any amount thereof not to exceed the amount specified in section 216 *[section 16]* of this title.

SEC. 262 *[Section 13]* **Definitions**

(a) When the terms "employer," "employee," and "wage" are used in this chapter in relation to the Fair Labor Standards Act of 1938, as amended, *[29 U.S.C. 201 et seq.]* they shall have the same meaning as when used in such Act of 1938.

Not Reprinted in U.S. Code *[Section 14]* **Separability.**

If any provision of this Act or the application of such provision to any person or circumstance is held invalid, the remainder of this Act and the application of such provision to other persons or circumstances shall not be affected thereby.

Not Reprinted in U.S. Code *[Section 15]* **Short Title.**

This Act may be cited as the "Portal-to-Portal Act of 1947."

Approved May 14, 1947.

AGE DISCRIMINATION IN EMPLOYMENT ACT OF 1967 (ADEA)

The Age Discrimination in Employment Act protects individuals who are 40 years of age or older from employment discrimination based on age. The ADEA's protection applies to both employees and job applicants. Under the ADEA, it is unlawful to discriminate against a person because of his/her age with respect to any term condition, or privilege or employment - including, but not included to hiring, firing, promotion, layoffs, compensation, benefits, job assignments, and training.

It is also unlawful to retaliate against an individual for opposing employment practices that discriminate based on age or for filing an age in any way in an investigation, proceeding, or litigation under ADEA.

The ADEA applies to employers with 20 or more employees, including state and local governments. It also applies to employment agencies and to labor organizations, as well as to the federal government.

AGE DISCRIMINATION IN EMPLOYMENT ACT OF 1967 (ADEA)

EDITOR'S NOTE: The following is the text of the Age Discrimination in Employment Act of 1967 (Pub. L. 90-202) (ADEA), as amended, as it appears in volume 29 of the United States Code, beginning at section 621. The ADEA prohibits employment discrimination against persons 40 years of age or older. The Older Workers Benefit Protection Act (Pub. L. 101-433) amends several sections of the ADEA. In addition, section 115 of the Civil Rights Act of 1991 (P.L. 102-166) amends section 7(e) of the ADEA (29 U. S.C. 626(e)). These amendments appear in boldface type. Cross references to the ADEA as enacted appear in italics following each section heading. Editor's notes also appear in italics

---

An Act

To prohibit age discrimination in employment.

Be it enacted by the Senate and House of Representatives of the United States of America in Congress assembled, that this Act may be cited as the "Age Discrimination in Employment Act of 1967".

* * *

Statement of Findings and Purpose

SEC. 621. *[Section 2]*

(a) The Congress hereby finds and declares that-

(1) in the face of rising productivity and affluence, older workers find themselves disadvantaged in their efforts to retain employment, and especially to regain employment when displaced from jobs;

(2) the setting of arbitrary age limits regardless of potential for job performance has become a common practice, and certain otherwise desirable practices may work to the disadvantage of older persons;

(3) the incidence of unemployment, especially long-term unemployment with resultant deterioration of skill, morale, and employer acceptability is, relative to the younger ages, high among older workers; their numbers are great and growing; and their employment problems grave;

(4) the existence in industries affecting commerce, of arbitrary discrimination in employment because of age, burdens commerce and the free flow of goods in commerce.

(b) It is therefore the purpose of this chapter to promote employment of older persons based on their ability rather than age; to prohibit arbitrary age discrimination in employment; to help employers and workers find ways of meeting problems arising from the impact of age on employment.

Education and Research Program

SEC. 622. *[Section 3]*

(a) The Secretary of Labor *[EEOC]* shall undertake studies **and provide** information to labor unions, management, and the general public concerning the needs and abilities of older workers, and their potentials for continued employment and contribution to the economy. In order to achieve the purposes of this chapter, the Secretary of Labor *[EEOC]* shall carry on a continuing program of education and information, under which he may, among other measures-

(1) undertake research, and promote research, with a view to reducing barriers to the employment of older persons, and the promotion of measures for utilizing their skills;

(2) publish and otherwise make available to employers, professional societies, the various media of communication, and other interested persons the findings of studies and other materials for the promotion of employment;

(3) foster through the public employment service system and through cooperative effort the development of facilities of public and private agencies for expanding the opportunities and potentials of older persons;

(4) sponsor and assist State and community informational and educational programs.

(b) Not later than six months after the effective date of this chapter, the Secretary shall recommend to the Congress any measures he may deem desirable to change the lower or upper age limits set forth in section 631 of this title *[section 12]*.

Prohibition of Age Discrimination

SEC. 623. *[Section 4]*

(a) It shall be unlawful for an employer-

(1) to fail or refuse to hire or to discharge any individual or otherwise discriminate against any individual with respect to his compensation, terms, conditions, or privileges of employment, because of such individual's age;

(2) to limit, segregate, or classify his employees in any way which would deprive or tend to deprive any individual of employment opportunities or otherwise adversely affect his status as an employee, because of such individual's age; or

(3) to reduce the wage rate of any employee in order to comply with this chapter.

(b) It shall be unlawful for an employment agency to fail or refuse to refer for employment, or otherwise to discriminate against, any individual because of such individual's age, or to classify or refer for employment any individual on the basis of such individual's age.

(c) It shall be unlawful for a labor organization-

(1) to exclude or to expel from its membership, or otherwise to discriminate against, any individual because of his age;

(2) to limit, segregate, or classify its membership, or to classify or fail or refuse to refer for employment any individual, in any way which would deprive or tend to deprive any individual of employment opportunities, or would limit such employment opportunities or otherwise adversely affect his status as an employee or as an applicant for employment, because of such individual's age;

(3) to cause or attempt to cause an employer to discriminate against an individual in violation of this section.

(d) It shall be unlawful for an employer to discriminate against any of his employees or applicants for employment, for an employment agency to discriminate against any individual, or for a labor organization to discriminate against any member thereof or applicant for membership, because such individual, member or applicant for membership has opposed any practice made unlawful by this section, or because such individual, member or applicant for membership has made a charge, testified, assisted, or participated in any manner in an investigation, proceeding, or litigation under this chapter.

(e) It shall be unlawful for an employer, labor organization, or employment agency to print or publish, or cause to be printed or published, any notice or advertisement relating to employment by such an employer or membership in or any classification or referral for employment by such a labor organization, or relating to any classification or referral for employment by such an employment agency, indicating any preference, limitation, specification, or discrimination, based on age.

(f) It shall not be unlawful for an employer, employment agency, or labor organization-

(1) to take any action otherwise prohibited under subsections (a), (b), (c), or (e) of this section where age is a bona fide occupational qualification reasonably necessary to the normal operation of the particular business, or where the differentiation is based on reasonable factors other than age, or where such practices involve an employee in a workplace in a foreign country, and compliance with such subsections would cause such employer, or a corporation controlled by such employer, to violate the laws of the country in which such workplace is located;

(2) to take any action otherwise prohibited under subsection (a), (b), (c), or (e) of this section-

(A) to observe the terms of a bona fide seniority system that is not intended to evade the purposes of this chapter, except that no such seniority system shall require or permit the involuntary retirement of any individual specified by section 631(a) of this title because of the age of such individual; or

(B) to observe the terms of a bona fide employee benefit plan-

(i) where, for each benefit or benefit package, the actual amount of payment made or cost incurred on behalf of an older worker is no less than that made or incurred on behalf of a younger

worker, as permissible under section 1625.10, title 29, Code of Federal Regulations (as in effect on June 22, 1989); or

(ii) that is a voluntary early retirement incentive plan consistent with the relevant purpose or purposes of this chapter.

Notwithstanding clause (i) or (ii) of subparagraph (B), no such employee benefit plan or voluntary early retirement incentive plan shall excuse the failure to hire any individual, and no such employee benefit plan shall require or permit the involuntary retirement of any individual specified by section 631(a) of this title, because of the age of such individual. An employer, employment agency, or labor organization acting under subparagraph (A), or under clause (i) or (ii) of subparagraph (B), shall have the burden of proving that such actions are lawful in any civil enforcement proceeding brought under this chapter; or

(3) to discharge or otherwise discipline an individual for good cause.

(g) *[Repealed]*

(h) (1) If an employer controls a corporation whose place of incorporation is in a foreign country, any practice by such corporation prohibited under this section shall be presumed to be such practice by such employer.

(2) The prohibitions of this section shall not apply where the employer is a foreign person not controlled by an American employer.

(3) For the purpose of this subsection the determination of whether an employer controls a corporation shall be based upon the-

(A) interrelation of operations,

(B) common management,

(C) centralized control of labor relations, and

(D) common ownership or financial control, of the employer and the corporation.

(i) It shall not be unlawful for an employer which is a State, a political subdivision of a State, an agency or instrumentality of a State or a political subdivision of a State, or an interstate agency to fail or refuse to hire or to discharge any individual because of such individual's age if such action is taken-

(1) with respect to the employment of an individual as a firefighter or as a law enforcement officer and the individual has attained the age of hiring or retirement in effect under applicable State or local law on March 3, 1983, and

(2) pursuant to a bona fide hiring or retirement plan that is not a subterfuge to evade the purposes of this chapter.

(j) (1) Except as otherwise provided in this subsection, it shall be unlawful for an employer, an employment agency, a labor organization, or any combination thereof to establish or maintain an employee pension benefit plan which requires or permits-

(A) in the case of a defined benefit plan, the cessation of an employee's benefit accrual, or the reduction of the rate of an employee' benefit accrual, because of age, or

(B) in the case of a defined contribution plan, the cessation of allocations to an employee's account, or the reduction of the rate at which amounts are allocated to an employee's account, because of age.

(2) Nothing in this section shall be construed to prohibit an employer, employment agency, or labor organization from observing an provision of an employee pension benefit plan to the extent that such provision imposes (without regard to age) a limitation on the amount of benefits that the plan provides or a limitation on the number of years of service or years of participation which are taken into account for purposes of determining benefit accrual under the plan.

(3) In the case of any employee who, as of the end of any plan year under a defined benefit plan, has attained normal retirement age under such plan-

(A) if distribution of benefits under such plan with respect to such employee has commenced as of the end of such plan year, then any requirement of this subsection for continued accrual of benefits under such plan with respect to such employee during such plan year shall be treated as satisfied to the extent of the actuarial equivalent of in-service distribution of benefits, and

(B) if distribution of benefits under such plan with respect to such employee has not commenced as of the end of such year in accordance with section 1056(a)(3) of this title *[section 206(a)(3) of the Employee Retirement Income Security Act of 1974]* and section 401(a)(14)(C) of title 26 *[the Internal Revenue Code of 1986]*, and the payment of benefits under such plan with respect to such employee is not suspended during such plan year pursuant to section 1053(a)(3)(B) of this title *[section 203(a)(3)(B) of the Employee Retirement Income Security Act of 1974]* or section 411(a)(3)(B) of title 26 *[the Internal Revenue Code of 1986]*, then any requirement of this subsection for continued accrual of benefits under such plan with respect to such employee during such plan year shall be treated as satisfied to the extent of any adjustment in the benefit payable under the plan during such plan year attributable to the delay in the distribution of benefits after the attainment of normal retirement age.

The provisions of this paragraph shall apply in accordance with regulations of the Secretary of the Treasury. Such regulations shall provide for the application of the preceding provisions of this paragraph to all employee pension benefit plans subject to this subsection and may provide for the application of such provisions, in the case of any such employee, with respect to any period of time within a plan year.

(4) Compliance with the requirements of this subsection with respect to an employee pension benefit plan shall constitute compliance with the requirements of this section relating to benefit accrual under such plan.

(5) Paragraph (1) shall not apply with respect to any employee who is a highly compensated employee (within the meaning of section 414(q) of title 26 *[the Internal Revenue Code of 1986]*) to the extent provided in regulations prescribed by the Secretary of the Treasury for purposes of precluding discrimination in favor of highly compensated employees within the meaning of subchapter D of chapter 1 of title 26 *[the Internal Revenue Code of 1986]*.

(6) A plan shall not be treated as failing to meet the requirements of paragraph (1) solely because the subsidized portion of any early retirement benefit is disregarded in determining benefit accruals.

(7) Any regulations prescribed by the Secretary of the Treasury pursuant to clause (v) of section 411(b)(1)(H) of title 26 *[the Internal Revenue Code of 1986]* and subparagraphs (C) and (D) of section 411(b)(2) of title 26 *[the Internal Revenue Code of 1986]* shall apply with respect to the requirements of this subsection in the same manner and to the same extent as such regulations apply with respect to the requirements of such sections 411(b)(1)(H) and 411(b)(2).

(8) A plan shall not be treated as failing to meet the requirements of this section solely because such plan provides a normal retirement age described in section 1002(24)(B) of this title *[section 3(24)(B) of the Employee Retirement Income Security Act of 1974]* and section 411(a)(8)(B) of title 26 *[the Internal Revenue Code of 1986]*.

(9) For purposes of this subsection-

(A) The terms “employee pension benefit plan,” “defined benefit plan,” “defined contribution plan,” and “normal retirement age” have the meanings provided such terms in section 1002 of this title *[Section 3 of the Employee Retirement Income Security Act of 1974]*.

(B) The term “compensation” has the meaning provided by section 414(s) of title 26 *[the Internal Revenue Code of 1986]*.

(k) A seniority system or employee benefit plan shall comply with this chapter regardless of the date of adoption of such system or plan.

(l) Notwithstanding clause (i) or (ii) of subsection (f)(2)(B) of this section-

(1) It shall not be a violation of subsection (a), (b), (c), or (e) of this section solely because-

(A) an employee pension benefit plan (as defined in section 1002(2) of this title *[section 3(2) of the Employee Retirement Income Security Act of 1974]*) provides for the attainment of a minimum age as a condition of eligibility for normal or early retirement benefits; or

(B) a defined benefit plan (as defined in section 1002(35) of this title *[section 3(35) of such Act]*) provides for-

(i) payments that constitute the subsidized portion of an early retirement benefit; or

(ii) social security supplements for plan participants that commence before the age and terminate at the age (specified by the plan) when participants are eligible to receive reduced or unreduced old-age insurance benefits under title II of the Social Security Act (42 U.S.C. 401 et seq.), and that do not exceed such old-age insurance benefits.

(2) (A) It shall not be a violation of subsection (a), (b), (c), or (e) of this section solely because following a contingent event unrelated to age

(i) the value of any retiree health benefits received by an individual eligible for an immediate pension;

(ii) the value of any additional pension benefits that are made available solely as a result of the contingent event unrelated to

age and following which the individual is eligible for not less than an immediate and unreduced pension; or

(iii) the values described in both clauses (i) and (ii); are deducted from severance pay made available as a result of the contingent event unrelated to age.

(B) For an individual who receives immediate pension benefits that are actuarially reduced under subparagraph (A)(i), the amount of the deduction available pursuant to subparagraph (A)(i) shall be reduced by the same percentage as the reduction in the pension benefits.

(C) For purposes of this paragraph, severance pay shall include that portion of supplemental unemployment compensation benefits (as described in section 501(c)(17) of title 26 *[the Internal Revenue Code of 1986]*) that-

(i) constitutes additional benefits of up to 52 weeks;

(ii) has the primary purpose and effect of continuing benefits until an individual becomes eligible for an immediate and unreduced pension; and

(iii) is discontinued once the individual becomes eligible for an immediate and unreduced pension.

(D) For purposes of this paragraph and solely in order to make the deduction authorized under this paragraph, the term "retiree health benefits" means benefits provided pursuant to a group health plan

covering retirees, for which (determined as of the contingent event unrelated to age)-

(i) the package of benefits provided by the employer for the retirees who are below age 65 is at least comparable to benefits provided under title XVIII of the Social Security Act (42 U.S.C. 1395 et seq.);

(ii) the package of benefits provided by the employer for the retirees who are age 65 and above is at least comparable to that offered under a plan that provides a benefit package with one-fourth the value of benefits provided under title XVIII of such Act; or

(iii) the package of benefits provided by the employer is as described in clauses (i) and (ii).

(E) (i) If the obligation of the employer to provide retiree health benefits is of limited duration, the value for each individual shall be calculated at a rate of $3,000 per year for benefit years before age 65, and $750 per year for benefit years beginning at age 65 and above.

(ii) If the obligation of the employer to provide retiree health benefits is of unlimited duration, the value for each individual shall be calculated at a rate of $48,000 for individuals below age 65, and $24,000 for individuals age 65 and above.

(iii) The values described in clauses (i) and (ii) shall be calculated based on the age of the individual as of the date of the contingent

event unrelated to age. The values are effective on October 16, 1990, and shall be adjusted on an annual basis, with respect to a contingent event that occurs subsequent to the first year after October 16, 1990, based on the medical component of the Consumer Price Index for all-urban consumers published by the Department of Labor.

(iv) If an individual is required to pay a premium for retiree health benefits, the value calculated pursuant to this subparagraph shall be reduced by whatever percentage of the overall premium the individual is required to pay.

(F) If an employer that has implemented a deduction pursuant to subparagraph (A) fails to fulfill the obligation described in subparagraph (E), any aggrieved individual may bring an action for specific performance of the obligation described in subparagraph (E). The relief shall be in addition to any other remedies provided under Federal or State law.

(3) It shall not be a violation of subsection (a), (b), (c), or (e) of this section solely because an employer provides a bona fide employee benefit plan or plans under which long-term disability benefits received by an individual are reduced by any pension benefits (other than those attributable to employee contributions)-

(A) paid to the individual that the individual voluntarily elects to receive; or

(B) for which an individual who has attained the later of age 62 or normal retirement age is eligible.

Study by Secretary of Labor

SEC. 624. *[Section 5]*

(a) (1) The Secretary of Labor *[EEOC]* is directed to undertake an appropriate study of institutional and other arrangements giving rise to involuntary retirement, and report his findings and any appropriate legislative recommendations to the President and to the Congress. Such study shall include-

(A) an examination of the effect of the amendment made by section 3(a) of the Age Discrimination in Employment Act Amendments of 1978 in raising the upper age limitation established by section 631(a) of this title *[section 12(a)]* to 70 years of age;

(B) a determination of the feasibility of eliminating such limitation;

(C) a determination of the feasibility of raising such limitation above 70 years of age; and

(D) an examination of the effect of the exemption contained in section 631(c) of this title *[section 12(c)]*, relating to certain executive employees, and the exemption contained in section 631(d) of this title *[section 12(d)]*, relating to tenured teaching personnel.

(2) The Secretary *[EEOC]* may undertake the study required by paragraph (1) of this subsection directly or by contract or other arrangement.

(b) The report required by subsection (a) of this section shall be transmitted to the President and to the Congress as an interim report not later than January 1, 1981, and in final form not later than January 1, 1982.

Transfer of Functions

[All functions relating to age discrimination administration and enforcement vested by Section 6 in the Secretary of Labor or the Civil Service Commission were transferred to the Equal Employment Opportunity Commission effective January 1, 1979 under the President's Reorganization Plan No. 1.]

Administration

SEC. 625. *[Section 6]*

The Secretary *[EEOC]* shall have the power-

(a) to make delegations, to appoint such agents and employees, and to pay for technical assistance on a fee for service basis, as he deems necessary to assist him in the performance of his functions under this chapter;

(b) to cooperate with regional, State, local, and other agencies, and to cooperate with and furnish technical assistance to employers, labor organizations, and employment agencies to aid in effectuating the purposes of this chapter.

Recordkeeping, Investigation, and Enforcement

SEC. 626. *[Section 7]*

(a) The Equal Employment Opportunity Commission shall have the power to make investigations and require the keeping of records necessary or appropriate for the administration of this chapter in accordance with the powers and procedures provided in sections 209 and 211 of this title *[sections 9 and 11 of the Fair Labor Standards Act of 1938, as amended]*.

(b) The provisions of this chapter shall be enforced in accordance with the powers, remedies, and procedures provided in sections 211(b), 216 (except for subsection (a) thereof), and 217 of this title *[sections 11(b), 16 (except for subsection (a) thereof), and 17 of the Fair Labor Standards Act of 1938, as amended]*, and subsection (c) of this section. Any act prohibited under section 623 of this title *[section 4]* shall be deemed to be a prohibited act under section 215 of this title *[section 15 of the Fair Labor Standards Act of 1938, as amended]*. Amounts owing to a person as a result of a violation of this chapter shall be deemed to be unpaid minimum wages or unpaid overtime compensation for purposes of sections 216 and 217 of this title *[sections 16 and 17 of the Fair Labor Standards Act of 1938, as amended]*: Provided, That liquidated damages shall be payable only in cases of willful violations of this chapter. In any action brought to enforce this chapter the court shall have jurisdiction to grant such legal or equitable relief as may be appropriate to effectuate the purposes of this chapter, including without limitation judgments compelling employment, reinstatement or promotion, or enforcing the liability for amounts deemed to be unpaid minimum wages or unpaid overtime compensation under this section. Before instituting any action under this section, the Equal Employment Opportunity Commission shall attempt to eliminate the discriminatory practice or practices alleged, and to effect voluntary compliance with the requirements of this chapter through informal methods of conciliation, conference, and persuasion.

(c) (1) Any person aggrieved may bring a civil action in any court of competent jurisdiction for such legal or equitable relief as will effectuate the purposes of this chapter: Provided, That the right of any person to bring such action shall terminate upon the commencement of an action by the Equal Employment Opportunity Commission to enforce the right of such employee under this chapter.

(2) In an action brought under paragraph (1), a person shall be entitled to a trial by jury of any issue of fact in any such action for recovery of amounts owing as a result of a violation of this chapter, regardless of whether equitable relief is sought by any party in such action.

(d) No civil action may be commenced by an individual under this section until 60 days after a charge alleging unlawful discrimination has been filed with the Equal Employment Opportunity Commission. Such a charge shall be filed-

(1) within 180 days after the alleged unlawful practice occurred; or

(2) in a case to which section 633(b) of this title applies, within 300 days after the alleged unlawful practice occurred, or within 30 days after receipt by the individual of notice of termination of proceedings under State law, whichever is earlier.

Upon receiving such a charge, the Commission shall promptly notify all persons named in such charge as prospective defendants in the action and shall promptly seek to eliminate any alleged unlawful practice by informal methods of conciliation, conference, and persuasion.

(e) **Section 259 of this title *[section 10 of the Portal-to-Portal Act of 1947]* shall apply to actions under this chapter. If a charge filed with the Commission under this chapter is dismissed or the proceedings of the Commission are otherwise terminated by the Commission, the Commission shall notify the person aggrieved. A civil action may be brought under this section by a person defined in section 630(a) of this title *[section 11(a)]* against the respondent named in the charge within 90 days after the date of the receipt of such notice.**

(f) **(1) An individual may not waive any right or claim under this chapter unless the waiver is knowing and voluntary. Except as provided in paragraph (2), a waiver may not be considered knowing and voluntary unless at a minimum-**

(A) the waiver is part of an agreement between the individual and the employer that is written in a manner calculated to be understood by such individual, or by the average individual eligible to participate;

(B) the waiver specifically refers to rights or claims arising under this chapter;

(C) the individual does not waive rights or claims that may arise after the date the waiver is executed;

(D) the individual waives rights or claims only in exchange for consideration in addition to anything of value to which the individual already is entitled;

(E) the individual is advised in writing to consult with an attorney prior to executing the agreement;

(F) (i) the individual is given a period of at least 21 days within which to consider the agreement; or

(ii) if a waiver is requested in connection with an exit incentive or other employment termination program offered to a group or class of employees, the individual is given a period of at least 45 days within which to consider the agreement;

(G) the agreement provides that for a period of at least 7 days following the execution of such agreement, the individual may revoke the agreement, and the agreement shall not become effective or enforceable until the revocation period has expired;

(H) if a waiver is requested in connection with an exit incentive or other employment termination program offered to a group or class of employees, the employer (at the commencement of the period specified in subparagraph (F) informs the individual in writing in a manner calculated to be understood by the average individual eligible to participate, as to-

(i) any class, unit, or group of individuals covered by such program, any eligibility factors for such program, and any time limits applicable to such program; and

(ii) the job titles and ages of all individuals eligible or selected for the program, and the ages of all individuals in the same job classification or organizational unit who are not eligible or selected for the program.

(2) A waiver in settlement of a charge filed with the Equal Employment Opportunity Commission, or an action filed in court by the individual or the individual's representative, alleging age discrimination of a kind prohibited under section 623 or 633a of this title *[section 4 or 15]* may not be considered knowing and voluntary unless at a minimum-

(A) subparagraphs (A) through (E) of paragraph (1) have been met; and

(B) the individual is given a reasonable period of time within which to consider the settlement agreement.

(3) In any dispute that may arise over whether any of the requirements, conditions, and circumstances set forth in subparagraph (A), (B), (C), (D), (E), (F), (G), or (H) of paragraph (1), or subparagraph (A) or (B) of paragraph (2), have been met, the party asserting the validity of a waiver shall have the burden of proving in a court of competent jurisdiction that a waiver was knowing and voluntary pursuant to paragraph (1) or (2).

(4) No waiver agreement may affect the Commission's rights and responsibilities to enforce this chapter. No waiver may be used to justify interfering with the protected right of an employee to file a charge or participate in an investigation or proceeding conducted by the Commission.

Notice to be Posted

SEC. 627. *[Section 8]*

Every employer, employment agency, and labor organization shall post and keep posted in conspicuous places upon its premises a notice to be prepared or approved by the Equal

Employment Opportunity Commission setting forth information as the Commission deems appropriate to effectuate the purposes of this chapter.

Rules and Regulations

SEC. 628. *[Section 9]*

In accordance with the provisions of subchapter II of chapter 5 of title 5 *[United States Code]*, the Equal Employment Opportunity Commission may issue such rules and regulations as it may consider necessary or appropriate for carrying out this chapter, and may establish such reasonable exemptions to and from any or all provisions of this chapter as it may find necessary and proper in the public interest.

Criminal Penalties

SEC. 629. *[Section 10]*

Whoever shall forcibly resist, oppose, impede, intimidate or interfere with a duly authorized representative of the Equal Employment Opportunity Commission while it is engaged in the performance of duties under this chapter shall be punished by a fine of not more than $500 or by imprisonment for not more than one year, or by both: Provided, however, that no person shall be imprisoned under this section except when there has been a prior conviction hereunder.

Definitions

SEC. 630. *[Section 11]*

For the purposes of this chapter-

(a) The term “person” means one or more individuals, partnerships, associations, labor organizations, corporations, business trust, legal representatives, or any organized groups of persons.

(b) The term "employer" means a person engaged in an industry affecting commerce who has twenty or more employees for each working day in each of twenty or more calendar weeks in the current or preceding calendar year: Provided, That prior to June 30, 1968, employers having fewer than fifty employees shall not be considered employers. The term also means (1) any agent of such a person, and (2) a State or political subdivision of a State and any agency or instrumentality of a State or a political subdivision of a State, and any interstate agency, but such term does not include the United States, or a corporation wholly owned by the Government of the United States.

(c) The term "employment agency" means any person regularly undertaking with or without compensation to procure employees for an employer and includes an agent of such a person; but shall not include an agency of the United States.

(d) The term "labor organization" means a labor organization engaged in an industry affecting commerce, and any agent of such an organization, and includes any organization of any kind, any agency, or employee representation committee, group, association, or plan so engaged in which employees participate and which exists for the purpose, in whole or in part, of dealing with employers concerning grievances, labor disputes, wages, rates of pay, hours, or other terms or conditions of employment, and any conference, general committee, joint or system board, or joint council so engaged which is subordinate to a national or international labor organization.

(e) A labor organization shall be deemed to be engaged in an industry affecting commerce if (1) it maintains or operates a hiring hall or hiring office which procures employees for an employer or procures for employees opportunities to work for an employer, or (2) the number of its members (or, where it is a labor organization composed of other labor organizations or their representatives, if the aggregate number of the members of such other labor organization) is fifty or more prior to July 1, 1968, or twenty-five or more on or after July 1, 1968, and such labor organization-

(1) is the certified representative of employees under the provisions of the National Labor Relations Act, as amended *[29 U.S.C.151 et seq.]*, or the Railway Labor Act, as amended *[45 U.S.C. 151 et seq.]*; or

(2) although not certified, is a national or international labor organization or a local labor organization recognized or acting as the representative of employees of an employer or employers engaged in an industry affecting commerce; or

(3) has chartered a local labor organization or subsidiary body which is representing or actively seeking to represent employees of employers within the meaning of paragraph (1) or (2); or

(4) has been chartered by a labor organization representing or actively seeking to represent employees within the meaning of paragraph (1) or (2) as the local or subordinate body through which such employees may enjoy membership or become affiliated with such labor organization; or

(5) is a conference, general committee, joint or system board, or joint council subordinate to a national or international labor organization, which includes a labor organization engaged in an industry affecting commerce within the meaning of any of the preceding paragraphs of this subsection.

(f) The term "employee" means an individual employed by any employer except that the term "employee" shall not include any person elected to public office in any State or political subdivision of any State by the qualified voters thereof, or any person chosen by such officer to be on such officer's personal staff, or an appointee on the policymaking level or an immediate adviser with respect to the exercise of the constitutional or legal powers of the office. The exemption set forth in the preceding sentence shall not include employees subject to the civil service laws of a State government, governmental agency, or political subdivision. The term ``employee'' includes any individual who is a citizen of the United States employed by an employer in a workplace in a foreign country.

[The exclusion from the term "employee" of any person chosen by an elected official "to be on such official's personal staff, or an appointee on the policymaking level or an immediate advisor with respect to the exercise of the constitutional or legal powers of the office," remains in section 11(f). However, the Civil Rights Act of 1991 now provides special procedures for such persons who feel they are victims of age and other types of discrimination prohibited by EEOC enforced statutes. <u>See</u> *section 321 of the Civil Rights Act of 1991.]*

(g) The term "commerce" means trade, traffic, commerce, transportation, transmission, or communication among the several States; or between a State and any place outside thereof; or within the District of Columbia, or a possession of the United States; or between points in the same State but through a point outside thereof.

(h) The term "industry affecting commerce" means any activity, business, or industry in commerce or in which a labor dispute would hinder or obstruct commerce or the free flow of commerce and includes any activity or industry "affecting commerce" within the meaning of the Labor-Management Reporting and Disclosure Act of 1959 *[29 U.S.C. 401 et seq.]*.

(i) The term "State" includes a State of the United States, the District of Columbia, Puerto Rico, the Virgin Islands, American Samoa, Guam, Wake Island, the Canal Zone, and Outer Continental Shelf lands defined in the Outer Continental Shelf Lands Act *[43 U.S.C. 1331 et seq.]*.

(j) The term "firefighter" means an employee, the duties of whose position are primarily to perform work directly connected with the control and extinguishment of fires or the maintenance and use of firefighting apparatus and equipment, including an employee engaged in this activity who is transferred to a supervisory or administrative position.

(k) The term "law enforcement officer" means an employee, the duties of whose position are primarily the investigation, apprehension, or detention of individuals suspected or convicted of offenses against the criminal laws of a State, including an employee engaged in this activity who is transferred to a supervisory or administrative position. For the purpose of this subsection, ``detention'' includes the duties of employees assigned to guard individuals incarcerated in any penal institution.

(l) The term "compensation, terms, conditions, or privileges of employment" encompasses all employee benefits, including such benefits provided pursuant to a bona fide employee benefit plan.

Age Limitation

SEC. 631. *[Section 12]*

(a) The prohibitions in this chapter *[except the provisions of section 4(g)]* shall be limited to individuals who are at least 40 years of age.

(b) In the case of any personnel action affecting employees or applicants for employment which is subject to the provisions of section 633a of this title *[section 15]*, the prohibitions established in section 633a of this title *[section 15]* shall be limited to individuals who are at least 40 years of age.

(c) (1) Nothing in this chapter shall be construed to prohibit compulsory retirement of any employee who has attained 65 years of age and who, for the 2-year period immediately before retirement, is employed in a bona fide executive or a high policymaking position, if such employee is entitled to an immediate nonforfeitable annual retirement benefit from a pension, profit-sharing, savings, or deferred compensation plan, or any combination of such plans, of the employer of such employee, which equals, in the aggregate, at least $44,000.

(2) In applying the retirement benefit test of paragraph (1) of this subsection, if any such retirement benefit is in a form other than a straight life annuity (with no ancillary benefits), or if employees contribute to any such plan or make rollover contributions, such benefit shall be adjusted in accordance with regulations prescribed by the Equal Employment Opportunity Commission, after consultation with the Secretary of the Treasury, so that the benefit is the equivalent of a straight life annuity (with no ancillary benefits) under a plan to

which employees do not contribute and under which no rollover contributions are made.

(d) Nothing in this chapter shall be construed to prohibit compulsory retirement of any employee who has attained 70 years of age, and who is serving under a contract of unlimited tenure (or similar arrangement providing for unlimited tenure) at an institution of higher education (as defined by section 1141(a) of title 20 *[section 1201(a) of the Higher Education Act of 1965]*).

Annual Report

SEC. 632. *[Section 13]*

The Equal Employment Opportunity Commission shall submit annually in January a report to the Congress covering its activities for the preceding year and including such information, data and recommendations for further legislation in connection with the matters covered by this chapter as it may find advisable. Such report shall contain an evaluation and appraisal by the Commission of the effect of the minimum and maximum ages established by this chapter, together with its recommendations to the Congress. In making such evaluation and appraisal, the Commission shall take into consideration any changes which may have occurred in the general age level of the population, the effect of the chapter upon workers not covered by its provisions, and such other factors as it may deem pertinent.

Federal-State Relationship

SEC. 633. *[Section 14]*

(a) Nothing in this chapter shall affect the jurisdiction of any agency of any State performing like functions with regard to discriminatory employment practices on account of age except that upon commencement of action under this chapter such action shall supersede any State action.

(b) In the case of an alleged unlawful practice occurring in a State which has a law prohibiting discrimination in employment because of age and establishing or authorizing a State authority to grant or seek relief from such discriminatory practice, no suit may be brought under section 626 of this title *[section 7]* before the expiration of sixty days after proceedings have been commenced under the State law, unless such proceedings have been earlier terminated: Provided, That such sixty-day period shall be extended to one hundred and twenty days during the first year after the effective date of such State law. If any requirement for the commencement of such proceedings is imposed by a State authority other than a requirement of the filing of a written and signed statement of the facts upon which the proceeding is based, the proceeding shall be deemed to have been commenced for the purposes of this subsection at the time such statement is sent by registered mail to the appropriate State authority.

Nondiscrimination on Account of Age in Federal Government Employment

SEC. 633a. *[Section 15]*

(a) All personnel actions affecting employees or applicants for employment who are at least 40 years of age (except personnel actions with regard to aliens employed outside the limits of the United States) in military departments as defined in section 102 of title 5 *[United States Code]*, in executive agencies as defined in section 105 of title 5 *[United States Code]* (including employees and applicants for employment who are paid from nonappropriated funds), in the United States Postal Service and the Postal

Rate Commission, in those units in the government of the District of Columbia having positions in the competitive service, and in those units of the legislative and judicial branches of the Federal Government having positions in the competitive service, and in the Library of Congress shall be made free from any discrimination based on age.

(b) Except as otherwise provided in this subsection, the Equal Employment Opportunity Commission is authorized to enforce the provisions of subsection (a) of this section through appropriate remedies, including reinstatement or hiring of employees with or without backpay, as will effectuate the policies of this section. The Equal Employment Opportunity Commission shall issue such rules, regulations, orders, and instructions as it deems necessary and appropriate to carry out its responsibilities under this section. The Equal Employment Opportunity Commission shall-

(1) be responsible for the review and evaluation of the operation of all agency programs designed to carry out the policy of this section, periodically obtaining and publishing (on at least a semiannual basis) progress reports from each department, agency, or unit referred to in subsection (a) of this section;

(2) consult with and solicit the recommendations of interested individuals, groups, and organizations relating to nondiscrimination in employment on account of age; and

(3) provide for the acceptance and processing of complaints of discrimination in Federal employment on account of age.

The head of each such department, agency, or unit shall comply with such rules, regulations, orders, and instructions of the Equal Employment Opportunity

Commission which shall include a provision that an employee or applicant for employment shall be notified of any final action taken on any complaint of discrimination filed by him thereunder. Reasonable exemptions to the provisions of this section may be established by the Commission but only when the Commission has established a maximum age requirement on the basis of a determination that age is a bona fide occupational qualification necessary to the performance of the duties of the position. With respect to employment in the Library of Congress, authorities granted in this subsection to the Equal Employment Opportunity Commission shall be exercised by the Librarian of Congress.

(c) Any person aggrieved may bring a civil action in any Federal district court of competent jurisdiction for such legal or equitable relief as will effectuate the purposes of this chapter.

(d) When the individual has not filed a complaint concerning age discrimination with the Commission, no civil action may be commenced by any individual under this section until the individual has given the Commission not less than thirty days' notice of an intent to file such action. Such notice shall be filed within one hundred and eighty days after the alleged unlawful practice occurred. Upon receiving a notice of intent to sue, the Commission shall promptly notify all persons named therein as prospective defendants in the action and take any appropriate action to assure the elimination of any unlawful practice.

(e) Nothing contained in this section shall relieve any Government agency or official of the responsibility to assure nondiscrimination on account of age in employment as required under any provision of Federal law.

(f) Any personnel action of any department, agency, or other entity referred to in subsection (a) of this section shall not be subject to, or affected by, any provision of this chapter, other than the provisions of section 631(b) of this title *[section 12(b)]* and the provisions of this section.

(g) (1) The Equal Employment Opportunity Commission shall undertake a study relating to the effects of the amendments made to this section by the Age Discrimination in Employment Act Amendments of 1978, and the effects of section 631(b) of this title *[section 12(b)]*, as added by the Age Discrimination in Employment Act Amendments of 1978.

(2) The Equal Employment Opportunity Commission shall transmit a report to the President and to the Congress containing the findings of the Commission resulting from the study of the Commission under paragraph (1) of this subsection. Such report shall be transmitted no later than January 1, 1980.

Effective Date

[Section 16 of the ADEA (not reproduced in the U.S. Code)]

This Act shall become effective one hundred and eighty days after enactment, except (a) that the Secretary of Labor may extend the delay in effective date of any provision of this Act up to an additional ninety days thereafter if he finds that such time is necessary in permitting adjustments to the provisions hereof, and (b) that on or after the date of enactment the Secretary of Labor [EEOC] is authorized to issue such rules and regulations as may be necessary to carry out its provisions.]

Appropriations

SEC. 634. *[Section 17]*

There are hereby authorized to be appropriated such sums as may be necessary to carry out this chapter.

[Approved December 15, 1967]

THE REHABILITATION ACT OF 1973

The Rehabilitation Act of 1973 was the first legislation to prohibit discrimination against people with disabilities. However, this law applied to programs conducted by federal agencies, those receiving federal funds, such as colleges participating in federal student loan programs, federal employment, and employment practices of businesses with federal contracts. The standards for determining employment discrimination under the Rehabilitation Act are the same as those used in Title I of the Americans With Disabilities Act.

THE REHABILITATION ACT OF 1973, SECTIONS 501 AND 505

EDITOR'S NOTE: The following is the text of Sections 501 and 505 of the Rehabilitation Act of 1973 (Pub. L. 93-112) (Rehab. Act), as amended, as these sections appear in volume 29 of the United States Code, beginning at section 791. Section 501 prohibits employment discrimination against individuals with disabilities in the federal sector. Section 505 contains provisions governing remedies and attorney's fees under Section 501. Relevant definitions that apply to sections 501 and 505 precede these sections. Section 512 of the Americans with Disabilities Act of 1990 (Pub. L. 101-336) (ADA) amends definitions applicable to the Rehab. Act. The Rehabilitation Act Amendments of 1992 (Pub. L. 102-559) further amends the definition of "individual with a disability" and Section 501. These amendments appear in boldface type. In addition, section 102 of the Civil Rights Act of 1991 (Pub. L. 102-166 (CRA) (which is printed elsewhere in this publication) amends the Revised Statutes by adding a new section following section 1977 (42 U.S.C. 1981), to provide for the recovery of compensatory and punitive damages in cases of intentional violations of Title VII, the Americans with Disabilities Act of 1990, and section 501 of the Rehabilitation Act of 1973. Cross references to the Rehabilitation Act as enacted appear in italics following each section heading. Editor's notes also appear in italics.

Definitions

SEC. 706 *[Section 7]*

For the purposes of this chapter:

(4) (A) **The term "drug" means a controlled substance, as defined in schedules I through V of section 202 of the Controlled Substances Act (21 U.S.C. 812).**

(B) **The term "illegal use of drugs" means the use of drugs, the possession or distribution of which is unlawful under the Controlled Substances Act *[21 U.S.C. 801 et seq.]*. Such term does not include the use of a drug taken under supervision by a licensed health care professional, or other uses authorized by the Controlled Substances Act *[21 U.S.C. 801 et seq.]* or other provisions of Federal law.**

(8) (B) Subject to subparagraphs (C)..., **(E), and (F)**, the term "individual with **a disability**" means ... any person who (i) has a physical or mental impairment which substantially limits one or more of such person's major life activities, (ii) has a record of such an impairment, or (iii) is regarded as having such an impairment.

(C) (i) [T]he term "individual with a disability" does not include an individual who is currently engaging in the illegal use of drugs, when a covered entity acts on the basis of such use. (ii) Nothing in clause (i) shall be construed to exclude as an individual with a disability an individual who –

(I) has successfully completed a supervised drug rehabilitation program and is no longer engaging in the illegal use of drugs, or has otherwise been rehabilitated successfully and is no longer engaging in such use;

(II) is participating in a supervised rehabilitation program and is no longer engaging in such use; or

(III) is erroneously regarded as engaging in such use, but is not engaging in such use;

except that it shall not be a violation of this chapter for a covered entity to adopt or administer reasonable policies or procedures, including but not limited to drug testing, designed to ensure that an individual described in subclause (I) or (II) is no longer engaging in the illegal use of drugs.

(E) For the purposes of [section 501] ... -

(i) for purposes of the application of subparagraph (B) to such [section], the term "impairment" does not include homosexuality or bisexuality; and

(ii) therefore the term "individual with a disability" does not include an individual on the basis of homosexuality or bisexuality.

(F) For the purposes of [section 501] ..., the term "individual with a disability" does not include an individual on the basis of - (i) transvestism, transsexualism, pedophilia, exhibitionism, voyeurism, gender identity disorders not resulting from physical impairments, or other sexual behavior disorders;

(ii) compulsive gambling, kleptomania, or pyromania; or

(iii) psychoactive substance use disorders resulting from current illegal use of drugs.

Employment of Individuals With Disabilities

SEC. 791. *[Section 501]*

(a) There is established within the Federal Government an Interagency Committee on **Employees who are Individuals with Disabilities** (hereinafter in this section referred to as the "Committee"), comprised of such members as the President may select, including the following (or their designees whose positions are Executive Level IV or higher): the Chairman of the Equal Employment Opportunity Commission (hereinafter in this section referred to as the "Commission"), **the Director of the Office of Personnel Management**, the Secretary of Veterans

Affairs, and the Secretary of Labor, the Secretary of Education, and the Secretary of Health and Human Services. **Either the Director of the Office of Personnel Management and the Chairman of the Commission shall serve as co-chairpersons of the Committee or the Director or Chairman shall serve as the sole chairperson of the Committee, as the Director and Chairman jointly determine, from time to time, to be appropriate.** The resources of the President's Committees on Employment of People with Disabilities and on Mental Retardation shall be made fully available to the Committee. It shall be the purpose and function of the Committee (1) to provide a focus for Federal and other employment of individuals with **disabilities,** and to review, on a periodic basis, in cooperation with the Commission, the adequacy of hiring, placement, and advancement practices with respect to individuals with **disabilities** by each department, agency, and instrumentality in the executive branch of Government, and to insure that the special needs of such individuals are being met; and (2) to consult with the Commission to assist the Commission to carry out its responsibilities under subsections (b), (c), and (d) of this section. On the basis of such review and consultation, the Committee shall periodically make to the Commission such recommendations for legislative and administrative changes as it deems necessary or desirable. The Commission shall timely transmit to the appropriate committees of Congress any such recommendations.

(b) Each department, agency, and instrumentality (including the United States Postal Service and the Postal Rate Commission) in the executive branch shall, within one hundred and eighty days after September 26, 1973, submit to the Commission and to the Committee an affirmative action program plan for the hiring, placement, and advancement of individuals with **disabilities** in such department, agency, or instrumentality. Such plan shall include a description of the extent to which and methods whereby the special needs of employees **who are individuals with disabilities** are being met. Such plan shall be updated annually, and shall be reviewed annually and approved by the Commission if the Commission determines, after consultation with the Committee, that such plan provides sufficient assurances, procedures and commitments to provide adequate hiring, placement, and advancement opportunities for individuals with **disabilities**.

(c) The Commission, after consultation with the Committee, shall develop and recommend to the Secretary for referral to the appropriate State agencies, policies and procedures which will facilitate the hiring, placement, and advancement in employment of individuals who have received rehabilitation services under State vocational rehabilitation programs, veterans' programs, or any other program for individuals with **disabilities**, including the promotion of job opportunities for such individuals. The Secretary shall encourage such State agencies to adopt and implement such policies and procedures.

(d) The Commission, after consultation with the Committee, shall, on June 30, 1974, and at the end of each subsequent fiscal year, make a complete report to the appropriate committees of the Congress with respect to the practices of and achievements in hiring, placement, and advancement of individuals with **disabilities** by each department, agency, and instrumentality and the effectiveness of the affirmative action programs required by subsection (b) of this section, together with recommendations as to legislation which have been submitted to the Commission under subsection (a) of this section, or other appropriate action to insure the adequacy of such practices. Such report shall also include an evaluation by the Committee of the effectiveness of the activities of the Commission under subsections (b) and (c) of this section.

(e) An individual who, as a part of an individualized written rehabilitation program under a State plan approved under this chapter, participates in a program of unpaid work experience in a Federal agency, shall not, by reason thereof, be considered to be a Federal employee or to be subject to the provisions of law relating to Federal employment, including those relating to hours of work, rates of compensation, leave, unemployment compensation, and Federal employee benefits.

(f) (1) The Secretary of Labor and the Secretary of Education are authorized and directed to cooperate with the President's Committee on Employment of People With Disabilities in carrying out its functions.

(2) In selecting personnel to fill all positions on the President's Committee on Employment of People with Disabilities, special consideration shall be given to qualified individuals with **disabilities**.

(g) The standards used to determine whether this section has been violated in a complaint alleging nonaffirmative action employment discrimination under this section shall be the standards applied under title I of the Americans with Disabilities Act of 1990 (42 U.S.C. 12111 et seq.) and the provisions of sections 501 through 504, and 510, of the Americans with Disabilities Act of 1990 (42 U.S.C. 12201-12204 and 12210), as such sections relate to employment.

Remedies and Attorney's Fees

SEC. 794a. *[Section 505]*

(a) (1) The remedies, procedures, and rights set forth in section 717 of the Civil Rights Act of 1964 (42 U.S.C. 2000e-16), including the application of sections 706(f) through 706(k) (42 U.S.C. 2000e-5(f) through (k)), shall be available, with respect to any complaint under section 791 of this title, to any employee or applicant for employment aggrieved by the final disposition of such complaint, or by the failure to take final action on such complaint. In fashioning an equitable or affirmative action remedy under such section, a court may take into account the reasonableness of the cost of any necessary work place accommodation, and the availability of alternatives therefore or other appropriate relief in order to achieve an equitable and appropriate remedy.

(2) The remedies, procedures, and rights set forth in title VI of the Civil Rights Act of 1964 *[42 U.S.C. 2000d et seq.]* shall be available to any person aggrieved by any act or failure to act by any recipient of Federal assistance or Federal provider of such assistance under section 794 of this title.

(b) In any action or proceeding to enforce or charge a violation of a provision of this subchapter, the court, in its discretion, may allow the prevailing party, other than the United States, a reasonable attorney's fee as part of the costs.

THE AMERICANS WITH DISABILITIES ACT (ADA)

The Americans with Disabilities Act prohibits discrimination against people with disabilities in employment, transportation, public accommodation, communications, and governmental activities. The ADA also established requirements for telecommunication relay services.

TITLES I AND V OF THE

AMERICANS WITH DISABILITIES ACT OF 1990 (ADA)

EDITOR'S NOTE: The following is the text of Titles I and V of the Americans with Disabilities Act of 1990 (Pub. L. 101-336) (ADA), as amended, as these titles appear in volume 42 of the United States Code, beginning at section 12101. Title I of the ADA, which became effective for employers with 25 or more employees on July 26, 1992, prohibits employment discrimination against qualified individuals with disabilities. Title I will apply to employers with 15 or more employees beginning on July 26, 1994. Title V contains miscellaneous provisions which apply to EEOC's enforcement of Title I. The Civil Rights Act of 1991 (Pub. L. 102-166) (CRA) amends sections 101(4), 102 and 509 of the ADA. These amendments appear in boldface type. In addition, section 102 of the CRA (which is printed elsewhere in this publication) amends the Revised Statutes by adding a new section following section 1977 (42 U.S.C. 1981) to provide for the recovery of compensatory and punitive damages in cases of intentional violations of Title VII, the Americans with Disabilities Act of 1990, and section 501 of the Rehabilitation Act of 1973. Cross references to the ADA as enacted appear in italics following each section heading. Editor's notes also appear in italics.

An Act

To establish a clear and comprehensive prohibition of discrimination on the basis of disability.

Be it enacted by the Senate and House of Representatives of the United States of America assembled, that this Act may be cited as the "Americans with Disabilities Act of 1990".

* * *

Findings and Purpose

SEC. 12101. *[Section 2]*

(a) Findings. - The Congress finds that-

(1) some 43,000,000 Americans have one or more physical or mental disabilities, and this number is increasing as the population as a whole is growing older;

(2) historically, society has tended to isolate and segregate individuals with disabilities, and, despite some improvements, such forms of discrimination against individuals with disabilities continue to be a serious and pervasive social problem;

(3) discrimination against individuals with disabilities persists in such critical areas as employment, housing, public accommodations, education, transportation, communication, recreation, institutionalization, health services, voting, and access to public services;

(4) unlike individuals who have experienced discrimination on the basis of race, color, sex, national origin, religion, or age, individuals who have experienced discrimination on the basis of disability have often had no legal recourse to redress such discrimination;

(5) individuals with disabilities continually encounter various forms of discrimination, including outright intentional exclusion, the discriminatory effects of architectural, transportation, and communication barriers, overprotective rules and policies, failure to make modifications to existing facilities and practices, exclusionary qualification standards and criteria, segregation, and relegation to lesser services, programs, activities, benefits, jobs, or other opportunities;

(6) census data, national polls, and other studies have documented that people with disabilities, as a group, occupy an inferior status in our society, and are severely disadvantaged socially, vocationally, economically, and educationally;

(7) individuals with disabilities are a discrete and insular minority who have been faced with restrictions and limitations, subjected to a history of purposeful unequal treatment, and relegated to a position of political powerlessness in our society, based on characteristics that are beyond the control of such individuals and resulting from stereotypic assumptions not truly indicative of the individual ability of such individuals to participate in, and contribute to, society;

(8) the Nation's proper goals regarding individuals with disabilities are to assure equality of opportunity, full participation, independent living, and economic self sufficiency for such individuals; and

(9) the continuing existence of unfair and unnecessary discrimination and prejudice denies people with disabilities the opportunity to compete on an equal basis and to pursue those opportunities for which our free society is justifiably famous, and costs the United States billions of dollars in unnecessary expenses resulting from dependency and nonproductivity.

(b) Purpose. - It is the purpose of this chapter-

(1) to provide a clear and comprehensive national mandate for the elimination of discrimination against individuals with disabilities;

(2) to provide clear, strong, consistent, enforceable standards addressing discrimination against individuals with disabilities;

(3) to ensure that the Federal Government plays a central role in enforcing the standards established in this chapter on behalf of individuals with disabilities; and

(4) to invoke the sweep of congressional authority, including the power to enforce the fourteenth amendment and to regulate commerce, in order to address the major areas of discrimination faced day-to-day by people with disabilities.

Definitions

SEC. 12102. *[Section 3]*

As used in this chapter:

(1) Auxiliary aids and services. - The term ``auxiliary aids and services" includes-

(A) qualified interpreters or other effective methods of making aurally delivered materials available to individuals with hearing impairments;

(B) qualified readers, taped texts, or other effective methods of making visually delivered materials available to individuals with visual impairments;

(C) acquisition or modification of equipment or devices; and

(D) other similar services and actions.

(2) Disability. - The term "disability" means, with respect to an individual-

(A) a physical or mental impairment that substantially limits one or more of the major life activities of such individual;

(B) a record of such an impairment; or

(C) being regarded as having such an impairment.

(3) State. - The term "State" means each of the several States, the District of Columbia, the Commonwealth of Puerto Rico, Guam, American Samoa, the Virgin Islands, the Trust Territory of the Pacific Islands, and the Commonwealth of the Northern Mariana Islands.

SUBCHAPTER I [*TITLE I*] – EMPLOYMENT

Definitions

SEC. 12111. *[Section 101]*

As used in this subchapter:

(1) Commission. - The term ``Commission'' means the Equal Employment Opportunity Commission established by section 2000e-4 of this title *[section 705 of the Civil Rights Act of 1964]*.

(2) Covered entity. - The term "covered entity" means an employer, employment agency, labor organization, or joint labor-management committee.

(3) Direct threat. - The term "direct threat" means a significant risk to the health or safety of others that cannot be eliminated by reasonable accommodation.

(4) Employee. - The term "employee" means an individual employed by an employer. **With respect to employment in a foreign country, such term includes an individual who is a citizen of the United States.**

(5) Employer. –

(A) In general. - The term "employer" means a person engaged in an industry affecting commerce who has 15 or more employees for each working day in each of 20 or more calendar weeks in the current or preceding calendar year, and any agent of such person, except that, for two years following the effective date of this subchapter, an employer means a person engaged in an industry affecting commerce who has 25 or more employees for each working day in each of 20 or more calendar weeks in the current or preceding year, and any agent of such person.

(B) Exceptions. - The term ``employer'' does not include-

(i) the United States, a corporation wholly owned by the government of the United States, or an Indian tribe; or

(ii) a bona fide private membership club (other than a labor organization) that is exempt from taxation under section 501(c) of Title 26 *[the Internal Revenue Code of 1986]*.

(6) Illegal use of drugs. –

(A) In general. - The term "illegal use of drugs" means the use of drugs, the possession or distribution of which is unlawful under the Controlled Substances Act [21 U.S.C. 801 et seq.]. Such term does not include the use of a drug taken under supervision by a licensed health care professional, or other uses authorized by the Controlled Substances Act or other provisions of Federal law.

(B) Drugs. - The term ``drug'' means a controlled substance, as defined in schedules I through V of section 202 of the Controlled Substances Act [21 U.S.C. 812].

(7) Person, etc. - The terms "person," "labor organization", "employment agency", "commerce", and "industry affecting commerce", shall have the same meaning given such terms in section 2000e of this title *[section 701 of the Civil Rights Act of 1964]*.

(8) Qualified individual with a disability. - The term "qualified individual with a disability" means an individual with a disability who, with or without reasonable accommodation, can perform the essential functions of the

employment position that such individual holds or desires. For the purposes of this subchapter, consideration shall be given to the employer's judgment as to what functions of a job are essential, and if an employer has prepared a written description before advertising or interviewing applicants for the job, this description shall be considered evidence of the essential functions of the job.

(9) Reasonable accommodation. - The term "reasonable accommodation" may include-

(A) making existing facilities used by employees readily accessible to and usable by individuals with disabilities; and

(B) job restructuring, part-time or modified work schedules, reassignment to a vacant position, acquisition or modification of equipment or devices, appropriate adjustment or modifications of examinations, training materials or policies, the provision of qualified readers or interpreters, and other similar accommodations for individuals with disabilities.

(10) Undue hardship. –

(A) In general. - The term "undue hardship" means an action requiring significant difficulty or expense, when considered in light of the factors set forth in subparagraph

(B) Factors to be considered. - In determining whether an accommodation would impose an undue hardship on a covered entity, factors to be considered include-

(i) the nature and cost of the accommodation needed under this chapter;

(ii) the overall financial resources of the facility or facilities involved in the provision of the reasonable accommodation; the number of persons employed at such facility; the effect on expenses and resources, or the impact otherwise of such accommodation upon the operation of the facility;

(iii) the overall financial resources of the covered entity; the overall size of the business of a covered entity with respect to the number of its employees; the number, type, and location of its facilities; and

(iv) the type of operation or operations of the covered entity, including the composition, structure, and functions of the workforce of such entity; the geographic separateness, administrative, or fiscal relationship of the facility or facilities in question to the covered entity.

Discrimination

SEC. 12112. *[Section 102]*

(a) General rule. - No covered entity shall discriminate against a qualified individual with a disability because of the disability of such individual in regard to job application procedures, the hiring, advancement, or discharge of employees, employee compensation, job training, and other terms, conditions, and privileges of employment.

(b) Construction. - As used in subsection (a) of this section, the term "discriminate" includes-

(1) limiting, segregating, or classifying a job applicant or employee in a way that adversely affects the opportunities or status of such applicant or employee because of the disability of such applicant or employee;

(2) participating in a contractual or other arrangement or relationship that has the effect of subjecting a covered entity's qualified applicant or employee with a disability to the discrimination prohibited by this subchapter (such relationship includes a relationship with an employment or referral agency, labor union, an organization providing fringe benefits to an employee of the covered entity, or an organization providing training and apprenticeship programs);

(3) utilizing standards, criteria, or methods of administration-

(A) that have the effect of discrimination on the basis of disability; or

(B) that perpetuate the discrimination of others who are subject to common administrative control

(4) excluding or otherwise denying equal jobs or benefits to a qualified individual because of the known disability of an individual with whom the qualified individual is known to have a relationship or association;

(5) (A) not making reasonable accommodations to the known physical or mental limitations of an otherwise qualified individual with a disability who is an applicant or employee, unless such covered entity can demonstrate that the accommodation would impose an undue hardship on the operation of the business of such covered entity; or

(B) denying employment opportunities to a job applicant or employee who is an otherwise qualified individual with a disability, if such denial is based on the need of such covered entity to make reasonable accommodation to the physical or mental impairments of the employee or applicant;

(6) using qualification standards, employment tests or other selection criteria that screen out or tend to screen out an individual with a disability or a class of individuals with disabilities unless the standard, test or other selection criteria, as used by the covered entity, is shown to be job-related for the position in question and is consistent with business necessity; and

(7) failing to select and administer tests concerning employment in the most effective manner to ensure that, when such test is administered to a job applicant or employee who has a disability that impairs sensory, manual, or speaking skills, such test results accurately reflect the skills, aptitude, or whatever other factor of such applicant or employee that such test purports to measure, rather than reflecting the impaired sensory, manual, or speaking skills of such employee or applicant (except where such skills are the factors that the test purports to measure).

(c) Covered entities in foreign countries. -

(1) In general. - It shall not be unlawful under this section for a covered entity to take any action that constitutes discrimination under this section with respect to an employee in a workplace in a foreign country if compliance with this section would cause such covered entity to violate the law of the foreign country in which such workplace is located.

(2) Control of corporation

(A) Presumption. - If an employer controls a corporation whose place of incorporation is a foreign country, any practice that constitutes discrimination under this section and is engaged in by such corporation shall be presumed to be engaged in by such employer.

(B) Exception. - This section shall not apply with respect to the foreign operations of an employer that is a foreign person not controlled by an American employer.

(C) Determination. - For purposes of this paragraph, the determination of whether an employer controls a corporation shall be based on-

(i) the interrelation of operations;

(ii) the common management;

(iii) the centralized control of labor relations; and

(iv) the common ownership or financial control, of the employer and the corporation.

(d) Medical examinations and inquiries. -

(1) In general. - The prohibition against discrimination as referred to in subsection (a) of this section shall include medical examinations and inquiries.

(2) Preemployment. –

(A) Prohibited examination or inquiry. - Except as provided in paragraph (3), a covered entity shall not conduct a medical examination or make inquiries of a job applicant as to whether such applicant is an individual with a disability or as to the nature or severity of such disability.

(B) Acceptable inquiry. - A covered entity may make preemployment inquiries into the ability of an applicant to perform job-related functions.

(3) Employment entrance examination. - A covered entity may require a medical examination after an offer of employment has been made to a job applicant and prior to the commencement of the employment duties of such applicant, and may condition an offer of employment on the results of such examination, if-

(A) all entering employees are subjected to such an examination regardless of disability;

(B) information obtained regarding the medical condition or history of the applicant is collected and maintained on separate forms and in separate medical files and is treated as a confidential medical record, except that_

(i) supervisors and managers may be informed regarding necessary restrictions on the work or duties of the employee and necessary accommodations;

(ii) first aid and safety personnel may be informed, when appropriate, if the disability might require emergency treatment; and

(iii) government officials investigating compliance with this chapter shall be provided relevant information on request; and

(C) the results of such examination are used only in accordance with this subchapter.

(4) Examination and inquiry. –

(A) Prohibited examinations and inquiries. - A covered entity shall not require a medical examination and shall not make inquiries of an employee as to whether such employee is an individual with a disability or as to the nature or severity of the disability, unless such examination or inquiry is shown to be job-related and consistent with business necessity.

(B) Acceptable examinations and inquiries. - A covered entity may conduct voluntary medical examinations, including voluntary medical histories, which are part of an employee health program available to employees at that work site. A covered entity may make inquiries into the ability of an employee to perform job-related functions.

(C) Requirement. - Information obtained under subparagraph (B) regarding the medical condition or history of any employee are subject to the requirements of subparagraphs (B) and (C) of paragraph (3).

Defenses

SEC. 12113. *[Section 103]*

(a) In general. - It may be a defense to a charge of discrimination under this chapter that an alleged application of qualification standards, tests, or selection criteria that screen out or tend to screen out or otherwise deny a job or benefit to an individual with a disability has been shown to be job-related and consistent with business necessity, and such performance cannot be accomplished by reasonable accommodation, as required under this subchapter.

(b) Qualification standards. - The term "qualification standards" may include a requirement that an individual shall not pose a direct threat to the health or safety of other individuals in the workplace.

(c) Religious entities. -

(1) In general. - This subchapter shall not prohibit a religious corporation, association, educational institution, or society from giving preference in employment to individuals of a particular religion to perform work connected with the carrying on by such corporation, association, educational institution, or society of its activities.

(2) Religious tenets requirement. - Under this subchapter, a religious organization may require that all applicants and employees conform to the religious tenets of such organization.

(d) List of infectious and communicable diseases. -

(1) In general. - The Secretary of Health and Human Services, not later than 6 months after July 26, 1990 *[the date of enactment of this Act]*, shall-

(A) review all infectious and communicable diseases which may be transmitted through handling the food supply;

(B) publish a list of infectious and communicable diseases which are transmitted through handling the food supply;

(C) publish the methods by which such diseases are transmitted; and

(D) widely disseminate such information regarding the list of diseases and their modes of transmissibility to the general public. Such list shall be updated annually.

(2) Applications. - In any case in which an individual has an infectious or communicable disease that is transmitted to others through the handling of food, that is included on the list developed by the Secretary of Health and Human Services under paragraph (1), and which cannot be eliminated by reasonable accommodation, a covered entity may refuse to assign or continue to assign such individual to a job involving food handling.

(3) Construction. - Nothing in this chapter shall be construed to preempt, modify, or amend any State, county, or local law, ordinance, or regulation applicable to food handling which is designed to protect the public health from individuals who pose a significant risk to the health or safety of others, which cannot be eliminated by reasonable accommodation, pursuant to the list of infectious or communicable diseases and the modes of transmissibility published by the Secretary of Health and Human Services.

Illegal Use of Drugs and Alcohol

SEC. 12114. *[Section 104]*

(a) Qualified individual with a disability. - For purposes of this subchapter, the term "qualified individual with a disability" shall not include any employee or applicant who is currently engaging in the illegal use of drugs, when the covered entity acts on the basis of such use.

(b) Rules of construction. - Nothing in subsection (a) of this section shall be construed to exclude as a qualified individual with a disability an individual who-

(1) has successfully completed a supervised drug rehabilitation program and is no longer engaging in the illegal use of drugs, or has otherwise been rehabilitated successfully and is no longer engaging in such use;

(2) is participating in a supervised rehabilitation program and is no longer engaging in such use; or

(3) is erroneously regarded as engaging in such use, but is not engaging in such use; except that it shall not be a violation of this chapter for a covered entity to adopt or administer reasonable policies or procedures, including but not limited to drug testing, designed to ensure that an individual described in paragraph (1) or (2) is no longer engaging in the illegal use of drugs.

(c) Authority of covered entity. -

A covered entity-

(1) may prohibit the illegal use of drugs and the use of alcohol at the workplace by all employees;

(2) may require that employees shall not be under the influence of alcohol or be engaging in the illegal use of drugs at the workplace;

(3) may require that employees behave in conformance with the requirements established under the Drug-Free Workplace Act of 1988 (41 U.S.C. 701 et seq.);

(4) may hold an employee who engages in the illegal use of drugs or who is an alcoholic to the same qualification standards for employment or job performance and behavior that such entity holds other employees, even if any unsatisfactory performance or behavior is related to the drug use or alcoholism of such employee; and

(5) may, with respect to Federal regulations regarding alcohol and the illegal use of drugs, require that-

(A) employees comply with the standards established in such regulations of the Department of Defense, if the employees of the covered entity are employed in an industry subject to such regulations, including complying with regulations (if any) that apply to employment in sensitive positions in such an industry, in the case of employees of the covered entity who are employed in such positions (as defined in the regulations of the Department of Defense);

(B) employees comply with the standards established in such regulations of the Nuclear Regulatory Commission, if the employees of the covered entity are employed in an industry subject to such regulations, including complying with regulations (if any) that apply to employment in sensitive positions in such an industry, in the case of employees of the covered entity who are employed in such positions (as defined in the regulations of the Nuclear Regulatory Commission); and

(C) employees comply with the standards established in such regulations of the Department of Transportation, if the employees of the covered entity are employed in a transportation industry subject to such regulations, including complying with such regulations (if any) that apply to employment in sensitive positions in such an industry, in the case of employees of the covered entity who are employed in such positions (as defined in the regulations of the Department of Transportation).

(d) Drug testing. -

(1) In general. - For purposes of this subchapter, a test to determine the illegal use of drugs shall not be considered a medical examination.

(2) Construction. - Nothing in this subchapter shall be construed to encourage, prohibit, or authorize the conducting of drug testing for the illegal use of drugs by job applicants or employees or making employment decisions based on such test results.

(e) Transportation employees. - Nothing in this subchapter shall be construed to encourage, prohibit, restrict, or authorize the otherwise lawful exercise by entities subject to the jurisdiction of the Department of Transportation of authority to-

(1) test employees of such entities in, and applicants for, positions involving safety-sensitive duties for the illegal use of drugs and for on-duty impairment by alcohol; and

(2) remove such persons who test positive for illegal use of drugs and on-duty impairment by alcohol pursuant to paragraph (1) from safety-sensitive duties in implementing subsection (c) of this section.

Posting Notices

SEC. 12115. *[Section 105]*

Every employer, employment agency, labor organization, or joint labor-management committee covered under this subchapter shall post notices in an accessible format to applicants, employees, and members describing the applicable provisions of this chapter, in the manner prescribed by section 2000e-10 of this title *[section 711 of the Civil Rights Act of 1964]*.

Regulations

SEC. 12116. *[Section 106]*

Not later than 1 year after July 26, 1990 *[the date of enactment of this Act]*, the Commission shall issue regulations in an accessible format to carry out this subchapter in accordance with subchapter II of chapter 5 of title 5 *[United States Code]*.

Enforcement

SEC. 12117. *[Section 107]*

(a) Powers, remedies, and procedures. - The powers, remedies, and procedures set forth in sections 2000e-4, 2000e-5, 2000e-6, 2000e-8, and 2000e-9 of this title *[sections 705, 706, 707, 709 and 710 of the Civil Rights Act of 1964]* shall be the powers, remedies, and procedures this subchapter provides to the Commission, to the Attorney General, or to any person alleging discrimination on the basis of disability in violation of any provision of this chapter, or regulations promulgated under section 12116 of this title *[section 106]*, concerning employment.

(b) Coordination. - The agencies with enforcement authority for actions which allege employment discrimination under this subchapter and under the Rehabilitation Act of 1973 *[29 U.S.C. 701 et seq.]* shall develop procedures to ensure that administrative complaints filed under this subchapter and under the Rehabilitation Act of 1973 are dealt with in a manner that avoids duplication of effort and prevents imposition of inconsistent or conflicting standards for the same requirements under this subchapter and the Rehabilitation Act of 1973. The Commission, the Attorney General, and the Office of Federal Contract Compliance Programs shall establish such coordinating mechanisms (similar to provisions contained in the joint regulations promulgated by the Commission and the Attorney General at part 42 of title 28 and part 1691 of title 29, Code of Federal Regulations, and the Memorandum of Understanding between the Commission and the Office of Federal Contract Compliance Programs dated January 16, 1981 (46 Fed. Reg. 7435, January 23, 1981)) in regulations implementing this subchapter and Rehabilitation Act of 1973 not later than 18 months after July 26, 1990 *[the date of enactment of this Act]*.

SUBCHAPTER IV [*TITLE V*] - MISCELLANEOUS PROVISIONS

Construction

SEC. 12201. *[Section 501]*

(a) In general. - Except as otherwise provided in this chapter, nothing in this chapter shall be construed to apply a lesser standard than the standards applied under title V of the Rehabilitation Act of 1973 (29 U.S.C. 790 et seq.) or the regulations issued by Federal agencies pursuant to such title.

(b) Relationship to other laws. - Nothing in this chapter shall be construed to invalidate or limit the remedies, rights, and procedures of any Federal law or law of any State or political subdivision of any State or jurisdiction that provides greater or equal protection for the rights of individuals with disabilities than are afforded by this chapter. Nothing in this chapter shall be construed to preclude the prohibition of, or the imposition of restrictions on, smoking in places of employment covered by subchapter I of this chapter *[title I]*, in transportation covered by subchapter II or III of this chapter *[Title II or III]*, or in places of public accommodation covered by subchapter III of this chapter *[title III]*.

(c) Insurance. - Subchapters I through III of this chapter *[titles I through III]* and title IV of this Act shall not be construed to prohibit or restrict-

   (1) an insurer, hospital or medical service company, health maintenance organization, or any agent, or entity that administers benefit plans, or similar organizations from underwriting risks, classifying risks, or administering such risks that are based on or not inconsistent with State law; or

(2) a person or organization covered by this chapter from establishing, sponsoring, observing or administering the terms of a bona fide benefit plan that are based on underwriting risks, classifying risks, or administering such risks that are based on or not inconsistent with State law; or

(3) a person or organization covered by this chapter from establishing, sponsoring, observing or administering the terms of a bona fide benefit plan that is not subject to State laws that regulate insurance.

Paragraphs (1), (2), and (3) shall not be used as a subterfuge to evade the purposes of subchapter I and III of this chapter *[titles I and III]*.

(d) Accommodations and services. - Nothing in this chapter shall be construed to require an individual with a disability to accept an accommodation, aid, service, opportunity, or benefit which such individual chooses not to accept.

State Immunity

SEC. 12202. *[Section 502]*

A State shall not be immune under the eleventh amendment to the Constitution of the United States from an action in Federal or State court of competent jurisdiction for a violation of this chapter. In any action against a State for a violation of the requirements of this chapter, remedies (including remedies both at law and in equity) are available for such a violation to the same extent as such remedies are available for such a violation in an action against any public or private entity other than a State.

Prohibition Against Retaliation and Coercion

SEC. 12203. *[Section 503]*

(a) Retaliation. - No person shall discriminate against any individual because such individual has opposed any act or practice made unlawful by this chapter or because such individual made a charge, testified, assisted, or participated in any manner in an investigation, proceeding, or hearing under this chapter.

(b) Interference, coercion, or intimidation. - It shall be unlawful to coerce, intimidate, threaten, or interfere with any individual in the exercise or enjoyment of, or on account of his or her having exercised or enjoyed, or on account of his or her having aided or encouraged any other individual in the exercise or enjoyment of, any right granted or protected by this chapter.

(c) Remedies and procedures. - The remedies and procedures available under sections 12117, 12133, and 12188 of this title *[sections 107, 203 and 308]* shall be available to aggrieved persons for violations of subsections (a) and (b) of this section, with respect to subchapter I, subchapter II and subchapter III, respectively, of this chapter *[title I, title II and title III, respectively]*.

Regulations by the Architectural and Transportation Barriers Compliance Board

SEC. 12204. *[Section 504]*

(a) Issuance of guidelines. - Not later than 9 months after July 26, 1990 *[the date of enactment of this Act]*, the Architectural and Transportation Barriers Compliance Board shall issue minimum guidelines that shall supplement the existing Minimum Guidelines and Requirements for Accessible Design for purposes of subchapters II and III of this chapter *[titles II and III]*.

(b) Contents of guidelines. - The supplemental guidelines issued under subsection (a) of this section shall establish additional requirements, consistent with this chapter, to ensure that buildings, facilities, rail passenger cars, and vehicles are accessible, in terms of architecture and design, transportation, and communication, to individuals with disabilities.

(c) Qualified historic properties. -

(1) In general. - The supplemental guidelines issued under subsection (a) of this section shall include procedures and requirements for alterations that will threaten or destroy the historic significance of qualified historic buildings and facilities as defined in 4.1.7(1)(a) of the Uniform Federal Accessibility Standards.

(2) Sites eligible for listing in National Register. - With respect to alterations of buildings or facilities that are eligible for listing in the National Register of Historic Places under the National Historic Preservation Act (16 U.S.C. 470 et seq.), the guidelines described in paragraph (1) shall, at a minimum, maintain the procedures and requirements established in 4.1.7(1) and (2) of the Uniform Federal Accessibility Standards.

(3) Other sites. - With respect to alterations of buildings of facilities designated as historic under State or local law, the guidelines described in paragraph (1) shall establish procedures equivalent to those established by 4.1.7(1)(b) and (c) of the Uniform Federal Accessibility Standards, and shall require, at a minimum, compliance with the requirements established in 4.1.7(2) of such standards.

Attorney's Fees

SEC. 12205. *[Section 505]*

In any action or administrative proceeding commenced pursuant to this chapter, the court or agency, in its discretion, may allow the prevailing party, other than the United States, a reasonable attorney's fee, including litigation expenses, and costs, and the United States shall be liable for the foregoing the same as a private individual.

Technical Assistance

SEC. 12206. *[Section 506]*

(a) Plan for assistance. -

(1) In general. - Not later than 180 days after July 26, 1990 *[the date of enactment of this Act]*, the Attorney General, in consultation with the Chair of the Equal Employment Opportunity Commission, the Secretary of Transportation, the Chair of the Architectural and Transportation Barriers Compliance Board, and the Chairman of the Federal Communications Commission, shall develop a plan to assist entities covered under this chapter, and other Federal agencies, in understanding the responsibility of such entities and agencies under this chapter.

(2) Publication of plan. - The Attorney General shall publish the plan referred to in paragraph (1) for public comment in accordance with subchapter II of chapter 5 of title 5 *[United States Code]* (commonly known as the Administrative Procedure Act).

(b) Agency and public assistance. - The Attorney General may obtain the assistance of other Federal agencies in carrying out subsection (a) of this section, including the National Council on Disability, the President's Committee on Employment of People with Disabilities, the Small Business Administration, and the Department of Commerce.

(c) Implementation. -

(1) Rendering assistance. - Each Federal agency that has responsibility under paragraph (2) for implementing this chapter may render technical assistance to individuals and institutions that have rights or duties under the respective subchapter or subchapters of this chapter for which such agency has responsibility.

(2) Implementation of subchapters. –

(A) Subchapter I *[Title I]*. - The Equal Employment Opportunity Commission and the Attorney General shall implement the plan for assistance developed under subsection (a) of this section, for subchapter I of this chapter *[title I]*.

(B) Subchapter II *[Title II]*. –

(i) Part A *[Subtitle A]*. - The Attorney General shall implement such plan for assistance for part A of subchapter II of this chapter *[subtitle A of title II]*.

(ii) Part B *[Subtitle B]*. - The Secretary of Transportation shall implement such plan for assistance for part B of subchapter II of this chapter *[subtitle B of title II]*.

(C) Subchapter III *[Title III]*. - The Attorney General, in coordination with the Secretary of Transportation and the Chair of the Architectural Transportation Barriers Compliance Board, shall implement such plan for assistance for subchapter III of this chapter, except for section 12184 of this title *[section 304]*, the plan for assistance for which shall be implemented by the Secretary of Transportation.

(D) Title IV. - The Chairman of the Federal Communications Commission, in coordination with the Attorney General, shall implement such plan for assistance for title IV.

(3) Technical assistance manuals. - Each Federal agency that has responsibility under paragraph (2) for implementing this chapter shall, as part of its implementation responsibilities, ensure the availability and provision of appropriate technical assistance manuals to individuals or entities with rights or duties under this chapter no later than six months after applicable final regulations are published under subchapters I, II, and III of this chapter *[titles I, II, and III]* and title IV.

(d) Grants and contracts. -

(1) In general. - Each Federal agency that has responsibility under subsection (c)(2) of this section for implementing this chapter may make grants or award contracts to effectuate the purposes of this section, subject to the availability of appropriations. Such grants and contracts may be awarded to individuals, institutions not organized for profit and no part of the net earnings of which inures to the benefit of any private shareholder or individual (including educational institutions), and associations representing individuals who have rights or duties under this chapter. Contracts may be awarded to entities

organized for profit, but such entities may not be the recipients or grants described in this paragraph.

(2) Dissemination of information. - Such grants and contracts, among other uses, may be designed to ensure wide dissemination of information about the rights and duties established by this chapter and to provide information and technical assistance about techniques for effective compliance with this chapter.

(e) Failure to receive assistance. - An employer, public accommodation, or other entity covered under this chapter shall not be excused from compliance with the requirements of this chapter because of any failure to receive technical assistance under this section, including any failure in the development or dissemination of any technical assistance manual authorized by this section.

Federal Wilderness Areas

SEC. 12207. *[Section 507]*

(a) Study. - The National Council on Disability shall conduct a study and report on the effect that wilderness designations and wilderness land management practices have on the ability of individuals with disabilities to use and enjoy the National Wilderness Preservation System as established under the Wilderness Act (16 U.S.C. 1131 et seq.).

(b) Submission of report. - Not later than 1 year after July 26, 1990 *[the date of enactment of this Act]*, the National Council on Disability shall submit the report required under subsection (a) of this section to Congress.

(c) Specific wilderness access. -

(1) In general. - Congress reaffirms that nothing in the Wilderness Act [16 U.S.C. 1131 et seq.] is to be construed as prohibiting the use of a wheelchair in a wilderness area by an individual whose disability requires use of a wheelchair, and consistent with the Wilderness Act no agency is required to provide any form of special treatment or accommodation, or to construct any facilities or modify any conditions of lands within a wilderness area in order to facilitate such use.

(2) Definition. - For purposes of paragraph (1), the term "wheelchair" means a device designed solely for use by a mobility-impaired person for locomotion, that is suitable for use in an indoor pedestrian area.

Transvestites

SEC. 12208. *[Section 508]*

For the purposes of this chapter, the term "disabled" or "disability" shall not apply to an individual solely because that individual is a transvestite.

Coverage of Congress and the Agencies of the Legislative Branch

SEC. 12209. *[Section 509]*

(a) Coverage of the Senate. -

(1) Commitment to Rule XLII. - The Senate reaffirms its commitment to Rule XLII of the Standing Rules of the Senate which provides as follows:

"No member, officer, or employee of the Senate shall, with respect to employment by the Senate or any office thereof-

"(a) fail or refuse to hire an individual;

"(b) discharge an individual; or

"(c) otherwise discriminate against an individual with respect to promotion, compensation, or terms, conditions, or privileges of employment on the basis of such individual's race, color, religion, sex, national origin, age, or state of physical handicap."

(2) Matters other than employment. –

(A) In general. - The rights and protections under this chapter shall, subject to subparagraph (B), apply with respect to the conduct of the Senate regarding matters other than employment.

(B) Remedies. - The Architect of the Capitol shall establish remedies and procedures to be utilized with respect to the rights and protections provided pursuant to subparagraph (A). Such remedies and procedures shall apply exclusively, after approval in accordance with subparagraph (C).

(C) Proposed remedies and procedures. - For purposes of subparagraph (B), the Architect of the Capitol shall submit proposed remedies and procedures to the Senate Committee on Rules and Administration. The remedies and procedures shall be effective upon the approval of the Committee on Rules and Administration.

(3) Exercise of rulemaking power. - Notwithstanding any other provision of law, enforcement and adjudication of the rights and protections referred to in paragraph **(2)(A)** shall be within the exclusive jurisdiction of the United States Senate. The provisions of paragraph (1), **(2)** are enacted by the Senate as an exercise of the rulemaking power of the Senate, with full recognition of the right of the Senate to change its rules, in the same manner, and to the same extent, as in the case of any other rule of the Senate.

(b) Coverage of the House of Representatives. -

(1) In general. - Notwithstanding any other provision of this chapter or of law, the purposes of this chapter shall, subject to paragraphs (2) and (3), apply in their entirety to the House of Representatives.

(2) Employment in the House. –

(A) Application. - The rights and protections under this chapter shall, subject to subparagraph (B), apply with respect to any employee in an employment position in the House of Representatives and any employing authority of the House of Representatives.

(B) Administration. –

(i) In general. - In the administration of this paragraph, the remedies and procedures made applicable pursuant to the resolution described in clause (ii) shall apply exclusively.

(ii) Resolution. - The resolution referred to in clause (i) is House Resolution 15 of the One Hundred First Congress, as agreed to January 3, 1989, or any other provision that continues in effect the provisions of, or is a successor to, the Fair Employment Practices Resolution (House Resolution 558 of the One Hundredth Congress, as agreed to October 4, 1988).

(C) Exercise of rulemaking power. - The provisions of subparagraph (B) are enacted by the House of Representatives as an exercise of the rulemaking power of the House of Representatives, with full recognition of the right of the House to change its rules, in the same manner, and to the same extent as in the case of any other rule of the House.

(3) Matters other than employment. –

(A) In general. - The rights and protections under this chapter shall, subject to subparagraph (B), apply with respect to the conduct of the House of Representatives regarding matters other than employment.

(B) Remedies. - The Architect of the Capitol shall establish remedies and procedures to be utilized with respect to the rights and protections provided pursuant to subparagraph (A). Such remedies and procedures shall apply exclusively, after approval in accordance with subparagraph (C).

(C) Approval. - For purposes of subparagraph (B), the Architect of the Capitol shall submit proposed remedies and procedures to the Speaker of the House of Representatives. The remedies and procedures shall be effective upon the approval of the Speaker, after consultation with the House Office Building Commission.

(c) Instrumentalities of Congress. -

(1) In general. - The rights and protections under this chapter shall, subject to paragraph (2), apply with respect to the conduct of each instrumentality of the Congress.

(2) Establishment of remedies and procedures by instrumentalities. - The chief official of each instrumentality of the Congress shall establish remedies and

procedures to be utilized with respect to the rights and protections provided pursuant to paragraph (1). Such remedies and procedures shall apply exclusively, **except for the employees who are defined as Senate employees, in section 201(c)(1) of the Civil Rights Act of 1991.**

(3) Report to Congress. - The chief official of each instrumentality of the Congress shall, after establishing remedies and procedures for purposes of paragraph (2), submit to the Congress a report describing the remedies and procedures.

(4) Definition of instrumentalities. - For purposes of this section, instrumentalities of the Congress include the following: the Architect of the Capitol, the Congressional Budget Office, the General Accounting Office, the Government Printing Office, the Library of Congress, the Office of Technology Assessment, and the United States Botanic Garden.

(5) Construction. - Nothing in this section shall alter the enforcement procedures for individuals with disabilities provided in the General Accounting Office Personnel Act of 1980 *[31 U.S.C. 731 et seq.]* and regulations promulgated pursuant to that Act.

Illegal Use of Drugs

SEC. 12210. *[Section 510]*

(a) In general. - For purposes of this chapter, the term "individual with a disability" does not include an individual who is currently engaging in the illegal use of drugs, when the covered entity acts on the basis of such use.

(b) Rules of construction. - Nothing in subsection (a) of this section shall be construed to exclude as an individual with a disability an individual who-

(1) has successfully completed a supervised drug rehabilitation program and is no longer engaging in the illegal use of drugs, or has otherwise been rehabilitated successfully and is no longer engaging in such use;

(2) is participating in a supervised rehabilitation program and is no longer engaging in such use; or

(3) is erroneously regarded as engaging in such use, but is not engaging in such use; except that it shall not be a violation of this chapter for a covered entity to adopt or administer reasonable policies or procedures, including but not limited to drug testing, designed to ensure that an individual described in paragraph (1) or (2) is no longer engaging in the illegal use of drugs; however, nothing in this section shall be construed to encourage, prohibit, restrict, or authorize the conducting of testing for the illegal use of drugs.

(c) Health and other services. - Notwithstanding subsection (a) of this section and section 12211(b)(3) of this title *[section 511(b)(3)]*, an individual shall not be denied health services, or services provided in connection with drug rehabilitation, on the basis of the current illegal use of drugs if the individual is otherwise entitled to such services.

(d) Definition of illegal use of drugs. -

(1) In general. - The term ``illegal use of drugs" means the use of drugs, the possession or distribution of which is unlawful under the Controlled Substances Act (21 U.S.C. 812). Such term does not include the use of a drug taken under supervision by a licensed health care professional, or other uses authorized by the Controlled Substances Act or other provisions of Federal law.

(2) Drugs - The term "drug" means a controlled substance, as defined in schedules I through V of section 202 of the Controlled Substances Act *[21 U.S.C. 812]*.

Definitions

SEC. 12211. *[Section 511]*

(a) Homosexuality and bisexuality. - For purposes of the definition of "disability" in section 12102(2) of this title *[section 3(2)]*, homosexuality and bisexuality are not impairments and as such are not disabilities under this chapter.

(b) Certain conditions. - Under this chapter, the term "disability" shall not include-

(1) transvestism, transsexualism, pedophilia, exhibitionism, voyeurism, gender identity disorders not resulting from physical impairments, or other sexual behavior disorders;

(2) compulsive gambling, kleptomania, or pyromania; or

(3) psychoactive substance use disorders resulting from current illegal use of drugs.

AMENDMENTS TO THE REHABILITATION ACT

[Section 512 of Title V of the ADA (42 U.S.C. 12115) amended two subsections of section 7 of the Rehabilitation Act of 1973 (29 U.S.C. 706(8)). These amendments are printed elsewhere in this publication.]

Alternative Means of Dispute Resolution

SEC. 12212. *[Section 513]*

Where appropriate and to the extent authorized by law, the use of alternative means of dispute resolution, including settlement negotiations, conciliation, facilitation, mediation, factfinding, minitrials, and arbitration, is encouraged to resolve disputes arising under this chapter.

Severability

SEC. 12213. *[Section 514]*

Should any provision in this chapter be found to be unconstitutional by a court of law, such provision shall be severed from the remainder of the chapter, and such action shall not affect the enforceability of the remaining provisions of the chapter.

[Approved July 26, 1990]

[1] So in original. Probably should be "subchapters."

[2] So in original. Probably should be "in a".

[3] So in original. Probably should be "of."

[4] So in original. Probably should be "paragraphs" (1) and (2).

THE CIVIL RIGHTS ACT OF 1991

The main focus of the amended section of the Civil Rights Act of 1964 was revised in 1991 to address the damages that may be awarded in cases on intentional discrimination.

Punitive damages may be awarded in intentional acts of discrimination against a company and not a government, government agency or political subdivision.

Compensatory damages may be awarded in all cases of discrimination and shall not include backpay, interest on backpay, or any other type of relief authorized by the Civil Rights Act of 1964.

The limited amount of compensatory damages may not exceed $300,000 in a current or preceding year that employs more than 500 persons in federal agencies.

A complainant may request a jury trial seeking compensatory or punitive damages.

THE CIVIL RIGHTS ACT OF 1991

EDITOR'S NOTE: The text of the Civil Rights Act of 1991 (Pub. L. 102-166), as enacted on November 21, 1991, appears below with the following modifications:

1. *The text of the sections of the CRA that amend the laws enforced by EEOC (i.e., Title VII of the Civil Rights Act of 1964, the Age Discrimination in Employment Act of 1967, the Americans with Disabilities Act of 1990) is not printed below. Instead, these amendments are printed elsewhere in this publication.*
2. *The following portions of the CRA that are not enforced by EEOC are referenced, but not reprinted here:*
   - *Section 117 (coverage of the U.S. House of Representatives and agencies of the Legislative Branch);*
   - *Title II (The Glass Ceiling Act); and*
   - *Portions of Title III (Establishing the Office of Senate Fair Employment Practices).*
3. *Title V, which amends the Civil War Sites Study Act of 1990 (Pub. L. 101-628) is not reprinted here.*
4. *Cross references to the U.S. Code, where applicable, appear in italics following each section heading. Editor's notes also appear in italics.*

An Act

To amend the Civil Rights Act of 1964 to strengthen and improve Federal civil rights laws, to provide for damages in cases of intentional employment discrimination, to clarify provisions regarding disparate impact actions, and for other purposes.

Be it enacted by the Senate and House of Representatives of the United States of America in Congress assembled, This Act may be cited as the "Civil Rights Act of 1991".

* * *

Findings

SEC. 2 *[42 U.S.C. 1981 note]*

The Congress finds that-

(1) additional remedies under Federal law are needed to deter unlawful harassment and intentional discrimination in the workplace;

(2) the decision of the Supreme Court in Wards Cove Packing Co. v. Atonio, 490 U.S. 642 (1989) has weakened the scope and effectiveness of Federal civil rights protections; and

(3) legislation is necessary to provide additional protection against unlawful discrimination in employment.

Purposes

SEC. 3 *[42 U.S.C. 1981 note]*

The purposes of this Act are-

(1) to provide appropriate remedies for intentional discrimination and unlawful harassment in the workplace;

(2) to codify the concepts of "business necessity" an "job related" enunciated by the Supreme Court in Griggs v. Duke Power Co., 401 U.S. 424 (1971), and in the other Supreme Court decisions prior to Wards Cove Packing Co. v. Atonio, 490 U.S. 642 (1989);

(3) to confirm statutory authority and provide statutory guidelines for the adjudication of disparate impact suits under title VII of the Civil Rights Act of 1964 (42 U.S.C. 2000e et seq.); and

(4) to respond to recent decisions of the Supreme Court by expanding the scope of relevant civil rights statutes in order to provide adequate protection to victims of discrimination.

TITLE I - FEDERAL CIVIL RIGHTS REMEDIES

Prohibition Against All Racial Discrimination in the Making and Enforcement of Contracts

SEC. 101

Section 1977 of the Revised Statutes (42 U.S.C. 1981) is amended-

(1) by inserting "(a)" before "All persons within"; and

(2) by adding at the end the following new subsections:

"(b) For purposes of this section, the term 'make and enforce contracts' includes the making, performance, modification, and termination of contracts, and the enjoyment of all benefits, privileges, terms, and conditions of the contractual relationship.

"(c) The rights protected by this section are protected against impairment by nongovernmental discrimination and impairment under color of State law."

Damages in Cases of Intentional Discrimination

SEC. 102

The Revised Statutes are amended by inserting after section 1977 (42 U.S.C. 1981) the following new section:

"SEC. 1977A. DAMAGES IN CASES OF INTENTIONAL DISCRIMINATION IN EMPLOYMENT. *[42 U.S.C. 1981a]*

(a) Right of Recovery. –

(1) Civil Rights. - In an action brought by a complaining party under section 706 or 717 of the Civil Rights Act of 1964 (42 U.S.C. 2000e-5) against a respondent who engaged in unlawful intentional discrimination (not an employment practice that is unlawful because of its disparate impact) prohibited under section 703, 704, or 717 of the Act (42 U.S.C. 2000e-2 or 2000e-3), and provided that the complaining party cannot recover under section 1977 of the Revised Statutes (42 U.S.C. 1981), the complaining party may recover compensatory and punitive damages as allowed in subsection (b), in addition to any relief authorized by section 706(g) of the Civil Rights Act of 1964, from the respondent.

(2) Disability. - In an action brought by a complaining party under the powers, remedies, and procedures set forth in section 706 or 717 of the Civil Rights Act of 1964 (as provided in section 107(a) of the Americans with Disabilities Act of 1990 (42 U.S.C. 12117 (a)), and section 505(a)(1) of the Rehabilitation Act of 1973 (29 U.S.C. 794a(a)(1)), respectively) against a respondent who engaged in unlawful intentional discrimination (not an employment practice that is unlawful because of its disparate impact) under section 501 of the Rehabilitation Act of 1973 (29 U.S.C. 791) and the regulations implementing section 501, or who violated the requirements of section 501 of the Act or the regulations implementing section 501 concerning the provision of a reasonable accommodation, or section 102 of the Americans with Disabilities Act of 1990 (42 U.S.C. 12112), or committed a violation of section 102(b)(5) of the Act, against an individual, the complaining party may recover compensatory and

punitive damages as allowed in subsection (b), in addition to any relief authorized by section 706(g) of the Civil Rights Act of 1964, from the respondent.

(3) Reasonable Accommodation and Good Faith Effort. – In cases where a discriminatory practice involves the provision of a reasonable accommodation pursuant to section 102(b)(5) of the Americans with Disabilities Act of 1990 or regulations implementing section 501 of the Rehabilitation Act of 1973, damages may not be awarded under this section where the covered entity demonstrates good faith efforts, in consultation with the person with the disability who has informed the covered entity that accommodation is needed, to identify and make a reasonable accommodation that would provide such individual with an equally effective opportunity and would not cause an undue hardship on the operation of the business.

(b) Compensatory and Punitive Damages. –

(1) Determination of punitive damages. - A complaining party may recover punitive damages under this section against a respondent (other than a government, government agency or political subdivision) if the complaining party demonstrates that the respondent engaged in a discriminatory practice or discriminatory practices with malice or with reckless indifference to the federally protected rights of an aggrieved individual.

(2) Exclusions from compensatory damages. – Compensatory damages awarded under this section shall not include backpay, interest on backpay, or any other type of relief authorized under section 706(g) of the Civil Rights Act of 1964.

(3) Limitations. - The sum of the amount of compensatory damages awarded under this section for future pecuniary losses, emotional pain, suffering, inconvenience, mental anguish, loss of enjoyment of life, and other nonpecuniary losses, and the amount of punitive damages awarded under this section, shall not exceed, for each complaining party –

(A) in the case of a respondent who has more than 14 and fewer than 101 employees in each of 20 or more calendar weeks in the current or preceding calendar year, $50,000;

(B) in the case of a respondent who has more than 100 and fewer than 201 employees in each of 20 or more calendar weeks in the current or preceding calendar year, $100,000; and

(C) in the case of a respondent who has more than 200 and fewer than 501 employees in each of 20 or more calendar weeks in the current or preceding calendar year, $200,000; and

(D) in the case of a respondent who has more than 500 employees in each of 20 or more calendar weeks in the current or preceding calendar year, $300,000.

(4) Construction. - Nothing in this section shall be construed to limit the scope of, or the relief available under, section 1977 of the Revised Statutes (42 U.S.C. 1981).

(c) Jury Trial. - If a complaining party seeks compensatory or punitive damages under this section -

(1) any party may demand a trial by jury; and

(2) the court shall not inform the jury of the limitations described in subsection (b)(3).

(d) Definitions. - As used in this section:

(1) Complaining party. - The term 'complaining party' means - “(A) in the case of a person seeking to bring an action under subsection (a)(1), the Equal Employment Opportunity Commission, the Attorney General, or a person who may bring an action or proceeding under title VII of the Civil Rights Act of 1964 (42 U.S.C. 2000e et seq.); or

(B) in the case of a person seeking to bring an action under subsection (a)(2), the Equal Employment Opportunity Commission, the Attorney General, a person who may bring an action or proceeding under section 505(a)(1) of the Rehabilitation Act of 1973 (29 U.S.C. 794a(a)(1)), or a person who may bring an action or proceeding under title I of the Americans with Disabilities Act of 1990 (42 U.S.C. 12101 et seq.).

(2) Discriminatory practice. - The term 'discriminatory practice' means the discrimination described in paragraph (1), or the discrimination or the violation described in paragraph (2), of subsection (a).

Attorney’s Fees

[This section amends section 722 of the Revised Statutes (42 U.S.C. 1988) by adding a reference to section 102 of the Civil Rights Act of 1991 to the list of civil rights actions in which reasonable attorney's fees may be awarded to the prevailing party, other than the United States.]

SEC. 103

The last sentence of section 722 of the Revised Statutes (42 U.S.C. 1988) is amended by inserting ",1977A" after "1977".

Definitions

SEC. 104

[This section amends section 701 of the Civil Rights Act of 1964 (42 U.S.C. 2000e) by adding the following new subsections: (l) "complaining party," (m) "demonstrates," and (n) "respondent."]

Burden of Proof in Disparate Impact Cases

SEC. 105

(a) *[This subsection amends section 703 of the Civil Rights Act of 1964 (42 U.S.C. 2000e-2) by adding a new subsection (k), on the burden of proof in disparate impact cases.]*

(b) No statements other than the interpretive memorandum appearing at Vol. 137 Congressional Record S 15276 (daily ed. Oct. 25, 1991) shall be considered legislative history of, or relied upon in any way as legislative history in construing or applying, any provision of this Act that relates to Wards Cove - Business necessity/ cumulation/alternative business practice. *[42 U.S.C. 1981 note]*

Prohibition Against Discriminatory Use of Test Scores

SEC. 106

[This section amends section 703 of the Civil Rights Act of 1964 (42 U.S.C. 2000e-2) by adding a new subsection (l), on the prohibition against discriminatory use of test scores.]

Clarifying Prohibition Against Impermissible Consideration of race, Color, Religion, Sex, or National Origin in Employment Practices

SEC. 107

(a) In general. *[This subsection amends section 703 of the Civil Rights Act of 1964 (42 U.S.C. 2000e-2) by adding a new subsection (m), clarifying the prohibition against consideration of race, color, religion, sex, or national origin in employment practices.]*

(b) Enforcement provisions. *[This subsection amends section 706(g) of the Civil Rights Act of 1964 (42 U.S.C. 2000e-5(g)) by renumbering existing subsection (g), and adding at the end a new subparagraph (B) to provide a limitation on available relief in "mixed motive" cases (where the employer demonstrates it would have made the same decision in the absence of discrimination).]*

Facilitating Prompt and Orderly Resolution of Challenges to Employment Practices Implementing Litigated or Consent Judgments or Orders

SEC. 108

[This section amends section 703 of the Civil Rights Act of 1964 (42 U.S.C. 2000e-2) by adding a new subsection (n), on the resolution of challenges to employment practices implementing litigated or consent judgments or orders.]

Protection of Extraterritorial Employment

SEC. 109

(a) Definition of Employee. *[This subsection amends the definition of "employee" in section 701(f) of the Civil Rights Act of 1964 (42 U.S.C. 2000e(f)) and section 101(4) of the Americans with Disabilities Act of 1990 (42 U.S.C. 12111(4)) by adding a sentence to the end of each definition to include U.S. citizens employed abroad within the laws' protections.]*

(b) Exemption. *[This subsection amends section 702 of the Civil Rights Act of 1964 (42 U.S.C. 2000e-1) by adding new subsections (b) (on compliance with the statute if violative of foreign law) and (c) (on the control of a corporation incorporated in a foreign country). This subsection similarly amends section 102 of the Americans with Disabilities Act of 1990 (42 U.S.C. 12112) by relettering the existing subsections and adding a new subsection (c) "Covered Entities in Foreign Countries."]*

(c) Application of Amendments. - The amendments made by this section shall not apply with respect to conduct occurring before the date of the enactment of this Act. *[42 U.S.C. 2000e note]*

Technical Assistance Training Institute

SEC. 110

(a) Technical Assistance. *[This subsection amends section 705 of the Civil Rights Act of 1964 (42 U.S.C. 2000e-4) by adding a new subsection (j), establishing the Technical Assistance Training Institute.]*

(b) Effective Date. - The amendment made by this section shall take effect on the date of enactment of this Act. *[42 U.S.C. 2000e-4 note]*

Education and Outreach

SEC. 111

[This section amends section 705(h) of the Civil Rights Act of 1964 (42 U.S.C. 2000e-4(h)) by renumbering the existing subsection and adding at the end a paragraph requiring the EEOC to engage in certain educational and outreach activities.]

Expansion of Right to Challenge Discriminatory Seniority Systems

SEC. 112

[This section amends section 706(e) of the Civil Rights Act of 1964 (42 U.S.C. 2000e-5(e)) by renumbering the subsection and adding at the end a paragraph to expand the right of claimants to challenge discriminatory seniority systems.]

Authorizing Award of Expert Fees

SEC. 113

(a) Revised Statutes. - Section 722 of the Revised Statutes is amended-

(1) by designating the first and second sentences as subsections (a) and (b), respectively, and indenting accordingly; and

(2) by adding at the end the following new subsection:

"(c) In awarding an attorney's fee under subsection (b) in any action or proceeding to enforce a provision of section 1977 or 1977A of the Revised Statutes, the court, in its discretion, may include expert fees as part of the attorney's fee." *[42 U.S.C. 1988]*

(b) Civil Rights Act of 1964. *[This section amends section 706(k) of the Civil Rights Act of 1964 (42 U.S.C. 2000e-5(k)) to provide for recovery of expert fees as part of an attorney's fees award.]*

Providing for Interest and Extending the Statute of Limitations in Actions Against the Federal Government

SEC. 114

[This section amends section 717 of the Civil Rights Act of 1964 (42 U.S.C. 2000e-16) by extending the time for federal employees or applicants to file a civil action from 30 to 90

days (from receipt of notice of final action taken by a department, agency or unit), and allowing federal employees or applicants the same interest to compensate for delay in payments as is available in cases involving nonpublic parties.]

Notice of Limitations Period Under the Age Discrimination in Employment Act of 1967

SEC. 115

[This section amends section 7(e) of the Age Discrimination in Employment Act of 1967 (ADEA) (29 U.S.C. 626(e)) by eliminating the two-and three-year statute of limitations and making ADEA suit- filing requirements the same as those under Title VII, and requiring the EEOC to provide notice to charging parties upon termination of the proceedings.]

Lawful, Court-Ordered Remedies, Affirmative Action, and Conciliation Agreement Not Affected

SEC. 116 *[42 U.S.C. 1981 note]*

Nothing in the amendments made by this title shall be construed to affect court-ordered remedies, affirmative action, or conciliation agreements, that are in accordance with the law.

Coverage of House of Representatives and the Agencies of the Legislative Branch

SEC. 117

(a) Coverage of the House of Representatives. *[This subsection extends the rights and protections of Title VII of the Civil Rights Act of 1964, as amended, to employees of the U.S. House of Representatives. Procedures for processing discrimination complaints are handled internally by the House, not by the EEOC.] [2 U.S.C. 60l]*

(b) Instrumentalities of Congress. *[This subsection extends the rights and protections of the Civil Rights Act of 1991 and Title VII of the Civil Rights Act of 1964, as amended, to "Instrumentalities of Congress," which are defined to include: the Architect of the Capitol, the Congressional Budget Office, the General Accounting Office, the Government Printing Office, the Office of Technology Assessment, and the United States Botanic Garden. Each agency is to establish its own remedies and procedures for enforcement.]*

Alternative Means of Dispute Resolution

SEC. 118 *[42 U.S.C. 1981 note]*

Where appropriate and to the extent authorized by law, the use of alternative means of dispute resolution, including settlement negotiations, conciliation, facilitation, mediation, factfinding, minitrials, and arbitration, is encouraged to resolve disputes arising under the acts or provisions of Federal law amended by this title.

TITLE II - GLASS CEILING

[This title sets up a "Glass Ceiling Commission" to focus attention on, and complete a study relating to, the existence of artificial barriers to the advancement of women and minorities in the workplace, and to make recommendations for overcoming such barriers. The Commission is to be composed of 21 members, with the Secretary of Labor serving as the Chairperson of the Commission. This title does not directly impose any responsibilities or obligations on the EEOC except to provide information and technical assistance as requested by the new Commission.] [42 U.S.C. 2000e note]

TITLE III - GOVERNMENT EMPLOYEE RIGHTS

Government Employee Rights Act of 1991

SEC. 301 *[2 U.S.C. 1201]*

(a) Short title. - This title may be cited as the "Government Employee Rights Act of 1991."

(b) Purpose. - The purpose of this title is to provide procedures to protect the right of Senate and other government employees, with respect to their public employment, to be free of discrimination on the basis of race, color, religion, sex, national origin, age, or disability.

(c) Definitions. - For purposes of this title:

(1) Senate employee. - The term “Senate employee” or “employee” means –

(A) any employee whose pay is disbursed by the Secretary of the Senate;

(B) any employee of the Architect of the Capitol who is assigned to the Senate Restaurants or to the Superintendent of the Senate Office Buildings;

(C) any applicant for a position that will last 90 days or more and that is to be occupied by an individual described in subparagraph (A) or (B); or

(D) any individual who was formerly an employee described in subparagraph (A) or (B) and whose claim of a violation arises out of the individual's Senate employment.

(2) Head of employing office. - The term "head of employing office" means the individual who has final authority to appoint, hire, discharge, and set the terms, conditions or privileges of the Senate employment of an employee.

(3) Violation. - The term "violation" means a practice that violates section 302 of this title.

Discriminatory Practices Prohibited

SEC. 302 *[2 U.S.C. 1202]*

[Sections 320 and 321 (which protect Presidential appointees and previously exempt state employees who may file complaints of discrimination with EEOC under this title) refer to the rights, protections and remedies of this section and section 307(h).]

All personnel actions affecting employees of the Senate shall be made free from any discrimination based on -

(1) race, color, religion, sex, or national origin, within the meaning of section 717 of the Civil Rights Act of 1964 (42 U.S.C. 2000e-16);

(2) age, within the meaning of section 15 of the Age Discrimination in Employment Act of 1967 (29 U.S.C. 633a); or

(3) handicap or disability, within the meaning of section 501 of the Rehabilitation Act of 1973 (29 U.S.C. 791) and sections 102-104 of the Americans with Disabilities Act of 1990 (42 U.S.C. 12112-14).

[SECTIONS 303 THROUGH 306: Section 303 (2 U.S.C. 1203) establishes the Office of Senate Fair Employment Practices, which will administer the procedures set forth in sections 304 through 307. Section 304 (2 U.S.C. 1204) outlines the four-step procedure described in Sections 305 through 309 for consideration of alleged violations. Section 305 (2 U.S.C. 1205) describes the Step I counseling procedures. Section 306 (2 U.S.C. 1206) describes the Step II mediation process. Section 307 (2 U.S.C. 1207), described fully below, sets forth the formal complaint and hearing procedures.]

Step III: Formal Complaint and Hearing

SEC. 307 *[2 U.S.C. 1207]*

[SECTION 307, SUBSECTIONS (a) THROUGH (g), AND (i): Subsections (a) through (g), and (i) of Section 307 describe the process from the formal complaint through the hearing stage.]

[Sections 320 and 321 (which protect Presidential appointees and previously exempt state employees who may file complaints of discrimination with EEOC under this title) refer to the rights, protections and remedies of section 302 and the following subsection.]

(h) Remedies. - If the hearing board determines that a violation has occurred, it shall order such remedies as would be appropriate if awarded under section 706 (g) and (k) of the Civil Rights Act of 1964 (42 U.S.C. 2000e-5 (g) and (k)), and may also order the award of such compensatory damages as would be appropriate if awarded under section 1977 and section 1977A (a) and (b)(2) of the Revised Statutes (42 U.S.C. 1981 and 1981A (a) and (b)(2)). In the case of a determination that a violation based on age has occurred, the hearing board shall order such remedies as would be appropriate if awarded under section 15(c) of the Age Discrimination in Employment Act of 1967 (29 U.S.C. 633a(c)). Any order requiring the payment of money must be approved by a Senate resolution reported by the Committee on Rules and Administration. The hearing board shall have no authority to award punitive damages.

[SECTIONS 308 THROUGH 313: Section 308 (2 U.S.C. 1208) describes the procedures by which a Senate employee or head of an employing office may request a review by the Select Committee on Ethics of a decision issued under Section 307. Section 309 (2

U.S.C. 1209) describes the circumstances under which a Senate employee or Member of the Senate may petition for a review by the United States Court of Appeals for the Federal Circuit. Section 310 (2 U.S.C. 1210) describes the procedures by which a complaint may be resolved. Section 311 (2 U.S.C. 1211) enumerates reimbursable costs of attending hearings. Section 312 (2 U.S.C. 1212) prohibits intimidation or reprisal against any employee because of the exercise of a right under this title. Section 313 (2 U.S.C. 1213) outlines confidentiality requirements for counseling, mediation, hearings, final decisions, and records.]

Exercise of Rulemaking Power

SEC. 314 *[2 U.S.C. 1214]*

The provisions of this title, except for sections 309, 320, 321, and 322, are enacted by the Senate as an exercise of the rulemaking power of the Senate, with full recognition of the right of the Senate to change its rules, in the same manner, and to the same extent, as in the case of any other rule of the Senate. Notwithstanding any other provision of law, except as provided in section 309, enforcement and adjudication with respect to the discriminatory practices prohibited by section 302, and arising out of Senate employment, shall be within the exclusive jurisdiction of the United States Senate.

Technical and Conforming Amendments

SEC. 315

[This section makes technical and conforming amendments to section 509 of the Americans with Disabilities Act of 1990 (ADA) (42 U.S.C. 12209) with respect to Senate employees.]

[SECTIONS 316 THROUGH 319: Section 316 (2 U.S.C. 1215) states that the consideration of political affiliation, domicile, and political compatibility with the employing office in an employment decision shall not be considered a violation of this title. Section 317 (2 U.S.C. 1216) states that a Senate employee may not commence a judicial proceeding to redress a prohibited discriminatory practice, except as provided in this title. Sec. 318 (2 U.S.C. 1217) expresses the Senate's view that legislation should be enacted to provide the same or comparable rights and remedies as are provided under this title to Congressional employees lacking such rights and remedies. Section 319 (2 U.S.C. 1218) reaffirms the Senate's commitment to Rule XLII of the Standing Rules of the Senate.]

Coverage of Presidential Appointees

SEC. 320 *[2 U.S.C. 1219]*

(a) In General. -

(1) Application. - The rights, protections, and remedies provided pursuant to section 302 and 307(h) of this title shall apply with respect to employment of Presidential appointees.

(2) Enforcement by administrative action. - Any Presidential appointee may file a complaint alleging a violation, not later than 180 days after the occurrence of the alleged violation, with the Equal Employment Opportunity Commission, or such other entity as is designated by the President by Executive Order, which, in accordance with the principles and procedures set forth in sections 554 through 557 of title 5, United States Code, shall determine whether a violation has occurred and shall set forth its determination in a final order. If the Equal

Employment Opportunity Commission, or such other entity as is designated by the President pursuant to this section, determines that a violation has occurred, the final order shall also provide for appropriate relief.

(3) Judicial review. –

(A) In general. - Any party aggrieved by a final order under paragraph (2) may petition for review by the United States Court of Appeals for the Federal Circuit.

(B) Law applicable. - Chapter 158 of title 28, United States Code, shall apply to a review under this section except that the Equal Employment Opportunity Commission or such other entity as the President may designate under paragraph (2) shall be an "agency" as that term is used in chapter 158 of title 28, United States Code.

(C) Standard of review. - To the extent necessary to decision and when presented, the reviewing court shall decide all relevant questions of law and interpret constitutional and statutory provisions. The court shall set aside a final order under paragraph (2) if it is determined that the order was -

(i) arbitrary, capricious, an abuse of discretion, or otherwise not consistent with law;

(ii) not made consistent with required procedures; or

(iii) unsupported by substantial evidence.

In making the foregoing determinations, the court shall review the whole record or those parts of it cited by a party, and due account shall be taken of the rule of prejudicial error

(D) Attorney's fees. - If the presidential appointee is the prevailing party in a proceeding under this section, attorney's fees may be allowed by the court in accordance with the standards prescribed under section 706(k) of the Civil Rights Act of 1964 (42 U.S.C. 2000e-5(k)).

(b) Presidential appointee. - For purposes of this section, the term "Presidential appointee" means any officer or employee, or an applicant seeking to become an officer or employee, in any unit of the Executive Branch, including the Executive Office of the President, whether appointed by the President or by any other appointing authority in the Executive Branch, who is not already entitled to bring an action under any of the statutes referred to in section 302 but does not include any individual -

(1) whose appointment is made by and with the advice and consent of the Senate;

(2) who is appointed to an advisory committee, as defined in section 3(2) of the Federal Advisory Committee Act (5 U.S.C. App.); or

(3) who is a member of the uniformed services.

Coverage of Previously Exempt State Employees

SEC. 321 *[2 U.S.C. 1220]*

(a) Application. - The rights, protections, and remedies provided pursuant to section 302 and 307(h) of this title shall apply with respect to employment of any individual chosen or appointed, by a person elected to public office in any State or political subdivision of any State by the qualified voters thereof -

(1) to be a member of the elected official's personal staff;

(2) to serve the elected official on the policymaking level; or

(3) to serve the elected official as an immediate advisor with respect to the exercise of the constitutional or legal powers of the office.

(b) Enforcement by administrative action. -

(1) In general. - Any individual referred to in subsection (a) may file a complaint alleging a violation, not later than 180 days after the occurrence of the alleged violation, with the Equal Employment Opportunity Commission, which, in accordance with the principles and procedures set forth in sections 554 through 557 of title 5, United States Code, shall determine whether a violation has occurred and shall set forth its determination in a final order. If the Equal Employment Opportunity Commission determines that a violation has occurred, the final order shall also provide for appropriate relief.

(2) Referral to state and local authorities. –

(A) Application. - Section 706(d) of the Civil Rights Act of 1964 (42 U.S.C. 2000e 5(d)) shall apply with respect to any proceeding under this section.

(B) Definition. - For purposes of the application described in subparagraph (A), the term "any charge filed by a member of the Commission alleging an unlawful employment practice" means a complaint filed under this section.

(c) Judicial review. - Any party aggrieved by a final order under subsection (b) may obtain a review of such order under chapter 158 of title 28, United States Code. For the purpose of this review, the Equal Employment Opportunity Commission shall be an "agency" as that term is used in chapter 158 of title 28, United States Code.

(d) Standard of review. - To the extent necessary to decision and when presented, the reviewing court shall decide all relevant questions of law and interpret constitutional and statutory provisions. The court shall set aside a final order under subsection (b) if it is determined that the order was -

(1) arbitrary, capricious, an abuse of discretion, or otherwise not consistent with law;

(2) not made consistent with required procedures; or

(3) unsupported by substantial evidence.

In making the foregoing determinations, the court shall review the whole record or those parts of it cited by a party, and due account shall be taken of the rule of prejudicial error.

(e) Attorney's fees. - If the individual referred to in subsection (a) is the prevailing party in a proceeding under this subsection, attorney's fees may be allowed by the court in accordance with the standards prescribed under section 706(k) of the Civil Rights Act of 1964 (42 U.S.C. 2000e-5(k)).

Severability

SEC. 322 *[2 U.S.C. 1221]*

Notwithstanding section 401 of this Act, if any provision of section 309 or 320(a)(3) is invalidated, both sections 309 and 320(a)(3) shall have no force and effect.

Payments by the President or a Member of the Senate

SEC. 323 *[2 U.S.C. 1222]*

The President or a Member of the Senate shall reimburse the appropriate Federal account for any payment made on his or her behalf out of such account for a violation committed under the provisions of this title by the President or Member of the Senate not later than 60 days after the payment is made.

Reports of Senate Committees

SEC. 324 *[2 U.S.C. 1223]*

(a) Each report accompanying a bill or joint resolution of a public character reported by any committee of the Senate (except the Committee on Appropriations and the Committee on the Budget) shall contain a listing of the provisions of the bill or joint resolution that apply to Congress and an evaluation of the impact of such provisions on Congress.

(b) The provisions of this section are enacted by the Senate as an exercise of the rulemaking power of the Senate, with full recognition of the right of the Senate to change its rules, in the same manner, and to the same extent, as in the case of any other rule of the Senate.

Intervention and Expedited Review of Certain Appeals

SEC. 325 *[2 U.S.C. 1224]*

(a) Intervention. - Because of the constitutional issues that may be raised by section 309 and section 320, any Member of the Senate may intervene as a matter of right in any proceeding under section 309 for the sole purpose of determining the constitutionality of such section.

(b) Threshold Matter. - In any proceeding under section 309 or section 320, the United States Court of Appeals for the Federal Circuit shall determine any issue presented concerning the constitutionality of such section as a threshold matter.

(c) Appeal. -

(1) In general. - An appeal may be taken directly to the Supreme Court of the United States from any interlocutory or final judgment, decree, or order issued by the United States Court of Appeals for the Federal Circuit ruling upon the constitutionality of section 309 or 320.

(2) Jurisdiction. - The Supreme Court shall, if it has not previously ruled on the question, accept jurisdiction over the appeal referred to in paragraph (1), advance the appeal on the docket and expedite the appeal to the greatest extent possible.

TITLE IV - GENERAL PROVISIONS

Severability

SEC. 401 *[42 U.S.C. 1981 note]*

If any provision of this Act, or an amendment made by this Act, or the application of such provision to any person or circumstances is held to be invalid, the remainder of this Act and the amendments made by this Act, and the application of such provision to other persons and circumstances, shall not be affected.

Effective Date

SEC. 402 *[42 U.S.C. 1981 note]*

(a) In General. - Except as otherwise specifically provided, this Act and the amendments made by this Act shall take effect upon enactment.

(b) Certain Disparate Impact Cases. Notwithstanding any other provision of this Act, nothing in this Act shall apply to any disparate impact case for which a complaint was filed before March 1, 1975, and for which an initial decision was rendered after October 30, 1983.

Approved November 21, 1991.

EEOC DECISION 1871264

CORBETT VS. DEPARTMENT OF THE ARMY

The following decision was won against the agency for the agency's failure to accept my allegations on my EEO complaint and for rejecting my allegations as being untimely.

This decision set the groundwork for winning my case against my employer because they were trying to deny me due process under the United States Constitution.

EQUAL EMPLOYMENT OPPORTUNITY COMMISSION
Office of Review and Appeals
5203 Leesburg Pike, Suite 900
Falls Church, Virginia 22041

87 JUL 31 11:43

John E. Corbett,
Appellant,

v.

Department of the Army,
Appellee.

Appeal No. 01871264
Agency No. 87-03-0092

DECISION

INTRODUCTION

On February 10, 1987, John E. Corbett (hereinafter referred to as appellant) initiated an appeal to the Equal Employment Opportunity Commission (EEOC) from the final decision of the Department of the Army (hereinafter referred to as the agency) issued on February 3, 1987 on his equal employment opportunity complaint. Appellant alleged that he was discriminated against because of his race (black) and sex (male) in violation of Title VII of the Civil Rights Act of 1964, as amended, 42 U.S.C. Section 2000e et seq. The appeal is accepted for decision by the Commission in accordance with the provisions of EEOC Order No. 960, as amended.

ISSUE PRESENTED

The issue presented by this appeal is whether the agency properly rejected the allegations of appellant's complaint for failure to contact an EEO counselor in a timely manner.

BACKGROUND

Appellant initially attempted to contact an EEO counselor on October 3, 1986. Due to the unavailability of a counselor at the time of this initial contact appellant did not actually meet with a counselor for informal counseling until November 19, 1986, 47 days after his attempted initial contact. Appellant's final interview with the EEO counselor was held on January 15, 1987. Appellant filed a formal EEO complaint, alleging discrimination on the basis of his race and sex, on January 30, 1987. The final agency decision rejected all of appellant's allegations for failure to contact an EEO counselor in a timely manner.

The record reflects that appellant's formal complaint form contained several inconsistencies in regard to the time frames involved with his allegations. In the blank space in which appellant was requested to state the date on which the most recent alleged discrimination occurred, appellant wrote "August 26, 1986." In appellant's explanation of the alleged discrimination, under allegation number 3, appellant wrote that the period in question was January 1, 1986 through December 31, 1986. In contrast, in the "Remarks" section for question number 20, under

8703 0092

allegation number 3, appellant wrote that one of his coworkers witnessed appellant's first and second level supervisors, the alleged discriminating officials (ADO), ignoring appellant's requests for assistance from "Oct. - Nov. 86." The agency did not ask appellant to clarify these conflicting dates.

Furthermore, the record reflects that in his formal complaint appellant listed only three allegations. First, appellant alleged that on August 26, 1986 the "Range Report" for which appellant was responsible was given to another employee and that the errors made by appellant in the report were not discussed with appellant. Second, appellant alleged that in March, 1986, when he reportedly sent incorrect data to the National Security Administration he was never notified that he had made any errors. Third, he alleged that he was "not informed or instructed on the major elements" of his "job performance planning worksheet." More specifically, appellant wrote that no instructions were given to him on how to properly prepare the final draft reports or on how to supply the "[r]outine 915 technical data receipt to DIA, monthly." In the EEO counselor's report, however, the counselor indicated that his discussions with appellant initially focused on management's failure to promote appellant. Their discussions also included a "year long chronology of events dealing with job assignments, reprimands, grievances, disciplinary actions, and a host of other problems ..." Neither the counselor nor the agency asked appellant to provide more specific information in regard to these matters. The record does contain, attached to the counselor's report, an undated, nine page document provided by appellant and entitled "Summary of Experiences Under the Direction ..." of the ADO. This document contains, among other things, a reference to a letter of suspension for three days which was reportedly delivered to appellant's desk on October 9, 1986. This more recent allegation of a discriminatory agency action was not addressed or further clarified by the agency.

In the final agency decision, the agency rejected the three allegations included in appellant's formal complaint. The first two allegations were rejected because the dates specified by appellant on which these matter occurred, were more than thirty days before appellant's initial attempt to contact an EEO counselor. The agency interpreted appellant's third allegation to mean that he was not informed as to what the major elements of his performance planning worksheet were. Accordingly, the agency concluded that as appellant had signed his performance planning worksheet on June 4, 1986, he was made aware on that date of what the major elements were and his third allegation was, therefore, untimely.

On appeal to this Commission, appellant asserts that when he attempted to initially contact an EEO counselor, on October 3, 1986, he was concerned about a proposed ten day suspension. Further, appellant asserts that by the time he finally spoke with the EEO counselor, more than a month later, so much had transpired in the interim that he had forgotten his initial concern.

87030092

ANALYSIS AND FINDINGS

EEOC Regulations provide that a complainant must contact an EEO counselor within thirty days of the alleged discriminatory act. 29 C.F.R. Section 1613.214. The agency concluded that none of appellant's allegations were timely raised with an EEO counselor. After a careful review of the record, this Commission finds that the agency's conclusion is not supported by the record.

The EEOC Regulations provide that EEO counselors must "counsel the aggrieved person concerning the issues in the matter". 29 C.F.R. Section 1613.213(a). Moreover, Federal Personnel Manual (FPM) Letter No. 713-21, which has been adopted by the EEOC, provides in pertinent part:

> Where issues are not clearly defined in those matters on which complainant has been counseled, the [agency] official should also contact the complainant and if necessary, assist him or her in amending the complaint ....

As can be seen from the above, the agency has a duty to aid the appellant in the articulation of his allegations. The law and the Commission's established policy does not require that lay complainants be able to articulate their complaint in the language specified in Title VII or the EEOC Regulations before they file a formal EEO complaint. A careful review of the record reveals that neither the agency nor the EEO counselor properly assisted appellant with the framing of his complaint.

Under allegation number 3, appellant alleged that he was not informed or instructed on the major elements of his job performance planning worksheet. Appellant further explained that no instructions were given to him on how to perform some of his assigned tasks. At one point in his complaint, he alleged that this occurred from January 1, 1986 to December 31, 1986. At another point in the complaint, he alleged that October to November, 1986, was the relevant time period. Neither the agency nor the EEO counselor asked appellant to clarify these contradictory dates. Moreover, appellant was given no assistance or advice on how to articulate this particular allegation. Instead, the agency narrowly redefined this allegation as appellant not being informed of the major elements of his job performance planning worksheet. Under this narrow redefinition, the agency rejected this allegation because appellant had signed a copy of the planning worksheet on June 4, 1986. The Commission finds that the agency's narrow redefinition does not accurately reflect the allegation as it was intended by appellant. June 4, 1986, is not the controlling date. It is, however, unclear from the present record on what date appellant was last denied training or instruction as to his job responsibilities and tasks.

Likewise, it is apparent from the counselor's report that appellant initially asserted that various disciplinary actions which had been taken against him by the ADO were discriminatory. Appellant referred specifically to a three day suspension letter he reportedly received on

87030092

October 9, 1986. On appeal, appellant asserts that he initially intended to include a proposed ten day suspension in his complaint.[1] Appellant was not advised by the agency to include specific information on this recent disciplinary action in his complaint. It is apparent from the above that both the agency and the counselor failed to meet their obligation to assist appellant in the articulation of his complaint.

In addition, it appears that appellant may be alleging a continuing violation. A continuing violation may be defined as an ongoing series of related discriminatory acts directed against an employee. When a continuing violation is properly alleged, the normal time limit for contacting an EEO counselor is suspended as to that particular allegation. If at least one of the acts complained of falls within the limitations period, all acts which are part of the continuing violation are timely. Clark v. Olinkraft, Inc., 556 F.2d 1219, 1221-22 (5th Cir. 1977), cert denied, 434 U.S. 1069 (1978); Rich v. Martin Marietta Corp., 522 F.2d 333 (10th Cir. 1975). The rationale underlying the continuing violation theory is that a remedy should be provided for "past actions which operate to discriminate against the complainant at the present time." Olson v. Rembrant Printing Co., 511 F.2d 1228, 1234 (8th Cir. 1975). If a continuing violation is involved, then appellant's first and second allegation may be timely as part of a related series of discriminatory acts by the ADO against appellant. It is unclear from the present record whether appellant's allegations constitute a continuing violation.

Accordingly, the final agency decision rejecting all of appellant's allegations as untimely must be vacated. The Commission finds that the agency failed to comply with its obligation to assist appellant in the clarification and articulation of his allegations. This case is remanded to the agency in accordance with this opinion. The agency must, at a minimum: clarify the time periods involved in appellant's allegation number 3; assist appellant in the articulation of his allegations including any allegations involving disciplinary actions taken against appellant; and determine whether appellant is alleging a continuing violation. After further clarification, the agency shall accept and process appellant's timely allegations and reject any untimely allegations.

CONCLUSION

For the reasons as set forth above, it is the decision of this Commission to vacate the final agency decision and to remand this case to the agency for processing in accordance with this opinion.

---

[1] It is unclear from the record whether this refers to one incident or two separate suspensions.

87030092

IMPLEMENTATION OF THE COMMISSION DECISION

Under EEOC regulations, compliance with the Commission's corrective action is mandatory. The agency must report to the Commission, within thirty (30) calendar days of receipt of the decision, that corrective action has been taken. The agency's report should be forwarded to the Compliance Office, Office of Review and Appeals, Equal Employment Opportunity Commission, 5203 Leesburg Pike, Falls Church, Virginia, 22041. A copy of the report should be sent to the appellant.

FOR THE COMMISSION:

28 JUL 1987

Date

Dolores L. Rozzi, Director
Office of Review and Appeals

87030092

EEOC DECISION 01934622

CORBETT VS. WEST, JR.

The following decision was won by me for the agency's continued violations for refusing to process my complaint and not complete a fair investigation on the stated allegations.

The agency vehemently refused to articulate my allegations into a formal complaint and accept them for investigation under the federal laws regarding processing federal EEO complaints. After many noncompliance decisions from EEOC, EEOC decided to articulate my complaint and issue a ruling.

U.S. EQUAL EMPLOYMENT OPPORTUNITY COMMISSION
Office of Federal Operations
P.O. Box 19848
Washington, D.C. 20036

John E. Corbett,
Appellant,

v.

Togo D. West, Jr.,
Secretary,
Department of the Army,
Agency.

Appeal No. 01934522
Agency No. 87-03-0092

DECISION

INTRODUCTION

On September 7, 1993, John E. Corbett (appellant) timely filed an appeal with the Equal Employment Opportunity Commission (Commission) from the final decision of the Secretary, Department of the Army (agency), received on September 3, 1993. Appellant alleged discrimination based on race (black) and sex (male) in violation of Title VII of the Civil Rights Act of 1964, as amended, 42 U.S.C. Section 2000e _et seq_. The appeal is accepted by the Commission in accordance with the provisions of EEOC Order No. 960.001.

ISSUE PRESENTED

The issue presented herein is whether the agency conducted a "complete and fair investigation" of certain allegations in accordance with 29 C.F.R. § 1613.216(a).

CONTENTIONS ON APPEAL

On appeal, appellant makes several contentions that shall be considered herein. The agency has offered no comments in response.

BACKGROUND

Appellant initially contacted an EEO counselor in October 1986, and filed his first formal complaint (Complaint-1) on January 15, 1987, alleging discrimination based on race (black) and sex (male) with regard to three issues. Thereafter, the agency issued a final decision (FAD-1) in which it rejected appellant's complaint based on untimeliness. Appellant appealed this dismissal to the Commission, and we determined that the agency had failed to comply with its obligation to assist appellant in the clarification and articulation of issues. _Corbett v. Dept. of the Army_, EEOC Appeal No. 01871264 (July 8, 1987). Specifically, we noted that, although appellant attempted to raise certain disciplinary actions with the EEO counselor, these were not subsequently raised in Complaint-1. We also determined that appellant appeared to be alleging a continuing violation. For these reasons, we remanded the complaint so that the agency could assist appellant in the full articulation of his allegations, and so that it could determine whether appellant had alleged a continuing violation. Thereafter, the agency provided appellant with additional EEO counseling, but determined that, because appellant had opted to file grievances with regard to three disciplinary actions, there were no allegations for a continuing violation.

Appellant contacted an EEO counselor in September 1987 and again attempted to raise adverse actions taken against him by the agency, including his removal in December 1986. However, the counselor's report indicates that these issues were not counselled because they either did not fall within the 30-day time period or had been addressed in the grievance process. Thereafter, appellant filed his second formal complaint (Complaint-2) on September 28, 1987, in which he alleged that he had been discriminated against when there was a delay in obtaining EEO counseling, and when the counselor failed to cover areas surrounding the adverse actions he had raised. The agency accepted Complaint-2 for investigation, and thereafter investigated the issues (Issues 1-5) raised in Complaints 1 and 2. These included whether appellant was discriminated against when: (1) he was held accountable for errors not reported to him; (2) other employees were allowed to correct his work without his knowledge; (3) he was not informed of the specific duties of his position; (4) he was not informed about the major elements of his performance appraisal; and (5) Complaint-1 was not properly processed. Following this investigation, the agency issued a proposed disposition finding no discrimination, and appellant requested an EEO administrative hearing. Appellant subsequently withdrew this request, and the agency issued a final decision (FAD-2) finding no discrimination with regard to Issues 1-5.

We initially affirmed FAD-2 (Corbett v. Dept. of the Army, EEOC Request No. 01913590, (January 31, 1992)), and appellant filed a request for reconsideration, arguing that, *inter alia*, the EEO counselor had not addressed his prior discipline and had not accepted his termination as an issue. Appellant also submitted a document entitled "Statement of Experiences," which documented nine incidents (Allegations 1-9) occurring between July 1985 and December 1986, including: (1) beginning in July 1985, [he] began being assigned the work of a clerical employee who had left the agency in addition to his own work; (2) in January 1986, [he] was told by his supervisor that he would not be promoted to a higher grade level; (3) after he told a senior employee to put a clerical task he wanted him to do in writing, he received a letter of reprimand in January 1986; (4) after a confrontation on or about January 1, 1986, appellant received a "DF" (identity of acronym not apparent) admonishing him not to make certain remarks to his supervisor or to a senior employee; (5) in March 1986, he received a "DF" stating that he was making continuous errors in a form used for data requests to the National Security Agency; (6) when he tried to defend himself by writing a letter indicating that he had not been informed of the alleged errors, he was reprimanded for mailing his letter through the government mails; (7) on October 9, 1986, he was given a three-day suspension by his supervisor; (8) he was never given guidance or direction about his work by his supervisor after he confronted him in early 1986; and (9) on December 11, 1986, he received a "DF" from his supervisor proposing his removal from Federal service. Appellant subsequently filed a request for reconsideration of this decision, which we granted. Corbett v. Dept. of Army, EEOC Request No. 05920407 (July 16, 1992).

In granting appellant's request for reconsideration, we concluded that the agency had not complied with our order in EEOC Appeal No. 01871264, to the extent the agency had ignored appellant's repeated attempts at raising a continuing violation. We also noted that, although the agency had indicated that appellant was precluded from raising certain disciplinary acts because he had filed grievances on these matters, the agency had provided nothing which supported this conclusion. For these reasons, we directed the agency to determine whether Issues 1-5 and Allegations 1-9 constituted a continuing violation, and to determine which allegations were acceptable for further processing.

In conjunction with our order, the agency determined that Allegations 1-9 had been treated as a continuing violation in the 1988 investigation to the extent the investigator had addressed them. However, a review of the investigative report indicates that, although the investigator questioned appellant about most of these allegations, they were treated as background information and not as separate issues. The agency also noted that two of the adverse actions set forth in Allegations 1-9 (3 and 6) had been addressed via the grievance procedure, and that appellant had filed an appeal with the Merit Systems Protection Board with regard to his termination (9). However, a review of the agency's regulations regarding the filing of grievances indicates that employees are not permitted to raise matters of discrimination in the grievance process.[1] Additionally, the record indicates that, while appellant did file an MSPB appeal with regard to his termination, this appeal

---

[1] Therefore, the fact that appellant had filed grievances with regard to these two allegations would not, pursuant to 29 C.F.R. 1613.219, preclude him from raising them in this forum.

was dismissed for lack of jurisdiction in June 1987. After the agency had completed its compliance report, it issued a third final decision (FAD-3) on August 23, 1993, finding no discrimination. It is from this decision that appellant now appeals.

ANALYSIS AND FINDINGS

Pursuant to 29 C.F.R. 1613.216(a), the regulation in effect during the period in question, the agency was required to thoroughly investigate the matter(s) complained of once the complaint had been accepted. In this case, the agency's position is that, because Allegations 1-9 were addressed during the course of its investigation, this was sufficient to satisfy the requirements of Section 1613.216(a). However, we disagree, and note that merely addressing these allegations as background information is not tantamount to accepting them as issues and investigating them. Therefore, we find that Allegations 1-9, to the extent the agency determined that they constitute a continuing violation, should be remanded for a proper investigation.[2] Accordingly, FAD-3 is VACATED, and Allegations 1-9 are REMANDED to the agency in accordance with this decision and the applicable regulations.

CONCLUSION

Based upon a review of the record, and for the foregoing reasons, it is the decision of the Commission to vacate the agency's final decision of no discrimination based on race and sex, and to remand Allegations 1-9 for further processing.

ORDER (E1092)

(1) The agency is ORDERED to process remanded Allegations 1-9 in accordance with 29 C.F.R. Section 1614.108. The agency shall acknowledge to appellant that it has received the remanded allegations within thirty (30) calendar days of the date this decision becomes final. The agency shall issue to appellant a copy of the investigative file and shall also notify appellant of the appropriate rights within one hundred fifty (150) calendar days of the date this decision becomes final, unless the matter is otherwise resolved prior to that time. If appellant requests a final decision without a hearing, the agency shall issue a final decision within sixty (60) days of receipt of appellant's request.

---

[2] Because the MSPB dismissed Allegation 9 based on lack of jurisdiction, appellant was not precluded from raising this allegation in the EEO process. <u>See</u> <u>Weaver v. Dept. of the Navy</u>, EEOC Request No. 05900230 (April 26, 1990).

A copy of the agency's letter of acknowledgement to appellant and a copy of the notice that transmits the investigative file and notice of rights must be sent to the Compliance Officer as referenced below.

IMPLEMENTATION OF THE COMMISSION'S DECISION (K1092)

Compliance with the Commission's corrective action is mandatory. The agency shall submit its compliance report within thirty (30) calendar days of the completion of all ordered corrective action. The report shall be submitted to the Compliance Officer, Office of Federal Operations, Equal Employment Opportunity Commission, P.O. Box 19848, Washington, D.C. 20036. The agency's report must contain supporting documentation, and the agency must send a copy of all submissions to the appellant.

STATEMENT OF RIGHTS - ON APPEAL

RECONSIDERATION (M1092)

The Commission may, in its discretion, reconsider the decision in this case if the appellant or the agency submits a written request containing arguments or evidence which tend to establish that:

1. New and material evidence is available that was not readily available when the previous decision was issued; or

2. The previous decision involved an erroneous interpretation of law, regulation or material fact, or misapplication of established policy; or

3. The decision is of such exceptional nature as to have substantial precedential implications.

Requests to reconsider, with supporting arguments or evidence, MUST BE FILED WITHIN THIRTY (30) CALENDAR DAYS of the date you receive this decision, or WITHIN TWENTY (20) CALENDAR DAYS of the date you receive a timely request to reconsider filed by another party. Any argument in opposition to the request to reconsider or cross request to reconsider MUST be submitted to the Commission and to the requesting party WITHIN TWENTY (20) CALENDAR DAYS of the date you receive the request to reconsider. *See* 29 C.F.R. § 1614.407. All requests and arguments must bear proof of postmark and be submitted to the Director, Office of Federal Operations, Equal Employment Opportunity Commission, P.O. Box 19848, Washington, D.C. 20036. In the absence of a legible postmark, the request to reconsider shall be deemed filed on the date it is received by the Commission.

RIGHT TO FILE A CIVIL ACTION (R0993)

This is a decision requiring the agency to continue its administrative processing of your complaint. However, if you wish to file a civil action, you have the right to file such action in an appropriate United States District Court. It is the position of the Commission that you have the right to file a civil action in an appropriate United States District Court WITHIN NINETY (90) CALENDAR DAYS from the date that you receive this decision. You should be aware, however, that courts in some jurisdictions have interpreted the Civil Rights Act of 1991 in a manner suggesting that a civil action must be filed WITHIN THIRTY (30) CALENDAR DAYS from the date that you receive this decision. To ensure that your civil action is considered timely, you are advised to file it WITHIN THIRTY (30) CALENDAR DAYS from the date that you receive this decision or to consult an attorney concerning the applicable time period in the jurisdiction in which your action would be filed. In the alternative, you may file a civil action AFTER ONE HUNDRED AND EIGHTY (180) CALENDAR DAYS of the date you filed your complaint with the agency, or filed your appeal with the Commission. If you file a civil action, **YOU MUST NAME AS THE DEFENDANT IN THE COMPLAINT THE PERSON WHO IS THE OFFICIAL AGENCY HEAD OR DEPARTMENT HEAD, IDENTIFYING THAT PERSON BY HIS OR HER FULL NAME AND OFFICIAL TITLE.** Failure to do so may result in the dismissal of your case in court. "Agency" or "department" means the national organization, and not the local office, facility or department in which you work. **Filing a civil action will terminate the administrative processing of your complaint.**

RIGHT TO REQUEST COUNSEL (Z1092)

If you decide to file a civil action, and if you do not have or cannot afford the services of an attorney, you may request that the Court appoint an attorney to represent you and that the Court permit you to file the action without payment of fees, costs, or other security. *See* Title VII of the Civil Rights Act of 1964, as amended, 42 U.S.C. §2000e *et seq.*; the Rehabilitation Act of 1973, as amended, 29 U.S.C. §§791, 794(c). **The grant or denial of the request is within the sole discretion of the Court.** Filing a request for an attorney does not extend your time in which to file a civil action. Both the request and the civil action must be filed within the time limits as stated in the paragraph above ("Right to File A Civil Action").

FOR THE COMMISSION:

JUN 24 1994

DATE

Ronnie Blumenthal

Ronnie Blumenthal, Director
Office of Federal Operations

JUDGMENT

CORBETT VS. RUMSFELD

A judgment was issued by a United States Court of Appeals after a United States District Court refused to adjudicate a judgment mandated by federal law after a favorable decision was rendered by a federal agency in a federal administrative complaint.

When the United States District Court refused to adjudicate a favorable decision required by federal law, they continued to deny me due process under the United States Constitution.

United States Court of Appeals
For the Eleventh Circuit

No. 03-14128

District Court Docket No.
01-01717-CV-BE-NE

FILED
U.S. COURT OF APPEALS
ELEVENTH CIRCUIT
Feb 27, 2004
THOMAS K. KAHN
CLERK

JOHN EDWARD CORBETT,

Plaintiff-Appellant,

versus

DONALD H. RUMSFELD, Secretary,
Department of Defense (Defense
Intelligence Agency),

Defendant-Appellee.

Appeal from the United States District Court
for the Northern District of Alabama

JUDGMENT

It is hereby ordered, adjudged, and decreed that the attached opinion included herein by reference, is entered as the judgment of this Court.

Entered: February 27, 2004
For the Court: Thomas K. Kahn, Clerk
By: Gilman, Nancy

ISSUED AS MANDATE
MAY 25 2004
U.S. COURT OF APPEALS
ATLANTA, GA.

REFERENCES

INFORMATION HAS BEEN PARAPHRASED FROM THE FOLLOWING

1. Robert A. Anderson and Walter A. Kump, Business Law, (Ohio: South-Western Publishing Company, 1973), pp. 17-25.
2. Gordon F. Bloom and Herbert R. Northrup, Economic of Labor Relations, (Ontario: Richard D. Irwin, Inc. 1971), pp. 712-714.
3. Marianne Lavelle, U. S. News and World Report, The New Rules of Sexual Harassment, July, 1998, pp. 30-31.
4. Barbara Lindemann Schlei, Paul Grossman, Employment Discrimination Law, 1988, pp. 1196-1198.
5. Mack A. Player, Elaine W. Shoben, Risa Liberwitz, Employment Discrimination Law, 2nd Edition, 1995, pp. 77-78.
6. Richard F. Richards, Charles Sullivan and Michael J. Zimmer, Federal Statutory Law of Discrimination, (New York: The Bobbs-Merrill Company, Inc., 1980), pp. 58-69.
7. U.S. Equal Employment Opportunity Commission, Resolving Federal EEO Complaints, 1995, pp. 1-67, pp. 5-6 through 5-11.
8. U.S. Equal Employment Opportunity Commission, Counseling Federal EEO Complaints, 1995, pp. 11-14, 31-33.
9. United States Merit Systems Protection Board, An Introduction To The MSPB, 1997, pp. 5-23.
10. United States Merit Systems Protection Board, Question And Answers About Whistleblower Appeals, 1997, pp. 5-21.

DOCUMENTED EVIDENCE OF FAVORABLE EVENTS

AND INCIDENTS CONCERNING YOUR CAREER

1.
2.
3.
4.
5.
6.
7.
8.
9.
10.
11.
12.
13.
14.
15.
16.
17.
18.
19.
20.
21.
22.
23.
24.
25.

DOCUMENTED EVIDENCE OF UNFAVORABLE EVENTS AND INCIDENTS CONCERNING YOUR CAREER

1.
2.
3.
4.
5.
6.
7.
8.
9.
10.
11.
12.
13.
14.
15.
16.
17.
18.
19.
20.
21.
22.
23.
24.
25.

EEOC DISTRICT OFFICES

The time limit for filing a claim with EEOC is within 180 days from the date of the alleged violation. This 180-day filing deadline may be extended to 300 days if the charge also is covered by a state or local anti-discrimination law. The 800 number for all offices is 1-800-669-4000.

ALABAMA
Birmingham District Office
Ridge Park Place
1130 22nd Street South
Suite 2000
Birmingham, AL 35205

Mobile Local Office
63 South Royal Street
Suite 504
Mobile, AL 36602

ARIZONA
3300 North Central Avenue
Suite 690
Phoenix, AZ 85012-2504

ARKANSAS
820 Louisiana Street
Suite 200
Little Rock, AR 72201

CALIFORNIA
Fresno Local Office
2300 Tulare Street
Suite 215
Fresno, CA 93721

Los Angeles District Office
255 East Temple Street
4th Floor
Los Angeles, CA 90012

Oakland Local Office
1301 Clay Street
Suite 1170-N
Oakland, CA 94612-5217

San Diego Local Office
401 B Street
Suite 510
San Diego, CA 92101

San Francisco District Office
350 The Embarcadero
Suite 500
San Francisco, CA 94105-1260

San Jose Local Office
96 North Third Street
Suite 200
San Jose, CA 95112

COLORADO
303 East 17th Avenue
Suite 510
Denver, CO 80203

DISTRICT OF COLUMBIA
1801 L Street, NW
Suite 100
Washington, DC 20507

FLORIDA
Miami District Office
One Biscayne Tower
2 South Biscayne Blvd
Suite 2700
Miami, FL 33131

Tampa Field Office
501 East Polk Street
Suite 1000
Tampa, FL 33602

GEORGIA
Atlanta District Office
Sam Nunn Atlanta Federal Center
100 Alabama Street, SW
Suite 4R30
Atlanta, GA 30303

Savannah Local Office
410 Mall Boulevard
Suite G
Savannah, GA 31406-4821

HAWAII
300 Ala Moana Boulevard
Room 7-127
PO Box 50082
Honolulu, HI 96850-0051

ILLINOIS
500 West Madison Street
Suite 2800
Chicago, IL 60661

INDIANA
101 West Ohio Street
Suite 1900
Indianapolis, IN 46204

KENTUCKY
600 Dr. Martin Luther King Jr. Place
Suite 268
Louisville, KY 40202

LOUISIANA
1555 Poydra Street
Suite 1900
New Orleans, LA 70112

MARYLAND
City Crescent Building
10 South Howard Street
3rd Floor
Baltimore, MD 21202

MASSACHUSETTS
John F. Kennedy Federal Building
475 Government Center
Boston, MA 02203

MICHIGAN
Patrick V. McNamara Building
477 Michigan Avenue
Room 865
Detroit, MI 48226

MINNESOTA
Towle Building
330 South Second Avenue
Suite 430
Minneapolis, MN 55401-2224

MISSISSIPPI
Dr. A.H. McCoy Federal Building
100 West capitol Street
Suite 207
Jackson, MS 39269

MISSOURI
Kansas City Area Office
4th & State Avenue
9th Floor
Kansas City, KS 66101

St. Louis District Office
Robert A. Young Federal Building
1222 Spruce Street
Room 8.100
St. Louis, MO 63103

NEVADA
333 Las Vegas Boulevard South
Suite 8112
Las Vegas, NV 89101

NEW JERSEY
One Newark Center
21st Floor
Raymond Boulevard at McCarter Hwy (Rt. 21)
Newark, NJ 07102-5233

NEW MEXICO
505 Marquette, NW
Suite 900, 9th Floor
Albuquerque, NM 87102

NEW YORK
Buffalo Local Office
6 Fountain Plaza
Suite 350
Buffalo, NY 14202

New York District Office
33 Whitehall Street
New York, NY 10004

NORTH CAROLINA
Charlotte District Office
129 West Trade Street
Suite 400
Charlotte, NC 28202

Greensboro Local Office
2303 West Meadowview Road
Suite 201
Greensboro, NC 27407

OHIO
Cincinnati Area Office
John W. Peck Federal Office Building
550 Main Street
10th Floor
Cincinnati, OH 45202

Cleveland Field Office
Anthony J. Celebreeze Federal Building
1240 East 9th Street
Suite 3001
Cleveland, OH 44199

OKLAHOMA
215 Dean A. McGee Avenue
5th Floor
Oklahoma City, OK 73102

PENNSYLVANIA
Philadelphia District Office
801 Market Street
Suite 1300
Philadelphia, PA 19107-3127

Pittsburgh Area Office
Liberty Center
1001 Liberty Avenue
Suite 300
Pittsburgh, PA 15222-4187

PUERTO RICO
525 F.D. Roosevelt Avenue
Plaza Las Americas
Suite 1202
San Juan, PR 00918-8001

SOUTH CAROLINA
301 North Main Street
Suite 1402
Greenville, SC 29601-9916

TENNESSEE
Memphis District Office
1407 Union Avenue
Suite 621
Memphis, TN 38104

Nashville Area Office
50 Vantage Way
Suite 202
Nashville, TN 37228-9940

TEXAS
Dallas District Office
Mickey Leland Federal Building
207 South Houston Street
3rd Floor
Dallas, TX 75202

El Paso Area Office
300 East Main Drive
Suite 500
El Paso, TX 79901

Houston District Office
1919 Smith Street
6th Floor
Houston, TX 77002-8049

San Antonio Field Office
Mockingbird Plaza II
5410 Fredericksburg Road
Suite 200
San Antonio, TX 78229

VIRGINIA
Norfolk Area Office
Federal Building
200 Granby Street
Suite 739
Norfolk, VA 23510

Richmond Local Office
830 East Main Street
6th Floor
Richmond, VA 23219

WASHINGTON
Federal Office Building
909 First Avenue
Suite 400
Seattle, WA 98104-1061

WISCONSIN
Milwaukee District Office
310 West Wisconsin Avenue
Suite 800
Milwaukee, WI 53203-2292

NOTE: All Letter Headings should start with the address, Equal Employment Opportunity Commission

MERIT SYSTEMS PROTECTION BOARD (MSPB)

REGIONAL AND FIELD OFFICES

Headquarters, Washington, DC
1615 M Street, NW
Washington, DC 20419
Phone: (202) 653-7200
Fax: (202) 653-7130

Atlanta Regional Office
401 West Peachtree Street, NW
Suite 1050
Atlanta, GA 30308
Phone: (404) 730-2751
Fax: (404) 730-2767

States Served:
Alabama, Florida, Georgia, Mississippi, South Carolina, and Tennessee

Central Regional Office
230 South Dearborn Street
Room 3100
Chicago, IL 60604
Phone: (312) 353-2923
Fax: (312) 886-4231

States Served:
Illinois, Indiana, Iowa, Kansas City-Kansas, Kentucky, Michigan, Minnesota, Missouri, Ohio, and Wisconsin

Dallas Field Office
1100 Commerce Street
Room 620
Dallas, TX 75242
Phone: (214) 761-0555
Fax: (214) 767-0102

States Served:
Arkansas, Louisiana, Oklahoma, and Texas

Denver Field Office
165 South Union Boulevard
Suite 318
Lakewood, CO 80228
Phone: (303) 969-5109
Fax: (303) 969-5109

States Served:
Arizona, Colorado, Kansas (except Kansas City), Montana, Nebraska, New Mexico, North Dakota, South Dakota, Utah, and Wyoming

New York Field Office
26 Federal Plaza
Room 3137 A
New York, NY 10278
Phone: (212) 264-9372
Fax: (212) 264-1417

States Served:
New Jersey (counties of Bergen, Essex, Hudson, and Union), New York, Puerto Rico, and Virgin Islands

Northeastern Regional Office
1601 Market Street
Suite 1700
Philadelphia, PA 19103
Phone: (215) 597-9960
Fax: (215) 597-3456

States Served:
Connecticut, Delaware, Maine, Maryland (except Montgomery and Prince George's counties), Massachusetts, New Hampshire, New Jersey (except Bergen, Essex, Hudson and Union counties), Pennsylvania, Rhode Island, Vermont, and West Virginia

Washington DC Regional Office
1800 Diagonal Road
Suite 205
Alexandria, VA 22314-2840
Phone: (703) 756-6250
Fax: (703) 756-7112

States Served:
Washington, DC, Maryland (counties of Montgomery and Prince George's), North Carolina, Virginia, and all overseas areas not otherwise covered

Western Regional Office
201 Mission Street
Suite 2310
San Francisco, CA 94105-1831
Phone: (415) 904-6772
Fax: (415) 904-0580

States Served:
Alaska, California, Hawaii, Idaho, Nevada, Oregon, Washington, and Pacific overseas

THINKING

If you think you are beaten, you are;
if you think you dare not, you don't
if you like to win but think you can't
it's almost a cinch you won't.

If you think you'll lose, you're lost,
for out in the world we find
success begins with a fellow's will
it's all in the state of mind.

If you think you are out-classed, you are
you've got to think high to rise;
you've got to be sure of yourself before
you can ever win a prize.

Life's battles don't always go
to the stronger or the faster man;
but sooner or later the man who wins
is the man who thinks he can.

--Walter D. Wintle

DON'T QUIT

When things go wrong, as they sometimes will;
When the road you're trudging seems all up hill,
When the funds are low and the debts are high,
And you want to smile, but you have to sigh,
When care is pressing you down a bit,
Rest, if you must – but don't you quit.

Life is queer with its twists and turns,
As everyone of us sometimes learns,
And many a failure turns about
When he might have won had he stuck it out;
Don't give up, though the pace seems slow –
You might succeed with another blow.

Often the goal is nearer than
It seems to a faint and faltering man,
Often the struggler has given up
When he might have captured the victor's cup.
And he learned too late, when the night slipped down,
How close he was to the golden crown.

Success is failure turned inside out –
The silver tint of the clouds of doubt –
And you never can tell how close you are,
It may be near when it seems afar;
So stick to the fight when you're hardest hit –
It's when things seem worst that you mustn't quit.

--Author Unknown

THE REASONS WHY I PUT THESE POEMS IN THE COURSE

The poems were given to me by a friend and a family member who witnessed my spirit being down and needed to be uplifted.

I consider myself to be a strong-willed person, but what I experienced took a toll on me some days mentally. I sought out people who I knew to give me inspiration and sometimes it wasn't enough.

When I read these poems, they helped me to rest my restless spirit. I placed them on my refrigerator so every time I opened it I would see the poems. They are still on my refrigerator today, and I still read them often.

If you have never seen these poems before, I hope they inspire you as they have inspired me.

CONCLUSION

This course was compiled and written to inspire, uplift, and inform those who may be affected by the number one social disease in our society, discrimination.

My reason for writing this course as noted in the introduction was due to my own personal experiences over about a 20-year period. I never have viewed anyone as a failure who has not had an equal opportunity to obtain a livelihood for them or their family. You will never fail in your efforts to maximize your success by being very honest with yourself. America as a whole, has refused to deal with racism in our society so your chances of being affected by it is very likely.

One of the other reasons for compiling this course is because the legal profession is also ignoring the cases involving discrimination. Many attorneys that I personally talked to informed me that discrimination cases do not make them money. They are mostly interested in criminal cases.

I believe that the best information in addressing any issue is first hand knowledge which is commonly referred to as experience. Experience is the best teacher in gaining knowledge. I made many mistakes in addressing my issues through lack of knowledge and receiving misguided advice from people who have never acted on their own. This material will serve as a roadmap for you to eliminate mistakes one will have in pursuing a case of discrimination. I wished I could have had this knowledge 20 years ago.

Our society will continue to rationalize away discrimination, but I say to you, do not fall in to this trap. Persevere in your beliefs, dreams and God's will and you will ultimately achieve your goal and be crowned the winner.

The best intentions of many groups who speak out against and fight discrimination will not stop the onslaught of cowardly discriminators. Discrimination in America is so culturally and historically rooted in American life. It will take many years in the future to completely turn it around and stop it. America invests in white America, simply put, Whiteness is favored. If you are white you automatically have financial clout. Black Americans and other minorities are disenfranchised and their skin color is a liability.

Fighting discrimination is profitable and in the best interest of all minorities who face it.

Your chance of winning your case of discrimination or sexual harassment is far greater when you are informed on how to proceed with your case. Your employer will thoroughly know their rights and you should thoroughly know yours. Always remember,

KNOWLEDGE IS POWER.

BUSINESS OPPORTUNITY

This course is offered as a unique opportunity to help others provide income who may suffer from being terminated from their employment. Word of mouth is foremost one of the best ways to market any product or information. Certainly, in today's society there are revolutionary ways to market a product over the computer using the internet.

Filing a complaint will be a very stressful time in your life and you will need all the financial assistance you can get.

You can supplement, increase, or establish a full-time income by marketing this course at a profit dependent on the number of books you sell. Simply fill out the purchase order provided with this information. The form may be copied for continued use.

When you have mastered the course and feel comfortable discussing discrimination law, you can teach the course, hold seminars or use the material anyway you want to advance your income while eradicating this cancer in our society.

I have no control on how you want to use this course to help yourself and others.

PURCHASE ORDER

Purchaser Information:

Name ____

Address ____

City ______________________________ State ______ Zip ____________

Ordering Information:

__________________ @ $____________________ = $________________________

Number of copies | Per Copy Price | Purchase Amount

Shipping Information:

Name ____

Address ____

City ______________________________ State ______ Zip ____________

______________________________________ ______________________

Purchaser's Signature | Date

Send This Form To The Publisher:

JUSTUS, John Corbett
PO Box 5960
Huntsville, Alabama 35814

Note:

- Please send money orders, bank cashier's checks, or certified checks only (**no personal or business checks**) for amount of purchase to the Publisher at the address listed above.
- Purchaser should retain a copy of this Purchase Order form for their records.
- Purchaser should copy this form to use for future orders.

INDEPENDENT SALES REPRESENTATIVE CHART

As an Independent Sales Representative, you will be marketing *Justice* by John Corbett to individuals seeking legal advice. This sale can earn you large profits based on the number of books ordered and sold. The minimum number of books per order is ten (10). Also, the publisher will pay all shipping charges and no sales tax will be added to any sales. A chart of your potential profits are as follows:

Books Ordered	Your Cost Per Book	Retail Price Per Book	Your Potential Profit
1-24	$170	$180	$10.00 to $240.00
25-49	$160	$180	$500.00 to $980.00
50-99	$150	$180	$1,500.00 to $2,970.00
100+	$140	$180	$4,000+

Sale example based on 100 books purchased and sold:

Books Sold at $180.00 Each	=	$18,000.00
Books Purchased at $140.00 Each	=	$14,000.00
Your Potential Profit	=	**$4,000.00**

Payment for book orders should be made directly to the publisher:

JUSTUS, John Corbett
PO Box 5960
Huntsville, Alabama 35814

Important Facts:

- Do not use your home mailbox to conduct your business.
- Always rent a PO Box when you start your business, especially when receiving large amounts of cash.
- Never discuss your finances with anyone you do not trust.

WAYS TO MARKET THIS INFORMATION

There are many low cost ways to advertise to sell this information that would bring many calls and direct sales to you.

Some of the ways to advertise are:

Newspapers
Magazines
Radio
Cable television advertisement
Tabloids
Community publications
Business publications
Phonebooks
Internet (e-mails, web page and eBay)
Writing letters to potential buyers (churches, social organizations, bookstores and privately owned businesses)
Make church fans advertising the book for sale and give them to churches
Making business cards in your name advertising the book for sale and give them away
Make tee – shirts, sweatshirts, flyers, and buttons advertising book for sale for family
Buy customized playing cards with advertised the book for sale and give them away
Make a voice-mail message advertising the book for sale
Advertise the book for sale on billboards, athletic fields, taxicabs and buses
Put on your personal profile when you visit internet sites you fight discrimination
Make a rubber portable advertisement for your vehicle advertising the book for sale
Make a politician styled lawn sign advertising the book for sale
Advertise the book for sale at employment career fairs and culture art festivals
Advertise the book for sale at large flea markets
Advertise the book for sale on city street level billboards and all transportation stops
Tell every member of your family tree about the book
Tell every person you meet that you have access to the information
Conduct workshops
Hold Seminars
Act as a consultant
Write newsletters
Use direct mail advertisements
Represent clients in the informal and formal process at hearings and mediations
Open an office as an equal employment opportunity counselor (EEO)

Note: *Anyone can act as an equal employment opportunity counselor in the informal and formal process of EEO complaints but not in a court of law.*

SAMPLE LETTER TO POTENTIAL CUSTOMERS

Date

Any Name
Street Address or PO Box
City, State, Zip Code

To Whom It May Concern:

Have you or somebody you know ever wondered what to do when faced with issues at work that would require legal assistance? Well, I'm writing to share that you can learn how to prepare and win cases of discrimination, sexual harassment, and whistleblowing related to employment and business matters through an exciting new book from JUSTUS Publishing.

Justice, by John Corbett, is an informative book that contains over 380 pages detailing steps on how to articulate, fill out forms, learn anti-discrimination laws, and maintain a discrimination case effective to win. Mr. Corbett has included his own personal experience and related legal documentation in his pursuit and winning of his own lawsuit for wrongful termination.

Not only is *Justice* an excellent resource for individuals, but could also be presented as an educational course or seminar to groups and organizations. Additionally, there is an excellent business opportunity to be found for those who may have lost their income related to civil right laws being violated, and others who want to start or advance their income.

If you are interested in learning more about *Justice* please contact me at (your number). Thank you and I look forward to hearing from you soon.

Sincerely,

Your signature

Type Your Name Here

Note: *This letter is just an example of how you might market* Justice *through the mail.*

THE AUTHORS TRAINING AND ACCOMPLISHMENTS IN EQUAL EMPLOYMENT OPPORTUNITY

.... Completed a course in personnel administration and personnel law at Alabama A& M University, Normal, Alabama

.... Received training from the United States Army Missile Command, Redstone Arsenal, Alabama as an Equal Employment Opportunity Counselor

.... Received training from the National Aeronautics and Space Administration (NASA), Marshall Space Flight Center, Huntsville, Alabama as an Equal Employment Opportunity Counselor (EEO)

.... Received training from the American Federation of Government Employees, Washington, D.C. on winning discrimination complaints in the federal sectors of employment

.... Studied in the law library for over 20 years in Huntsville, Alabama on winning complaints in the private and federal sectors of employment

.... Co- founder of the Back Federal Employees Association, Huntsville, Alabama

.... Consultant to the Redstone Arsenal Minority Employees Association (RAM), Huntsville, Alabama

.... Represented self and won EEO decision, Corbett vs. Department of the Army, Appeal No. 01871264

.... Represented self and won EEO decision, Corbett vs. Department of the Army, Appeal No. 01934622

.... Represented self and won federal court case, Corbett vs. Rumsfeld

www.ingramcontent.com/pod-product-compliance
Lightning Source LLC
LaVergne TN
LVHW080014210926
848481LV00011B/3020